"If you read only one book about
erudition, dark humor, and clarity

the prejudices which distort America's view of Pakistan. This is not the country of the U.S. imagination—a near-failed state where bearded fanatics and mad mullahs burn the American flag while darkly plotting to seize control of the nuclear bombs. Manan Ahmed's Pakistan is a diverse and dynamic country with a rich past and promising future. Its history is shaped by Islam, by British colonial rule, and, more recently, by American support for its military dictators. Its future lies in democracy. But this book is not only about Pakistan. It is also about the United States, and its peculiar blindness to the way it slips into the old habits of British colonial thinking. Creating a Pakistan in its imagination very different from reality, it convinces itself that without its firm guidance, the country would descend into chaos. Despite its professed commitment to democracy, America has never really learned to trust 'the masses' of Pakistan or, indeed, of other Muslim countries. This book should be compulsory reading for anyone interested in understanding why the United States has repeatedly failed to build an effective relationship with Pakistan."

—MYRA MACDONALD

senior Reuters journalist, blogger, author of *Heights of Madness*,
a book about the Siachen war

ABOUT

JUST WORLD BOOKS
"TIMELY BOOKS FOR CHANGING TIMES"

Just World Books produces excellent books on key international issues—and does so in a very timely fashion. Because of the agility of our process, we cannot give detailed advance notice of fixed, seasonal "lists." To learn about our existing and upcoming titles, to download author podcasts and videos, to learn our terms for bookstores or other bulk purchases, or to buy our books, visit our website:

www.justworldbooks.com

Our secure-purchase webstore is at:

justworldbooks.mybigcommerce.com.

Also check our updates on Facebook and Twitter!

Our first title was published in October 2010. By March 2012, we had published ten titles, including:

- *The Tragedy of Lebanon: Christian Warlords, Israeli Adventurers, and American Bunglers,* by Jonathan Randal

- *The General's Son: Journey of an Israeli in Palestine,* by Miko Peled

- *Troubled Triangle: The United States, Turkey, and Israel in the New Middle East,* edited by William B. Quandt

- *War Diary: Lebanon 2006,* by Rami Zurayk

- *Where the Wild Frontiers Are: Pakistan and the American Imagination,* by Manan Ahmed, with a Foreword by Amitava Kuma

WHERE THE WILD FRONTIERS ARE

WHERE THE
WILD FRONTIERS ARE

PAKISTAN AND THE
AMERICAN IMAGINATION

MANAN AHMED

WITH PAINTINGS BY DAISY ROCKWELL
AND A FOREWORD BY

AMITAVA KUMAR

CHARLOTTESVILLE, VIRGINIA

JUST WORLD
BOOKS

Third printing, 2012.

Cartography by Lewis Rector and Moacir P. de Sá Pereira and © Just World Publishing, LLC. Overall book design by Lewis Rector for Just World Publishing, LLC. Typesetting and design of chapter headings by Jane Sickon for Just World Publishing, LLC.

**Publisher's Cataloging-in-Publication
(Provided by Quality Books, Inc.)**

Ahmed, Manan.
   Where the wild frontiers are : Pakistan and the
American imagination / by Manan Ahmed ; with a foreword
by Amitava Kumar and illustrations by Daisy Rockwell.
   p. cm.
   Includes bibliographical references.
   LCCN 2011926654
   ISBN-13: 978-1-935982-21-0
   ISBN-10: 1-935982-21-4

   1. Pakistan—Politics and government—1988-
2. Pakistan—Foreign relations—United States. 3. United
States—Foreign relations—Pakistan. 4. Pakistan—Press
coverage. 5. Terrorism—Prevention.   I. Title.

DS389.A36 2011   954.9105'3
                         QBI11-600087

To all at Sarai Sultan, Lahore,
and Drexel Ave., Chicago

Contents

Foreword, by Amitava Kumar — 13

Preface — 21

Title image: "Goggles 1: U.S. President George W. Bush, sporting a pair of goggles."

Map — 24

1 Terra In/cognito — 25

The purpose of this chapter is to begin with a sample of the main concerns of the blog: commentaries on U.S. foreign policy, critiques of the narratives prevalent in mainstream media, and attempts to offer historical context for political happenings. The happenings inside the social, cultural, and political landscapes of the United States and South Asia remain the focus, and the entries in this chapter lay out that terrain.

Title image: "Portrait of Osama bin Laden with a magical curtain."

2 Observe — 53

The legal, military, and cultural innovations (so to speak) of the Iraq War cast a long, long shadow within and outside the United States. As such, it was important to collect most of the worthwhile posts that deal with the Iraq War—as a distant observer—at the front of the book.

Title image: "Goggles 2: U.S. Secretary of State Condoleezza Rice, resplendent in goggles."

3 Resist — 69

Speaking to the media, metaphorically speaking, is a particular obsession of Chapati Mystery (CM). . . . These entries represent the need to resist the overabundance of pablum, which

*newspapers and magazines . . . force onto the ill-informed and the
misinformed.*

Title image: "Tee Vee: General Pervez Musharraf, hands out-
stretched."

4 Debate   85

*The debate over the "empire-ness" of America seems never-ending,
because it is a debate not over history but over representation. Early
in the life of CM, I wrote a series of posts in an effort to engage with
historian Bernard Porter's work on the British Empire. Those posts
form the backbone of this chapter, but the last post . . . is really a
summation of my own reading of America's past.*

Title image: "Buri Nazar Wale Tera Munh Hara: Roadtrip Devi."

5 Support   105

*This chapter is a collection of posts dealing with the support the Bush
White House showed to Pervez Musharraf and the antidemocratic
agenda in Pakistan. Of particular interest should be "To Dream a
Man" as well as the "Round-Up" series, which tried to document the
protests against Musharraf's rule as they unfolded in 2007 and 2008.*

Title image: "Jacqueline Kennedy and her sister, Lee Radziwill, take a
camel ride in Karachi, 1962."

6 Deny   145

*In April 2007, I began the "Tick Tock" series, which was a
countdown to the ouster of President Musharraf. . . . As the events
spiraled out of U.S. control, the administration continued to deny
that it had no idea what was going on in Pakistan.*

Title image: "Benazir 8: Benazir Bhutto greets her admirers shortly
before the bomb goes off."

7 Ignore   165

*The idea of unknowing (or deliberate ignorance) is at the heart of the
empire—and arguably, specifically, the American Empire. . . . The
posts in this chapter are bits of knowledge about Pakistan—sketches
of personalities and events—which collectively remain out of purview
of the empire.*

Title images (clockwise from top left): "General Ayub Khan, President
of Pakistan 1958–1969," "General Yahya Khan, President of Pakistan
1969–1971," "General Zia-ul-Haq, President of Pakistan 1977–1988,"
and "General Pervez Musharraf, President of Pakistan 2001–2008."

8 Friend 195

These bits of profiles, studies of persons, were often meant to introduce the American reader to the contestations over public memory and the ways in which pasts are continually erased in contemporary Pakistani politics. . . .

Title images (clockwise from top left): "Liaquat Ali Khan, Prime Minister of Pakistan 1947–1951, assassinated in 1951," "Zulfiqar Ali Bhutto, Prime Minister of Pakistan 1973–1977," "Nawaz Sharif, Prime Minister of Pakistan 1990–1993 and 1997–1999," "Benazir Bhutto, Prime Minister of Pakistan 1988–1990 and 1993–1996," and (centered) "Yousuf Raza Gilani, Prime Minister of Pakistan 2008–present."

9 Wrong 219

The plight of the minority communities in Pakistan . . . is at the very heart of the ideology of this state. Most of the posts in this chapter were written after the terrorist attack on an Ahmadi mosque in Lahore, which killed nearly 100 worshippers. These same concerns . . . were behind the assassination of the governor of Punjab in January 2011.

Title image: "Portrait of the notorious Karnataka sandalwood smuggler Veerappan."

10 Closers 243

There are two clusters of essays here. The three on Pakistan . . . try to highlight the internal and external ways in which Pakistan is framed and curtailed. The three dealing with the United States . . . form the central critique that I tried to develop during 2010–2011. . . .

Title image: "Dance Fever: Barack Obama cuts a rug."

Epilogue 277

Glossary 283

Foreword

Where was I when I heard that Osama Bin Laden had been killed?

I'm glad you asked. I was on Twitter.

More on Twitter in a moment, but first this: The philosopher Judith Butler has written, "In the United States we begin the story by invoking a first-person narrative point of view, and telling what happened on September 11." There are very few other narrative options available—there weren't when Butler was writing, in the immediate aftermath of the attacks, and the situation hasn't improved much since—for those who want to frame the story in broader terms. What I admire about writers from *elsewhere* is the sense they bring of other places and other lives. Not where *I* was at such-and-such a time, but what are the other histories that were unfolding at that moment, in a universe whose center isn't so close to mine? That is what I have found most illuminating about reading writers from places where, for instance, a bomb is more likely than snow to fall from the sky.

"If we have actionable intelligence about high-value terrorist targets and President Musharraf won't act, we will." This was Barack Obama, in 2007, speaking during his campaign for president. In the same speech, Obama also declared his desire to see American forces "getting out of Iraq and onto the right battlefield in Afghanistan and Pakistan."

Speaking soon after, at the YearlyKos conference in Chicago, Manan Ahmed had some news for Senator Obama, which was reported thusly by Dennis Perrin at the *Huffington Post*:

> Manan Ahmed got the party started with a direct, detailed critique of Barack Obama's statements about bombing Pakistan. Manan gave a meticulous power point presentation illustrating just how craven and idiotic Obama's remarks were. Unlike the fantasy Pakistan that Obama depicted, where President Pervez Musharraf is dragging his heels on fighting extremism, and it might take U.S. air strikes to focus his attention, the Pakistani army is currently battling extremists in the North Waziristan region, fighting that is comparable to what's happening in Iraq. Also, U.S. has already hit Pakistan, on

November 10, 2006, shelling a madrassa in Bajaur, which resulted in zero al-Qaida dead, but did manage to kill some of the seminary's children.[1]

That piece of news is still news, alas, even several years later. On that occasion, after his YearlyKos speech, the Democratic politicos arranged for Ahmed to attend a blogger meet-up with Obama, but, disappointingly, there was no discussion of AfPak. How one wishes Ahmed had been more widely heard then! The hundreds of drone attacks that have taken place since Obama took office might still have been carried out, but not with the unique mixture of ignorance and hypocrisy that marks U.S. foreign policy in the subcontinent. At the current moment, an informed discussion is now all the more necessary, especially after all the finger-pointing at Pakistan following the events in Abbottabad. What does history look like from the other side? Well, one way to think of the situation is to recognize that there *is* no other side. We don't live in opposed worlds; in fact, our worlds are linked. They are linked by the violence of war, by terrorist acts, but also by tourism, trade, and global migration. Not least, our worlds are linked by the knowledge as well as misinformation we share about each other; and both aspects of this equation are captured in the report in the *New York Times* about President Obama and the Internet: "At night in the family residence, an adviser said, Mr. Obama often surfs the blogs of experts on Arab affairs or regional news sites to get a local flavor for events. He has sounded out prominent journalists like Fareed Zakaria of *Time* magazine and CNN and Thomas L. Friedman, a columnist at the *New York Times*, regarding their visits to the region." (Mr. President, allow me to introduce to you Manan Ahmed. Please read also his comments on Thomas Friedman on pages 73, 77, and 80.)

Back to Twitter—whose creators originally, lest we forget, described it as a "micro-blog," though it soon became much more than that. I first heard about the Bin Laden killing on Twitter; I began reading what people were posting, comments as well as links to blogs. I would sometimes switch to Facebook. Then, still sitting in front of my computer, I watched President Obama deliver the news about the operation in Abbottabad. I woke up my wife to tell her what had happened and then went back to Twitter. Through my keyboard, I felt the intense heat on my fingertips; there was so much speculation. I participated in it myself, wondering whether Bin Laden would be buried in Guantanamo. Bin Laden had been killed, but where were the details? A few details had been provided that night when the president spoke, and then they were altered the next day, and again the day after that. In that process, we learned that just as much care as had been invested in the execution of the operation (or, perhaps, the operation of the execution?) in Abbottabad was also put into managing the disclosure of information about it afterward—a cocktail of drugs released, in a time-controlled manner, into the body politic.

On the Monday after the story from Abbottabad first broke, Twitter sent me to a characteristically sharp piece by *New Yorker* writer Jane Mayer that began, "Well, that didn't take long. It may have taken nearly a decade to find and kill Osama bin Laden, but it took less than twenty-four hours for torture apologists to claim credit for his downfall." It was also on Twitter that a couple of days later I read the novelistic observation made by Walter Kirn that it appeared that the president, like Kirn, had allowed himself to regress into a state of euphoria over the killing of the National Enemy: "As he uttered the pitiless words 'at my direction' in reference to the lethal assault, his educated features hardened slightly. *Harvard Law Review,* first blood."

My Twitter feed led me to several excellent blog posts in those days but what stood out was one written by Manan Ahmed. It was titled, simply, "At Sea." It appears as the Epilogue in this volume. The text comprises five short parts. I shall not take from you the sharp stab of surprise you will likely feel as you read the first of them—go and read it yourself! That piece disturbs our expectations, making us sit up and take notice of the assumptions that shape our thinking. (This is a signature move by Manan Ahmed.) He repeats it to great effect in the second part. The dislocation this time is closer to the subject at hand: Instead of resurrecting Osama bin Laden, our commentator raises the ghosts of all the innocents killed in Bin Laden's name. The rest of the piece offers yet more surprises. So far, Ahmed has been functioning as a historian of the present, but in the third brief section, for the first time, he steps deeper into the past. The fact that Bin Laden's code name during the operation was "Geronimo" serves as a pretext for a lucid excursus not into what is obvious—the imperial history's long-pursued "forgetting" of the genocidal wars waged upon native peoples—but into the entanglement of academic histories in that historical violence. The foundations of prestigious Ivy League institutions were built with profits from colonial piracy, he reminds us. How to provincialize America? That is his question there. (How to introduce under the name "Pakistan" not a cipher for the projection of any random prejudice but, instead, a pretext for a return to stubborn, lived realities? That is another way of asking the same question.) In the fourth section, very quickly, we are told about the provenance of the name "Abbottabad"—the name that, for some reason, American commentators during that first day, in a keenly Orientalizing gesture, kept pronouncing as if it were a name like Peshawar or Rawalpindi. In the fifth and final section, Ahmed reveals his polemical prowess by nailing the lie behind Salman Rushdie's call for retribution against Pakistan. What Ahmed says is terribly important, because, in this instance as so many other times before, he reminds the pundits of the difference between the State and the people. Ahmed here is our very own Raymond Williams, his astute writing populated with the lived histories of marginalized peoples, producing in his deft cultural commentary a testimonial to the struggles of all the Geronimos of the world.

When you read a good practitioner of any form of writing, you are also provided a lesson in the practice of the art itself. Here's what you learn from Manan Ahmed about blogging: Blogs should be short to be true to their medium; bound to the every day, they should appear like fresh blood on the bandage. Ahmed's posts possess both these qualities. As a blogger, Ahmed has too much quickness and wit to sound sententious; he is also far too self-conscious, or just plain honest, to ever wrap himself in sanctimony. These qualities not only make him eminently readable, they also push his writings, which deal with grim issues of culture and bloody politics, toward a kind of startling poignancy. I know very few writers who lead us to rich sentiment as a refinement of thought itself. Ahmed is one of them. There is also something else in this writing: It is youthful, hip, eager to reach out to the world. I don't mean I see here a naive friendliness. No, as should be deduced from the idea of the blog, there is a desire to engage in a conversation, sure, but it is a critical conversation, full of attitude. Think of the young Los Angeles–based South Asian hip-hop artist Chee Malabar singing: ". . . From Madras to Mombasa, / they harass us in our casa sayin', 'You Hamas huh?' / 'Yeah, like I learned to rap in a fucking Madrasah.'" Lastly, the blog posts that have been assembled for this book do not have the Saran Wrap of retrospective packaging: They possess the immediacy of newborn hope, and of a fear that is more like foreboding than settled despair. As a reader, coming upon these entries again, I'm instantly transported to the moment of their making. Thanks to Ahmed, you and I are alive to history.

Manan Ahmed wrote some of the texts that are curated into this book in Chicago; he wrote some in Lahore—and many of the others, in other great world cities. He wrote them between April 2004 and April 2011. But the histories with which they resound—histories of Pakistan, of the West, of the world—drape a period that is closer to 7 or 27 centuries long, rather than 7 short years. Those were, however, 7 key years in the record of Pakistan's encounter with the West.

A couple of days after Bin Laden's killing, a link from @nybooks, the Twitterfeed of the *New York Review of Books*, sent me to the text of a letter about Saul Bellow in Africa. The letter's writer mentioned that Bellow hadn't ever visited Africa when he wrote about it in *Henderson the Rain King*; strapped for cash, Bellow used the library instead. Later, when he had the money, Bellow went on a trip to Kenya, but not before he had taken himself to Abercrombie and Fitch, where he bought "a suitable bush outfit including the solar topee." On his first day in Africa, Bellow put on his new outfit and stepped out into the city. The locals were wearing "ordinary business clothes, which often included jacket and tie." And then, he spotted someone in the distance. Another white person, also in a bush outfit, walking toward him under a similar solar topee. When the man came closer, Bellow found out it was his pal Saul Steinberg.

When I read that letter, which was not about Abbottabad, I thought about Abbottabad. This was because in the figure of the exotic visitor, who has a certain mental notion of the natives, I saw all the experts who had a lot to say about Pakistan on television in those days. How much did they really know about the country, much less about the city where Bin Laden had been discovered? Did they speak any of the languages spoken by Pakistan's 180 million people? Had any of them engaged in any sustained study of the place or the people? These questions arose for me because each of these so-called experts—whether it be Bernard Lewis, Tom Friedman, or Greg Mortenson—has long fascinated Manan Ahmed. One of the pleasures of reading Manan Ahmed, like the great Eqbal Ahmad before him, is to witness the empire striking back. Again and again, we find our commentator calling out each pretender to knowledge.

Another pleasure of reading Ahmed, if "pleasure" is the word we want, is his rage at the injustices, especially against women and minorities, in his homeland. To read him on the persecution of Ahmadis; or the crimes against Christians, like Samuel Masih or Asiya Bibi, who were accused of blasphemy; or the murder of the liberal politician Salman Taseer, is to encounter the sorrow not of an expert but of a fellow citizen and a brother. The expert speaks from a distance; the expert sees like the State.

Or like a drone.

In contrast, Ahmed's writings rely on shared histories and shared hopes, and this allows them to become a staging ground for discussions among the readers of his *Chapati Mystery* blog. It is the reason why, unlike the experts who call for state action, Ahmed in his blog posts often demands a response from sections of the civil society, urging them to protest, write letters, or post blogs.

A few weeks after the attacks of September 11, I was on a visit to Pakistan. One evening, I was in Lahore, on my way to a dinner. The car belonged to a friend of mine who is a well-known editor and journalist. I was being driven through a crowded street, and I began to look at the row of roadside flower shops. The vendors had arranged roses, lilies, and marigolds under the light of bright, naked bulbs. Currency notes of various denominations were woven into fat garlands of tuberoses that hung from bamboo poles. There were dainty bracelets, made from small *chameli* blossoms, for guests to wear during the weddings that were under way all over the city.

Earlier in the evening, I had made my first contact with a leader of the fundamentalist jihadi group that, a few weeks later, was responsible for the kidnapping and then the murder of Daniel Pearl. I had given the man my name—which would have revealed to him that I was an Indian and a Hindu—but I wasn't worried about it much. I had told myself that the "fundos" would not harm a journalist. As the hours passed, there were more calls and cell-phone numbers exchanged, and a little before midnight, anticlimactically, the meeting was cancelled.

If I remember that evening, it is for something more ordinary that happened as I was sitting in the car looking at the flowers outside. My host's driver, Qasim—a slight man, in his late twenties, with a thin moustache—quietly asked me where I was visiting from. I told him that I was a writer living in the United States. He turned to me and said in Urdu, "The Americans are the true Muslims." I did not understand the logic behind this statement. The attacks in New York and Washington, D.C., were still fresh in everyone's minds. I had also seen the images from the streets of Lahore and the rest of Pakistan, of bearded men shouting slogans in support of the Taliban. Qasim said, "The Americans have read and really understood the message of the *Qur'an*." I was still baffled. But Qasim explained his point to me. He said, "*Woh log apne mulaazimo ke saath sahi salook karte hain. Woh unko overtime dete hain*" ["The Americans treat their workers in the right way. They pay them overtime"].

Ah, overtime! Fair wages, just working conditions, true democracy. There was little place on American television, amidst all that talk about terrorism, for this plain man's sublime understanding [Islam?] in Pakistan had not freed Qasim, and he wanted the minimum wage that for him was a tenet of his religious belief. As far as Qasim was concerned, it was others in his own country, fellow Muslims, who were the oppressors. On the other hand, the fair-minded employers of the poor in America, such as they were, when they died, were going to be gathered in the arms of the angels and wafted to heaven.

I like to tell that story when I do readings in the United States, because it challenges our tendency, supported by the tenured elite in the West, to make vast, faceless generalizations about entire nations and whole peoples. Manan Ahmed's memorable epitaph for such moronic thinking: "You are a hammer and everything else is a nail." As Edward Said and others were so successful in showing, there has been a venerable old tradition in the West of manufacturing an idea of the East. But in the aftermath of the September 11 attacks, the Manichean ideology of a liberal West engaged in battle with a militant East has provided cover for U.S. occupation in places like Iraq. Islamophobia is a part of the reason why this has been possible and why, equating Islam with terror, it has been possible for the United States to take steps that have curtailed civil liberties in this country. Consider the Rand Corporation report that said that although the number of terrorist incidents in the United States since September 11 was less than 50, the number of *yearly* terrorist incidents in the 1970s was closer to 70. According to that report, "from January 1969 to April 1970 alone, the U.S. somehow managed to survive 4,330 bombings, 43 deaths, and $22 million of property damage."[2]

If Manan Ahmed is to go ahead and put into practice the idea he suggests in one of his blog posts, of standing at a street corner with a placard saying "Ask Me About History of Islam," he would no doubt be a good person to explain what distinguishes the 1970s from the brutal last decade under Bush and Obama. But if Ahmed is not found at a street corner near you, then without a doubt the best alternative is buying—and reading—this book.

Amitava Kumar
Vassar College
May 2011

Foreword Notes

1 Dennis Perrin, "My Yearly Kos Diary," August 6, 2007, archived at http://huff.to/37FHo.
2 Quoted in Stephan Salisbury, "Citizen Alioune," archived at http://bit.ly/kUOw4f.

Preface

It is fortuitous that I am writing this preface in Lahore, Pakistan. It was here in February 2004 that I decided to begin the blog *Chapati Mystery* (*CM*). I was, at the time, engaged in a lengthy research trip for my dissertation amid dusty archives and rabid photocopiers. Iraq loomed large in Pakistan at the time—as did the war on terror. Reading the daily press, speaking with my family and friends, I felt stymied. There was a queer distancing between history and event, between time and narrative, in the daily conversations. Muslims were perpetually under attack. America was seemingly new at this imperialism business.

My decision to start a blog focused on history and culture, media criticism, and commentary—and where "the empire is resisted" (as an early subtitle claimed) emerged out of those conversations. I wanted to elongate the time in daily discussions. I wanted also to insist that the genealogies in question were intricately intertwined—the ones between the so-called colony and the designated empire. My intended audience was my younger brother, Mukarram.

It is worth lingering on that initial impulse. My brother, then in his mid-20s, asked a lot of questions in our conversations. He wanted to know the historical dimensions of commonly recalled terms in contemporary political—madrasas, imperialism, Khilafat Movement, and so forth. The newspapers and magazines, whether in the United States or Pakistan, were filled with spurious history or decontextualized information that either did not make any sense or contributed to even greater misunderstanding. I kept telling him to read this or that book—ones that, I realized, were not easily available in Pakistan, and the capacity to read them was even less readily available. As a graduate student, I was used to summarizing books for discussion (argument, evidence, and critique), and I thought that this blog would do that for him: provide summaries of books and some mindless fun posts as glue.

Blogging was not new to me. Back in 1998–99, I was part of an early experiment to do a "Pakistan Site of the Day" project, where we trolled the Yahoo! and AltaVista directories, found websites dealing with Pakistan, and gave them a small .gif file to display on their pages. The format was very akin to blogging (single entries, reverse chronology, archives) but it was all hand-coded, and we soon ran out of websites to highlight. Soon thereafter, a few other friends joined to begin a group blog focused on literary gossip, which was intelligible to the five people writing and reading the blog. It was great fun.

A conversation with some senior faculty at the University of Chicago (where I was a graduate student) provided the other impetus. I mentioned to a small group of faculty at a gathering the need to disrupt the narratives being peddled in the media by the likes of Fouad Ajami, Kenan Makiya, or Bernard Lewis. What about writing some op-eds for the *Chicago Tribune*? I asked. Clearly, you have a great standing in the scholarly community, and your words about Iraq's colonial history or earlier British efforts to bring "freedom" in the Muslim world would be valuable. However, the response from the faculty was a little chilled. The public space is already lost, they argued back. Fox News is already dominant. The major newspapers—the *New York Times* (*NYT*) or the *Washington Post* (*WaPo*), or even the *New Yorker*—led the selling of the war and were now busy reporting on its success (or at least on the rightness of the decision). There is no gain from writing opinion pieces or letters to the editor or any other act of engaging the public opinion. Plus, one of the faculty reminded me with arched eyebrows, you should be concentrating on your dissertation even as we all are concentrating on our respective scholarship.

Well.

For all the dedication to politics in poststructuralist and postmodern scholarship (postcolonial or subaltern), there was a marked resistance to speaking beyond the academy. Indeed, there was also a lot of angst at that moment about academic bloggers. They (the blogs) were going to ruin us, distract our attention, and prevent us from finishing, prevent us from getting hired, or prevent our tenure. The basic, fundamental advice was: Wait until tenure. I will not lie or pretend that these concerns were not material to me or that I did not think that these warnings were without merit. However, I was not convinced that tenure itself was some magical pill that would provide me with the platform or moral rectitude to speak out. It was just a safety net. The effort to be ethical in the world we inhabit cannot wait for better times and milder risks. I was pretty convinced, and I remain convinced, that those who remain silent before tenure will remain silent after tenure. Tenure, then, is immaterial. As for the other concerns—not finishing, getting a job, or receiving tenure—well, those worries will keep us all awake at night, blog or no blog.

The blog took off pretty early. But it wasn't just the blog. I made an effort to find a place in the Chicago radio community and submitted op-eds for various newspapers. I was lucky enough to attract some attention from the media in Britain and in Pakistan, which helped me write more broadly and with a wider audience in my mind.

My efforts, however well intentioned, would never have gained any traction (and you certainly would not be reading this work) if it weren't for the kindness and help of many dear friends: Daisy Rockwell (whose art brilliantly illuminates these pages) and Stephen D. Marlowe (who forever remains my American lodestar), Salmaan Hussain (who is the head archivist of *CM* and who first helped curate these files), Rajeev Kinra, Prithvi Chandra Shobhi Datta, Whitney Cox, Blake T. Wentworth, Elizabeth Angell, Gerard Siarny, Bulbul Tiwari, Aaron Bady, Sarah Neilson, Anil Kalhan, Rebecca Goetz, Sabrina Small, Jonathan Shainin, Ralph Luker, Jonathan Dresner, and Jerome McDonald. The *CM* family, however, extends to everyone else who left nearly 10,000 comments and made it possible for *CM* to exist to this day. I especially want to note: Rob Priest, Caleb McDaniel, Zack Ajmal, Conrad Barwa, Desi Italiana, Quizman, Umair Muhajir, Akbar, Nitin Pai, Sharon Howard, AbdulWahab, Biryanilady, and SaviyaC. And, finally, my heartfelt thanks go to Helena Cobban for being an amazingly patient publisher and a believer, and to Lilly Frost, Andrea Hammer, and Heather Wilcox at Just World Books.

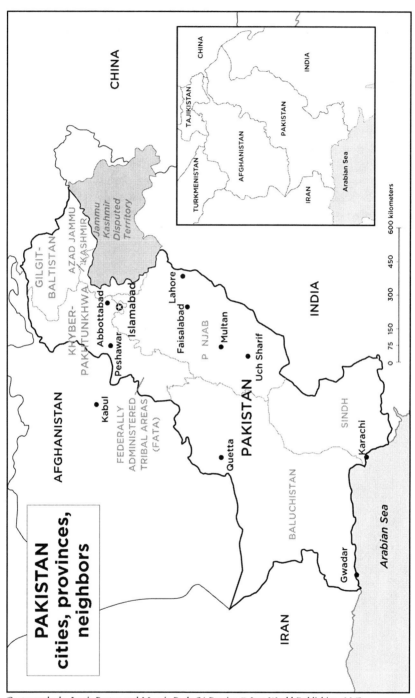

PAKISTAN
cities, provinces,
neighbors

CHINA

Jammu
Kashmir
Disputed
Territory

GILGIT-
BALTISTAN

AZAD JAMMU
KASHMIR

KHYBER-
PAKHTUNKHWA

Abbottabad

Peshawar

Islamabad

Lahore

Faisalabad

Multan

PUNJAB

Uch Sharif

INDIA

AFGHANISTAN

Kabul

FEDERALLY
ADMINISTERED
TRIBAL AREAS
(FATA)

Quetta

PAKISTAN

SINDH

Karachi

BALUCHISTAN

IRAN

Gwadar

Arabian Sea

0   75   150   300   450   600 kilometers

TURKMENISTAN

TAJIKISTAN

CHINA

AFGHANISTAN

PAKISTAN

INDIA

IRAN

Arabian Sea

Cartography by Lewis Rector and Moacir P. de Sá Pereira © Just World Publishing, LLC

1
Terra In/cognito

The first post on Chapati Mystery (CM), of course, is the point of entry, but the purpose of this chapter is to begin with a sample of the main concerns of the blog: commentaries on U.S. foreign policy, critiques of the narratives prevalent in mainstream media, and attempts to offer historical context for political happenings. The happenings inside the social, cultural, and political landscapes of the United States and South Asia remain the focus, and the entries in this chapter lay out that terrain. "God's Rule" and "Lawless in Pakistan" reveal the twin impulses behind CM, whereas "Objects in the Mirror" is a more reflective piece on my own stance and agency. "Strangers in the Night" is a summary of a talk I gave at a forum held at the University of Chicago in the aftermath of the Mumbai terror attacks.

Basmati Rice[1]
April 8, 2004

I had no idea Pakistan was important before September 11, 2001.

Listen to Condoleezza Rice's testimony before the Senate: "America's al-Qaida policy wasn't working because our Afghanistan policy wasn't working, and our Afghanistan policy wasn't working because our Pakistan policy wasn't working."

In fact, Pakistan was mentioned 27 times by Rice, while Iraq only got 26 shout-outs. So there. The World Trade Center in '93, the Kenya embassy bombings, the *Cole* attack in the Persian Gulf, and the Khartoum fiasco did not result in a comprehensive al-Qaida strategy. America had shoved Pakistan under the rug since 1989.

Indeed.

I am becoming a big fan of the various domino scenarios the administration brings out. Pakistan/Afghanistan/Taliban or Iraq/Syria/Iran/RestOfTheMiddleEast. States capitulate and change course, because the comprehensive game plan of the administration leaves them no recourse. Since when does Iraq invite Syria and Iran for democracy sleepovers?

More later.

Oh, and welcome to *Chapati Mystery*.

God's Rule[2]
July 26, 2004

There is a line uttered by a Texan candidate in the 2002 primary filmed in the PBS documentary *Last Man Standing: Politics—Texas Style*. Here is what the documentary shows him saying:

> Our God is not their God. First of all, the God of the Bible is a God of love and redemption, who sent His Son into the world to die for our sins. Allah tells people to die for him in order to get salvation. That is not our God.

The quote was summarized from Pat Robertson's rumination on Allah on CBN 700. As I watched him say it, I was reminded that, George W. Bush's rhetoric notwithstanding, the idea that the war on terror is a war between gods has taken root in the minds of most red-state Americans. I am not talking anything as sophisticated (ha!) as Sam Huntington's *Clash of Civilizations* but a simple dichotomous understanding of *Us v. Them*, where Us = Jesus, and Them = Allah.

My own rumination was sparked by Moacir's post on watching CNN's presentation on Flight 93 from *The 9/11 Commission Report*:

> Popularly, terrorism is connected (still) to the belief of Islam and the cultural identity/position of Arab/Middle-Easterner. In this case, the war on terror is no longer a posthistoricist war against a tactic (as conflict no longer exists). It is, instead, a cover for a good, old-fashioned kind of war against states (that have Arabs/Middle-Easterners) and based on beliefs (Islam, or, in the case of Iraq, a sort of perverted socialism).

The conservative argument, paraphrased by Dennis Miller nightly, is that we know *these* people attacked us. Why can't we call a spade a spade? They exclaim *Allah-o Akbar* and wage Jihad on us. Yet we are insisting on waging a secular, statist war on them. It makes no sense.

Is he right? Conventional wisdom (CW) is starting to tilt that way. And, in my opinion, nothing will shape CW on this topic more than *The 9/11 Commission Report*. Every pundit/politico is reading that to get the lowdown. Let us start there. In the "Why They Hate Us" section (written by B. Lewis, I am sure, because *no one else* is reading H. Pirenne anymore), they explain thusly the Islamic conception of "state":

> Islam is both a faith and a code of conduct for all aspects of life. For many Muslims, a good government would be one guided by the moral principles of their faith. This does not necessarily translate into a desire for clerical rule and the abolition of a secular state. It does mean that some Muslims tend to be uncomfortable with distinctions between religion and state, though Muslim rulers throughout history have readily separated the two.
>
> To extremists, however, such divisions, as well as the existence of parliaments and legislation, only prove these rulers to be false Muslims usurping God's authority over all aspects of life. Periodically, the Islamic world has seen surges of what, for want of a better term, is often labeled "fundamentalism."
>
> Denouncing waywardness among the faithful, some clerics have appealed for a return to observance of the literal teachings of the Qur'an and Hadith. One scholar from the fourteenth century from whom Bin Ladin selectively quotes, Ibn Taimiyyah, condemned both corrupt rulers and the clerics who failed to criticize them. He urged Muslims to read the Qur'an and the Hadith for themselves, not to depend solely on learned interpreters like himself but to hold one another to account for the quality of their observance.
>
> The extreme Islamist version of history blames the decline from Islam's golden age on the rulers and people who turned away from the true path of their religion, thereby leaving Islam vulnerable to encroaching foreign powers eager to steal their land, wealth, and even their souls.[3]

Muslims have no separation of Minbar and Throne. And parliaments/legislations somehow piss God off. Even this deeply informed panel cannot distinguish between Muslims or get a clear-headed picture of Islamic past. The reason is simple: Their job is to explain 9/11. Fourteen centuries of Islamic history have slowly and steadily built up to that exclamation point. The debates on Statehood, Role of Community, Pious Leadership, and Rights of Minorities that were fostered and cultivated over hundreds of years have only one question to answer: Why did 9/11 happen? And when you look at it this way, then all roads will indeed lead to Rome.

The intellectual origin of al-Qaida (Ibn Taymiyya and Sayyid Qutb) reflects a basic theme of the failure of an Islamic state and the intervention of a colonial empire. Yet the report avoids going into any of that. They hate us because the liberal-democratic state is un-Islamic. Can't get any more Clash of Civ than that, can you? Instead of being a war among states, this is a war on the conception of the state itself.

The blanket language of authority and *knowing* pervades the report. All Muslims have one idea—that the state should be God's Rule. There is still no way to avoid the *Jesus vs. Allah* scenario. Perhaps B. Lewis should have briefed the panel that such an Islamic state never existed. That there was no Golden Age. That rule and religion *have* been separate throughout the political history of Islam in the Middle East, North Africa, and South Asia. That all ancient and premodern kings and sultans proclaimed divine guidance—whether in Christian Europe, heathen Asia, or Kafir Africa. That Kingship and Godhead cannot part company. Our own president talks to God, for God's sake. That Muslims have sought legitimacy of rule in just as many diverse sources as Christians: mystics, custom, geography, and text. There is no recognition of that knowledge—or even how that complicates the debate on authority in Islam. Tragedy, they suppose, demands a straightforward answer from Islam. Yet no one simply asks what the conception of a Christian state had to do with the Jewish Holocaust caused by Catholic or Lutheran Germans.

Lawless in Pakistan[4]
March 21, 2007

The headlines everywhere in the United States are filled with the scandal of district attorneys fired for political reasons. The White House, the Justice Department, Congress, and pundits are immersed in pondering the consequences of such gross politicization of the law. Gone unnoticed, outside of a few reports, is another crisis involving the executive and the judicial branches that is tearing a nation apart. This one, though, has consequences far graver than Karl Rove's testimony before some committee. Two weeks ago, General Pervez Musharraf suspended the chief justice of the Supreme Court of Pakistan, Iftikhar Muhammad Chaudhry, on vague corruption charges. Since then, daily riots and protests have broken out in major cities; the government has tried to shut down TV stations that reported on these riots; the police have repeatedly assaulted the lawyers who are leading the process. Musharraf claims that this is much ado about nothing. But this crisis could bring down the government of General Musharraf of Pakistan.

I said government, but, of course, a more honest description of the state in Pakistan would be praetorianism, authoritarianism, or dictatorship. And no, I will not be crying if it does fall apart. The truth is, though, that with the support of freedom growers like Condi Rice and the White House, Musharraf is secure in doing what he can to stay in power. If that means turning Pakistan into a police state (if a sustainable argument can even be made that it is not already one) and imprisoning or vanishing his opponents, then he will do it. This is a pivotal year for him—2007. He has promised elections. He has promised to return democracy. He has promised to run in elections. But, like his earlier promises of shedding the military uniform or stepping down, he would have found a way—with the support of the White House—to keep himself in power as a military and civil commander while allowing some rudimentary nods toward electoral politics. How would he have managed that?

The same way that every single military regime in Pakistan has done it since 1958: with the support of an "independent judiciary," which would legitimize his actions as mere counterbalances to a "corrupt or runaway" legislature.

From Mohammad Ayub Khan to Mohammad Zia-ul-Haq to Musharraf, Pakistan's warrior-kings have made one fundamental claim to the public: that their particular act of suspension of democracy in Pakistan was ultimately *constitutional* and, hence, *for the benefit of the nation*. And they have had the support of the Supreme Court in making this claim—a support that gave them the necessary legitimacy to stay in power. To understand the current crisis in Pakistan—and *to recognize the ultimate blunder of Musharraf*—we have to look at the history and role of the Constitution in Pakistan, the historical involvement of the judiciary in the dismissal of democratic institutions, and the tensions between the three centers of power in Pakistani society that undergird this whole enterprise. Feel up to it?

It is all about the mythic Constitution.

It took nine years after independence, in 1956, for the Constitutional Assembly to come up with the first Constitution of Pakistan. That remarkable document survived a mere two years, as General Ayub Khan installed martial law in 1958. Another Constitution was drafted in 1962, suspended in 1969, and abrogated in 1972. Finally, the Constitution drafted in 1973 has held up to this day, albeit with this checkered past, summarized aptly by the CIA Factbook: suspended July 5, 1977; restored with amendments December 30, 1985; suspended October 15, 1999; restored in stages in 2002; amended December 31, 2003. It was Zia-ul-Haq who issued a dozen or so presidential ordinances, which were grafted as amendments to the Constitution in 1985. Among other things, they cemented the power of the executive to dismantle the legislative branch within the Constitution. Ask Benazir Bhutto and Nawaz Sharif about that.

It may appear counterintuitive from the teleology I give above, but the Constitution became an almost totemic document in the Pakistani political psyche. It may be that the very public and near-constant assaults increased its importance as a political document. Or, I can conjecture that it was one of the sole documents that sought to "define" Pakistan as a postindependent reality as opposed to a "once-future" promise of 1940. (Is it an Islamic state? a democratic republic? whose laws for whom? were all questions that had to be answered in that document. Of course they remain questions, still.) The keepers of this tattered almost-narrative—the Supreme Court of Pakistan—have built their own prestige on the back of this document by honing a unique relationship to Pakistan's self-identification.

The first blow was struck in 1954, when Governor General Ghulam Muhammad dissolved the Constituent Assembly. Maulvi Tamizuddin Khan, the president of the assembly, appealed to the Supreme Court, asking it rule on the legitimacy of such an action—was the legislative branch a legitimate member of the government? Chief Justice (CJ) Muhammad Munir sided with the executive and declared that the legislative served only at the pleasure of the executive, because Pakistan was a dominion state and the British Raj still applied. Four years later, in October 1958, President Iskander Mirza killed off the 1956 Constitution and declared martial law with General Ayub Khan as the martial law administrator. The case *State vs. Dosso* came before CJ Munir again. Using Hans Kelsen's *Grundnorm* thesis, the Supreme Court upheld the coup. The very next day, General Ayub Khan exiled the president, and the template was fixed for futures to come.

In 1977, the Supreme Court unanimously upheld martial law under General Zia-ul-Haq. In 1981, he instituted the Provisional Constitutional Order and asked all justices to retake their oaths. Those who refused were fired or retired. This was to ensure future accommodation of any wishes of the chief military officer of the country. The Supreme Court, for example, rejected all challenges and upheld the 1988 dissolution of the National Assembly by General Zia. In 2000, Musharraf stuck to the playbook by sacking any judge who refused to take his oath to his regime.

The basis of this symbiotic relationship between the general and the court lies in the structure of power and influence in Pakistani society. The tiers in this pyramid are the military, which is the largest employer, the largest landholder, and has the longest duration in power; the civil bureaucracy, which traces back to the Raj, though much weakened during Musharraf's tenure; and the largely land-based elite. Functioning between these tiers are functional classes, like the lawyers who have parlayed their unique access to military, civil, and landed elite into their necessary role as brokers. The court is apex of such brokerage. It has relied especially on the hagiography of the Constitution to bolster its power. The generals, eager to have any official stamps on their chests, have in turn portrayed the court as the last bastion of truly apolitical and patriotic actors in Pakistan—meaning that when scandal does erupt around the court, it has far greater reverberations.

To return to CJ Iftikhar Muhammad Chaudhry and Pervez Musharraf's blunder. A letter was circulated via emails and blogs that accused the CJ of corruption, cronyism, and abuse of public trust. There was nothing terribly unique in any of the assertions. In fact, upon first reading it, I was convinced that it was a satirical piece, because it perfectly described the behavior of every person of power in Pakistan. Surprisingly, the state seized this letter and filed a complaint against the CJ and, before any investigation was launched, removed him from office. The state, in fact, agreed that the CJ of Pakistan was corrupt and abused the public trust.

I can assume that CJ Chaudhry could not be fully trusted to toe the line in this crucial year and had to go in any case—the letter providing a handy excuse. The problem is that after years of building the judiciary as the last bastion of honesty, the state pulled the rug out under its own feet. It undermined its own claims and attacked the public trust in the Supreme Court. The reaction was swift and massive—with public protests and demonstrations and speeches. The state still could have contained the damage; instead it made all the wrong moves in the initial stages of the scandal. It made unsubstantiated charges, changed its own story, and attacked the press and the lawyers. In a very short period of time, it managed to delegitimize itself in the eyes of the public, create a sharp division with the judiciary and alienate, perhaps irrevocably, itself from the section of the population that has helped it maintain law and order—the brokering legal community.

This is perhaps the endgame for the general. However he survives this, he cannot rely on the legitimating authority of the Supreme Court. The street unrest will trigger other interests out as well—the Islamist parties, the dormant political opposition, the Muttahida Quami Movement (MQM), and, maybe, attention from the Democratic Congress of United States.

While in the United States, Alberto Gonzales wrote memos justifying torture and suspension of the Geneva Convention and habeas corpus and . . . nothing, there were no consequences. But when he fired eight lawyers, all voices proclaimed that he should be ex–attorney general in about 3 days. The general in Pakistan should have known: Do whatever, but don't fuck with the lawyers.

Wild Frontiers of Our Localized World[5]
August 2, 2007

How can Barack Obama be just as wrong as George W. Bush?

Yesterday, Obama delivered a major speech at the Woodrow Wilson International Center for Scholars.[6] I believe that, despite its virtues, it is overall an erroneous reading of the world's geo-political landscape, that his understanding of terrorism is deeply flawed, and that his specifics on action in Pakistan should bring a smile to any fellow at the American Enterprise Institute.

The speech contains Obama's boilerplate mixture of poetic flourishes, declarative statements, and heavy-handed hypotheticals (binary positions only, please). Here are his basic critiques of U.S. foreign policy: Iraq was the wrong war; we did not finish the job in Afghanistan; we lacked international cooperation and diplomacy; we lost the battle for the hearts and minds. In response to these failures, he provides a five-pronged policy for his presidency:

> When I am president, we will wage the war that has to be won, with a comprehensive strategy with five elements: getting out of Iraq and on to the right battlefield in Afghanistan and Pakistan; developing the capabilities and partnerships we need to take out the terrorists and the world's most deadly weapons; engaging the world to dry up support for terror and extremism; restoring our values; and securing a more resilient homeland.

I will largely restrict my comments to the first element—leaving Iraq for Pakistan. A couple of casual observations. First: This "getting out of Iraq" business is just not gonna happen as envisioned by many Democrats. Colin Powell told many deliberate lies to this world, but he said one thing right: You break it, you own it. However, once Obama suggests that we get our troops out of Iraq only to send them to Pakistan, it makes an ill-advised proposition calamitous. Normally, I would also have cheered the idealism in his speech. For example, he is surely picking up on something I wrote here many moons ago when he states:

> I will also launch a program of public diplomacy that is a coordinated effort across my administration, not a small group of political officials at the State Department explaining a misguided war. We will open "America Houses" in cities across the Islamic world, with Internet, libraries, English lessons, stories of America's Muslims and the strength they add to our country, and vocational programs. Through a new "America's Voice Corps," we will recruit, train, and send out into the field talented young Americans who can speak with—and listen to—the people who today hear about us only from our enemies.

But when read in the context of his whole speech, the idealism remains a plain contradiction. Which world will be receptive to America's Voice Corps after we would have invaded three countries in half a decade?

I have been a fan of Obama's candidacy for a long while—I am his constituent—but I would have expected this speech to come from Charles Krauthammer. For seven years, millions have been hoping that a change in the White House will be a change in our policies at home and abroad, the hope being that a democratic administration will not start preemptive wars nor freeze the world out from our deliberations. Yet, here we stand. Clinton wants to invade Iran, and Obama wants to invade Pakistan. It appears that there is unanimity in our political spectrum as far as global terrorism and our reaction to it is concerned. We clearly know and understand who our enemy is, what he wants, and how will we combat him—no inquiry, no analysis, no knowledge of the local is needed or required.

Point, if you can, to the difference between this spurious understanding of terrorism from Obama to anything you can find amid the neoconservative library. Compare, as well, the blanket and generalized statements, the assertions of fallacies, and the monolithic construction of "their" narratives:

> Al-Qaida's new recruits come from Africa and Asia, the Middle East, and Europe. Many come from disaffected communities and disconnected corners of our interconnected world. And it makes you stop and wonder: When those faces look up at an American helicopter, do they feel hope, or do they feel hate?
>
> We know where extremists thrive: in conflict zones that are incubators of resentment and anarchy. In weak states that cannot control their borders or territory or meet the basic needs of their people. From Africa to central Asia to the Pacific Rim—nearly 60

countries stand on the brink of conflict or collapse. The extremists encourage the exploitation of these hopeless places on their hate-filled websites.

And we know what the extremists say about us. America is just an occupying army in Muslim lands, the shadow of a shrouded figure standing on a box at Abu Ghraib, the power behind the throne of a repressive leader. They say we are at war with Islam. That is the whispered line of the extremist who has nothing to offer in this battle of ideas but blame—blame America, blame progress, blame Jews. And often he offers something along with the hate: a sense of empowerment and maybe an education at a madrasa, some charity for your family, some basic services in the neighborhood. And then, a mission and a gun.

We know we are not who they say we are. America is at war with terrorists who killed on our soil. We are not at war with Islam. America is a compassionate nation that wants a better future for all people. Most of the world's 1.3 billion Muslims have no use for bin Laden or his bankrupt ideas. But too often since September 11, the extremists have defined us, not the other way around.

This theory of global Islamic terrorism—poverty, chaos and conflict, disjunctive communities, the charismatic whisperer—is the one that Bernard Lewis has told and retold millions of times, despite all scholarship and evidence to the contrary. Lewis's model—derived from the Hashashin of Syria, a.k.a. the Old Man of the Mountain—has this narrative: Islamdom and Christendom are embroiled in a crusade. The charismatic Old Man of the Mountain takes poor and abandoned young Muslims and spirits them away to the mountain hiding ground, where he has built a paradise of beautiful girls and virginal waters. He feeds them, sends aid to their families, shows them tantalizing glimpses of "paradise," and brainwashes them with the help of hashish. Eventually, they are given a suicide mission to go kill and gain access to that paradise they briefly encountered—with virgins. Lewis had peddled this particular reading of Islamic terrorism as early as 1991, but it was only after September 2001 that this emerged as the definitive understanding of the "Why do they hate us?" mind bender. Despite being completely ahistorical, it cleverly explained the appeal and command of someone like Osama bin Laden, confirmed the basic truth of the civilizational clash, and also negated any culpability in the American history.

Needless to say, there is no place for facts in this narrative, and the underlining assumptions remain unshakeable. For example, our enemy cannot be rational or modern—Muhammad Atta or Shahzad Tanveer or Kafeel Ahmed notwithstanding. Why not? Because modernity and enlightenment are forces that, by definition, should have no space for such actions. Consider further that in Obama's retelling, Abu Ghraib is not an actual war crime but something extremists "say"—tripping on hashish, no doubt. Similarly, our occupation of Iraq is not an imperial reality but a mirage of elaborate lies. In effect, the "whispers" of the extremists, devoid of any truth, remain the hypnosis of the Old Man of the Mountain. All we have to do is to proclaim them as such—call them out as lies—and the spell will be broken. The unmistakable conclusion of that narrative, of course, escapes Obama and others who still cling to such theories. We will have to end the incubators in London, in Amsterdam, in Madrid, and in Bali—surely by invading these countries that provide safe havens to these terrorists.

This national discourse comes from a deep Orientalism that has been a staple of our political lives prior to and since that "bright and beautiful Tuesday morning." It is what enables us to question the sanity and the patriotism of anyone who dares raise the long history of American involvement across the globe as a contributing factor. It enables us to collapse real geographies from Leeds and Glasgow to Karachi and Islamabad into "wind-swept deserts and cave-dotted mountains."

Pakistan, of course, is the main thrust of Obama's speech. Here is his declaration: *Al-Qaida has a sanctuary in Pakistan.* Note that the word "sanctuary" necessarily implies state protection and safety and that "Pakistan" indeed refers to the entire country. To reinforce his point, he states again, "[Al-Qaida is] training new recruits in Pakistan." These could easily be the exact words used by Bush to describe Afghanistan right before the U.S. invasion in 2001. And *invasion* is the only conclusion one can reach when Obama states that he wants to "*deploy* troops to the "right battlefield in Afghanistan and Pakistan." The only way I know of deploying troops to a sovereign nation is by invading said nation.

Obama demands his preemptive strike both as justification for the World Trade Center attacks and because Pakistan has not proven a good enough ally:

> As president, I would make the hundreds of millions of dollars in U.S. military aid to Pakistan conditional, and I would make our conditions clear: Pakistan must make substantial progress in closing down the training camps, evicting foreign fighters, and preventing the Taliban from using Pakistan as a staging area for attacks in Afghanistan.
>
> I understand that President Musharraf has his own challenges. But let me make this clear. There are terrorists holed up in those mountains who murdered 3,000 Americans. They are plotting to strike again. It was a terrible mistake to fail to act when we had a chance to take out an al-Qaida leadership meeting in 2005. If we have actionable intelligence about high-value terrorist targets and President Musharraf won't act, we will.

One should remind Obama and the U.S. Congress, which just passed such a conditional bill, that Pakistan is, in clear and evident fact, fighting a war in Waziristan—with scores of military casualties seemingly every day. One can also remind him that since the Lal Masjid stand off—July 3—there have been a dozen suicide bombings across Pakistan killing more than 200 civilians, almost keeping pace with Baghdad. One can further remind him that Pakistan has indeed allowed U.S. military strikes on its sovereign territory, even with questionable intelligence. On November 10, 2006, U.S. missiles hit a madrasa in Bajaur aimed at killing the elusive No. 2 of al-Qaida but managed mainly to kill children. They must all be casualties of Pakistan's soft focus in the war on terror.

To be crystal clear, Obama suggests that a country that is a sovereign nation and ally, has full nuclear capability, has the ability to carry out nuclear attacks, has the ability to give nuclear technologies to the card-carrying-member-of-the-Axis-of-Evil-next-door Iran, has an unpopular dictator supported and maintained by the United States, has deployed 100,000 troops across its northwestern borders, has suffered thousands of casualties—army and civilians—carrying out the global war on terror, has seen its cities and deserts flood with the detritus from the forgotten war going on in Afghanistan but has nonetheless maintained complete compliance by killing and capturing many key members of al-Qaida . . . should be invaded.

I can only conclude that strategically, conceptually, operationally, and politically, this is as bad a policy statement as was introduced in March 2003. It ought to be self-evident, according to Obama even, that if invading a country of 30 million, who were under severe sanctions for more than a decade, at false pretense was a "wrong war," then invading a country of 165 million, with nuclear power, could prove a slightly more egregious blunder.

I could plumb further depths of this inanity by showing how flawed Obama is on his reading of Saudi Arabia, Israel, and Iran and how his diplomatically mature outlook fails to even mention India or China—two major powers of the region—but I will stop here.

Instead, let's go back and ask this simple question: How can Obama be just as wrong as Bush? Or, more specifically, why is it that the world from Obama's or Bush's eyes appears no different?

There is no doubt that there are very real enemies intent on carrying out their own civilizational mission. But instead of focusing on the historical, cultural, religious, or political specificities of these enemies, our public discourse remains intent on reproducing imagined entities—and the deep Orientalism I mentioned above surely plays a significant role in this. This discourse makes potent, global actors out of local thugs. More important, it obfuscates any distinction between the local thug and someone like Osama bin Laden. It keeps alive our prejudices and assumptions about Islam. The fact that Bush did not know of the presence of Shia and Sunni sects in Islam (in Iraq or in general) is not simply comment on his being dull. He is a sharp man. He has many, many advisers who know and can comprehend "difference." That fact is actually a revelation of our systematic conceptualization of that uniform Other—the Muslim Terrorist. The thought that there may be differences and details and histories simply *shouldn't* have occurred to him. It is no surprise that the clash of civilization operates not on differences but on sameness—whether in Us or Them. When Bush stated, "You are with us or you are against us," he was not being brash and belligerent—he was being honest.

Similarly, the hegemonized "imperialism" of America in the Islamist discourse cannot differentiate between actors near or far, nor can it understand any history or geo-political narrative. In their discourses, centuries of corruption and weakness in Islam will be swept away only by the cleansing power of their militant actions. The Muslim victims, Shia or Sunni or anything, are no different from the infidels, because they really are no *different* in their eyes. The West is just as monolithic and undifferentiated. Osama bin Laden will surely flunk a basic history or cultural test of United States. He cannot tell you the difference between a Protestant and a Roman Catholic or between the imperialisms of the Ottoman Empire, the British Empire, or the conceived American Empire. Such distinctions are immaterial to his Occidentalism.

All this is no great insight. We cannot explain how we are able to systematically generate a comprehension of the world we inhabit without examining the ways in which we construct our knowledge. Why are we, 4 years after our indefensible invasion of Iraq and nearly 6 years after the attack on us, still unable to comprehend our enemies as capable, rational, modern agents? Every new instance of a new cell in our modern cosmopolitans, of a doctor or an engineer blowing himself up, is met either with universal bewilderment or universal condemnation of the very soul of Islam. Our terrorists, even when they are born in Bradford or housed in Hamburg, remain in the wild frontier of our imagination. When terrorism happens in the domestic context, at Virginia Tech, for example, we seek pathologies and sickness and material differences. When the same act is repeated in a crowded Baghdad market or a fruit stand in Islamabad, we summarily assign blame to an ever-lengthening chain of transmission that inevitably goes back to the whisperer in caves afar. Islam, we conclude, is still medieval—it needs rationality, science, a reformation.

When Obama refuses to even *know* the facts of Pakistan or Iran or Saudi Arabia, he is not being careless; he is just reaffirming the dominant discourse of American imperialism. Our actions, preemptive or postpartum, leave us with nothing more than empty platitudes of God-given Freedom or New Hope. We are reluctant to know. We do not want to investigate, to learn, or to understand. We insist on our global, flat, and binary world, no matter how many facts pile up proving us wrong.

Unless we decide to get local, to pay attention to local narratives, facts, histories, realities, languages, religions, ethnicities, cultures, and so forth, we will remain in this deeply flawed discourse. So the answer to my question—How can Obama be just as wrong as Bush?—is simple enough: There is only one answer available at the moment.

Objects in the Mirror[7]
October 15, 2007

I.

But, another inflection, if the testament is always made in front of witnesses, a witness in front of witnesses, it is also to open and enjoin, it is also to confide in others the responsibility of their future. To bear witness, to test, to attest, to contest, to present oneself before witnesses. For Mandela, it was not only to show himself, to give himself to be known, him and his people, it was also to reinstitute the law for the future, as if, finally, it had never taken place. As if, having never been respected, it were to remain, this arch-ancient thing that had never been present, as the future even—still now invisible.

—Jacques Derrida[8]

Michael Rubin is coming to speak on our campus tomorrow. Rubin's presence on this campus is not really a surprise. We have hosted Richard Perle (twice), Doug Feith, Bill Kristol, and numerous other figures from the American Enterprise Institute. Whether the Straussian connection has anything to do this with or not is irrelevant, because these folks have enjoyed a prestigious platform for their ideas. I have avoided direct attendance in any of these talks. Largely because I knew what they would say (having read their copious public writings), and I knew that I had no patience to listen to them. I also didn't feel that it was my personal responsibility to provide a corrective to their view—that is why they tenure smart folks and area specialists, after all. Surely, they would take care of it.

Yet I felt an unusual amount of anger and frustration when I read this latest email announcing Rubin's talk, "Preventing a Nuclear Iran"—these people, having led us into one war on false pretenses, outright lies, and devious half-truths are now expecting us, again, to fall into line. But I was still not sure that I wanted to attend or do anything. I had plenty of rationalizations for ignoring Rubin. What difference does it really make? He has been consistent in his calls for invasion of Iran since 2002, so he won't say anything new. The Iraq War is plenty unpopular, so I am sure that campus lefties will grill him. The many experts of Middle East Studies on campus will surely hold a competing event—a teach-in, perhaps. There are many here who will do the needful. I further rationalized that my absence was, in itself, a protest (those embedded silences in the Foucault's discursive formations).

I am, myself, devoid of agency. I cannot vote for leaders who will come and restore sanity in the government. Sure, I can use the spending power of my wallet to support candidates, issues, and I do.

Maybe I will post something on my blog.

Enough?

The war against Iraq was not thrust upon this public. We were groomed by months of commentaries, Sunday talk-shows, op-eds, *New York Times* cover stories, *New Yorker* essays, *Washington Post* reports . . . pundithed to death by our public intellectuals. The alternatives were always grave and always noble. Terrorism. Democracy. Fear. Hope. Throughout it all, we were confronted with unassailable truths—about Saddam Hussein, about weapons of mass destruction (WMDs), about Iraqi desire for "freedom." Throughout it all, there was no history or any past that was relevant except the history and the past of tyranny.

The aftermath has not been so kind to these received wisdoms (though the wise men have escaped unscathed). But these same truths are being bandied about again. Iran is going to have nuclear capability; it cannot. It is interfering with our mission in Iraq; it mustn't. It is the source of all our troubles in Iraq, in Palestine, in Lebanon, in Afghanistan; it should be stopped. These truths can, at the very least, be contested. Yet the old hoary voices that screamed against the Iraq War are the only ones against opening the Iranian theater. The rest of the American public, expert or otherwise, plays mute witness.

II.

> *That's your answer to everything, Dude. And let me point out—pacifism is not— look at our current situation with that camelfucker in Iraq— pacifism is not something to hide behind.*
> —Walter Sobchak, *The Big Lebowski* (1998)

I was invited to speak at Edison, in Piqua, Ohio, in conjunction with the Dayton Literary Peace Prize—well, more like threatened. Steve Marlowe, a.k.a. Farangi, is a hard man to ignore. I was asked to speak on something that vaguely corresponded with the theme.

I chose to talk about Jamaluddin Afghani (1838–1897). Admittedly, this was outside my area of "expertise." I was, however, very clear with my audience. I told them that, insofar as one can accuse me of being a historian, I was a medievalist. My expertise was restricted to 13th-century Indo-Persian histories. Still, I wanted to do something topical, and Afghani's brand of violent anti-imperialism and his version of the "clash of civilizations" seemed a worthy topic for a 20-minute discussion—especially in a comparison of sorts with the Lewis/Huntington model. I told the audience to feel free to dismiss me.

My initial draft had perhaps too much navel gazing. I postulated that one can borrow and reapply Fukuyama's phrase "The End of History" to the ways in which Islam is dehistoricized in current discourse. I suggested that it is the task of the historians of Islam and the Middle East to insist on injecting history—however complicated or contradictory it may be—into our public lives. A friend, commenting on my draft, told me that it was more or less a rant. I agreed and excised it. Instead, I concentrated on the clash of narratives and the idea of neomedievalism, hoping to give the audience tools to see the structures that enable the same exact dialectic cast and recast again and again.

I can honestly admit that the Q&A was humbling. The questions were probing, direct, engaged with my material, and, often, difficult to answer. I realized as well that there is a lack of basic historical knowledge (Colonialism? Empires? Post World War II Asia?) that historians can very easily fill—without getting all "political" and stuff. Popular history print books, blogs, may not be the best vehicles for such dissemination. Why not bring back that late-19th and early-20th-century staple, public lectures and debates? Such events, when they currently happen, are tied mainly to authors plugging their books—academic or popular—or to the think-tank crowd. Why not untether that? I, for one, left feeling the need to strap on an "Ask Me About History of Islam" placard and stand on a street corner. Perhaps not my brightest idea.

III.

> *Bol, ki thoda waqt bahut hai/Jism-o-zuban ki maut se pehle*
> *(Speak, this brief hour is long enough/Before the death of body and tongue)*
> —Faiz Ahmed Faiz, revolutionary Urdu poet
> (translation by Agha Shahid Ali)

This past weekend, I attended half the Academic Freedom conference. Tony Judt's remarks—on the place of the university as the last bastion of "public intellectual"—impressed me the most. I didn't wholly agree with him that the university was the "only" such space (um, the Internet), but I see the need to protect the university as a sacred space wherein speech cannot be regulated, made to surrender to conformity or power. (Akeel Bilgrami gave a damning account of Columbia.) Judt also provided a cautionary tale on the lack of power that a typical nontenured academic has in today's climate. I took it to heart.

I must focus on the job market. A tenure-track gig at a Research I institute is surely what I need. Of course, I can keep this blog going. Do the odd political post. Rail about this or that comment from this or that politician about this or that war. It should be enough to give me a sense of moral smugness. And life is busy. And full. Must we all, individually, find time to do battle with information warriors like Michael Rubin? There always exists the possibility of inaction itself as a form of action. I know this. We all know this.

Right? I am not convinced.

I will set up shop outside Rubin's talk tomorrow. It is the least I can do. I will be joined by others, but no expert of Middle East history at Chicago has decided to historicize the present, so far.

Strangers in the Night[9]
January 15, 2009

I.

Yesterday, at her Senate confirmation hearing, Senator Hillary Clinton faced a number of questions about Pakistan and Afghanistan. Her most detailed conversation was with Senator John Kerry, who will head the powerful Senate Foreign Relations Committee. Senator Kerry spoke about his trip to South Asia, in the immediate aftermath of Mumbai attacks:

> We do not live there. We don't live in the community, in a hamlet, in a small town, pocket, whatever you want to call it. And so we're not there often at night. They are. And the night often rules with the insurgencies.[10]

It is a profoundly illuminating statement. The interplay of light and dark, day and night. The reference to hamlets and pockets. Insurgency—the lexical contribution of the Iraq War, which continues to hold sway. They live there. We don't. That language of globalization that rules the pages of the *Wall Street Journal* and the *New York Times* is distinctly absent. These are not interconnected communities that stretch across national borders—these are inwardly focused, premodern histories. To further explain, Senator Kerry mentioned that he has been doing a lot of reading recently—readings that impressed upon him the importance of "tribalism": "We honored tribalism when we dealt with the Northern Alliance and initially went in to Afghanistan. We really haven't adequately since." He recommended that Senator Clinton read Rory Stewart's travelogue of walking across Afghanistan and Pakistan, *The Places in Between.* And also Janet Wallach's biography of Gertrude Bell entitled *Desert Queen: The Extraordinary Life of Gertrude Bell: Adventurer, Advisor to Kings, Ally of Lawrence of Arabia.* Let that title wash all over you. Luxuriate in it.

Senator Clinton responded warmly to Kerry's literary suggestions:

> Sitting here today, when I think about my trips to Afghanistan, my flying over that terrain, my awareness of the history going back to Alexander the Great and certainly, the imperial British military and Rudyard Kipling's memorable poems about Afghanistan, the Soviet Union, which put in more troops than we're thinking about putting in—I mean, it calls for a large dose of humility about what it is we are trying to accomplish.[11]

The historian in me is fascinated by these teleologies at display: Alexander to the British to the Soviets to United States. A timeline of invaders and conquerors who, I assume, only abided [during] the day and not the night. There is the unapologetic emphasis on the romantic and the Orientalist—a vocabulary of time and space that does not mesh, at all, with our own. I do not know if our senators realized that this is also, explicitly, a teleology of failed imperial enterprises. Not the precedent, I am sure, they'd want to invoke.

But the tribalism espoused by Senator Kerry is also part of this now-defunct mode. It stands for those "Others" every colonial power has ever imagined into being. To fight their wars. The burden of tribalism is the burden of violence on colonial subjects—be they the Hindus and Muslims under British colonial rule in the early decades of the 20th century or the Sunnis and Shias in Baghdad under the surge. The colonial histories are written in that particular language of violence. These are the violent colonial solutions to political problems, to be exact.

II.

Reading the U.S. press and Senators Kerry and Clinton on Pakistan is to know that Pakistan does not exist as a coherent nation-state. It seems to comprise undifferentiated security actors (Musharraf/Kayani, Karzai, Northern Alliance, Taliban, Pakistan military, Inter-Services Intelligence [ISI]) operating in a volatile soup. It is constantly claimed that the state—whether civil or military—does not control its own western and southwestern territories, a claim that enables the United States to conduct drone attacks as well as military incursions into the country. In the first seven months of 2008, there were five drone strikes inside Pakistan. Since August, there have been more than 30, some as deep as 25 miles into Pakistani territory and deadly—killing 50 people in four attacks in September, alone.

But Pakistan does have a history as a nation-state, in fact. And it is not the history of Alexander's arrival to the Indus Valley in 326 BCE. Let me give you a brief recount. From 1999 to 2008, we supported the military dictatorship of General Pervez Musharraf—he was the devil we knew and liked. From 2002 to 2008, the same devil presided as vast swathes of his country were converted into a war zone. In 2005, to suppress the protonationalist uprising in Baluchistan, he used the same tactics that were being practiced across the border in Afghanistan: bombing civilian enclaves, missile assassinations, heavy military footprint. As he methodically destroyed the claimants for an engaged and equal partnership for Baluchistan in the federal regime, he created the political space for the emergence of new actors—the Mehsud tribe in Waziristan. As a result, Pakistan, by the end of 2008, faces several civil wars—in the northwest, it faces the development of self-declared Taliban regime, which is hoping to enforce Shari'a. In the southwest, it faces the proliferation of both protonationalist and terrorist groups. In the city of Karachi, there is the systematic effort to expel Afghan/Pakhtun immigrants by the ethnic party, MQM.

Previously, we supported two other decade-long military dictatorships: General Zia-ul-Haq (1977–1988); during whose tenure we fought our hot Cold War in Afghanistan and during whose tenure we excused a rampant policy of

Sunnification and militarization; and Field Marshal Mohammad Ayub Khan (1958–1969), whose tenure saw the effective killing of democratic institutions and the highlighting of Kashmir as the central issue of Pakistan. We supported all three men. They came to our capital, spoke to the Congress, enjoyed days and nights as our esteemed friends. Overall, in the 61 years of existence, we supported 30-plus years of military rule in Pakistan. Let me restate this: The United States has consistently supported the elimination of any democratic development in Pakistan since 1947. During the civilian administrations, we routinely ignored Pakistan or imposed sanctions. If Pakistan lacks coherence as a nation-state to Senators Kerry and Clinton, they can look to these specific histories for explanation. Alexander the Great cannot help them.

III.

In the aftermath of Mumbai attacks, the world has found yet another reason to doubt the sustainability of Pakistan, doubt the intentions of the people and the state, doubt their commitment to being peaceful global citizens. These doubts, those proclamations, some of the harsh denouncements of the Indian media were heard loudly and clearly across Pakistan. The bellicosity—apparent even in the flyer for this panel—generated its own predictable response. The military, which had finally lost all credence, is slowly coming back in business. It is the protector. It is the sustainer of the national myths.

The Pakistanis are also attuned to the silences. They note that in the teleology of modern terror—NYC, Madrid, London, and now Mumbai—there is no mention of Lahore and Islamabad. The September 20 blast at the Marriott, Islamabad, is a clear precursor to the tragedy at Taj, Mumbai. It, too, was a site where the local elite gathered for daily mingling. It, too, catered to the foreign visitors. It, too, was a sign of Pakistan's growing economy. Yet, while New York City and Mumbai are forever linked, the victims of Islamabad and Lahore find themselves on the other side of history.

The Obama administration will need to stop reading Rudyard Kipling and start reading even the wide-circulation daily Urdu and English press from Pakistan. It is quite easy—they are all online. It will have to know Pakistan's hopes lie with civilian institutions, civic bodies that protect women and minorities, elementary and secondary education for all, strengthening the judiciary, invoking land reform. It will have to know that the military is the largest land-owning entity, one of the biggest business entities, and the greatest consumer of the U.S. Agency for International Development (U.S. AID). The Obama administration needs to focus on the people of Pakistan, in the *present* and not in some distant past surrounded in unknown terrain, if it hopes to combat escalating extremism in the region. Collectively, there are more than 200 million inhabitants in Afghanistan and Pakistan. There are mega-cities like Karachi, with populations of more than 19 million. We are not dealing with hamlets and pockets. And the global context is certainly clear to the terrorists in Mumbai. In the violence they spread, during 3 days, and their targets and their statements, they drew upon this language of political violence. Nariman house to Gaza, Kashmir to Taj Hotel are not teleologies of tribalism, and we make a grave error if we read them wrongly.

Ironically, 2008 began with one of the greatest moments in the history of this nation. After a year-long civic protest, led by the lawyers' movement, the people of Pakistan democratically voted out this military dictator. The February elections in Pakistan were a resounding dismissal of a decade of military dominance as well as the religious parties. Yet we failed to engage with this flowering of democracy. And we need to engage with the civilian government of Zardari—however flawed that particular person is.

There are no military solutions to a decades-old political problem. Because military solutions mandate that the language of political violence be the only language left (be it in Kashmir or Islamabad or Mumbai).

The War Must Go On[12]
December 2, 2009

The safe havens must be eliminated. The corruption must be stopped. The infrastructures must be built. The people must be free. The allies must stand together. The nuclear arms must remain safe. The bombing must be stopped. The safe haven must be eliminated.

Thirty thousand, plus an exit date of June 2011. It's a safe bet that we will need some more troops. It's a safe bet that things will calm down before they become restive, once again. It's a safe bet that we will reevaluate before we redeploy.

A certain generation of Americans is heavily invested in the "Vietnam analogy," because that generation watches all the cable shows. Is Afghanistan like or unlike Vietnam? Afghanistan is like Afghanistan. Its majority population has been born and raised in the noise of bomb blasts and the heavy weight of an automatic weapon nearby—highly transient and shell-shocked. They say more Afghans are needed to fight for the future of Afghanistan. I'd say find more Afghans who are done fighting.

Obama said, "Since 9/11, al-Qaida's safe havens have been the source of attacks against London and Amman and Bali." See, again. There is no Islamabad. No Peshawar. No Lahore. No Lahore. No Lahore. Nor even Mumbai (though the Indian prime minister did get that nice dinner). No matter how much thoughtful and thorough review happens, some things are never questioned nor changed.

"Public opinion has turned," he said. Right. It was public opinion that kept us back from 2001 to 2008. We had a name for that public opinion, didn't we? Our moderately enlightened public opinion. "In the past, we too often defined our relationship with Pakistan narrowly. Those days are over." Ah, past. Let us not tarry there. Let us move on quickly and forcefully. But where? To fund and finance the capacity of Pakistanis to carry out bigger and more effective wars? How exactly is that a break from the past? Maybe the difference is that we are now going to drop night-vision goggles instead of a pellet full of dollars from the C-9 or C-7 or whatever big planes are called? Yes, that is indeed new. Because night-vision goggles can give you sight in the darkness. Essential.

We will support democracy. We supported the "flawed" election of Karzai. That, unfortunately, is not "the past." We supported Pervez Musharraf. He doesn't want to be "the past." And neither does "President Zardari"—who was bequeathed both a political party and a nation by a woman who last won an election in 1993 but was still the only possible future Pakistan was deemed to have. Sadly, she is also "the past."

Should I have been heartened, at least, by his [mention of] "concerns about our approach"? Yes, there are some concerns. In Islamabad. In Kabul. Maybe even in Khost and Karachi. Or in Kandahar and Lahore. We weren't told, but maybe those concerns were heard in the "review process." I am sure that the easy traffic of weapons and people across borders, the legitimate demands of disenfranchised in Swat or Baluchistan, the fear of everyday life in Lahore or Karachi were all heard and discussed. Could it be that this "let's send some more troops and help train some other more troops" strategy was developed with the political and civil leaders in Pakistan and Afghanistan at the table with the Iranian, Indian, and Chinese officials to address inter- and intraregional tactics? Maybe hidden in the fine print are new means of communication, new definitions of strategic aims and missions, and a much more harmonized action plan? It certainly never was in "the past."

We have to "go forward," "go forward" while "going forward," "going forward" and then "move forward" while "moving forward." And Afghanistan? It has "moved backward." Movement is key in a stateless country where the only anchored reference remains Alexander the Great. We will move forward. If it comes that these (safe?) havens also move, we will already be ahead of them. Or behind.

Here we go 'round the mulberry bush.

I Am a Bhains[13]
August 27, 2010

I am a *bhains*. I am now dead.

You must have read, recently, a particularly elegiac treatment of the last moments of a prostrate brown-and-white brindled cow in your favorite newspaper. I didn't read it, but I was told about it. Cow? I said to myself. Cow? We are talking about southern Punjab, yes? Sure there are cows here, but to use a cow as a crassly evocative narrative device seems akin to highlighting the Vespa scooter, when the Honda Hero is really the star of the show!

I mean, come on, I am here. Me. Use me. Punjab is unexplainable, unknowable, unthinkable without me. Speak about me, think about me, hear my voice.

You may have heard of me. They routinely say, *aql bari kay bhains* (a buffalo bigger or brains?). Am I right? What an insult. Of course, I am bigger than "intelligence." But these city folks who can only see me as a street nuisance, while they sip on the delicious milk I provide, are so very keen to make up insulting *proverbs* about me. Or you may have heard, *jis ki lathi uss ki bhains* (he who holds the stick, holds the buffalo). Another insult. Just because someone has a stick, I do not become his possession. I do have a functioning brain! I do recognize, know, and love my owner. The most insulting, however, is, *bhains kay aagay been bajana* (to play the flute in front of the buffalo). Insulting for the sad, pathetic human, of course. I am not sure why they think I am immune to the charms of a good tune on the flute. I love music.

Or you may heard of my genetic cousins in Kenya or Indonesia or wherever the Montgomery Breeding Techniques took my breed (we work well in tropical heat, they concluded)? Or maybe you heard of my cousins, Murrah, Kundhi, Nili, Ravi, here in Desh?

Oh, I know. You don't care about me. It is that farmer standing next to my dead carcass who interests you more, isn't it? You think that now that his life is ruined by this flood, his cattle is dead, his land is covered in waist-high mud and soil, his crops are ruined, his body is racked with dysentery and cholera, he will become a Taliban and attack America. Yes. That is who you really want to hear about. Sadly, even though I have a voice (beyond the carcass, even!), he doesn't. He needs someone else to speak for him. Someone with a more evocative touch than his illiterate, agrarian, yet highly combustible brain can possibly produce.

I hear you. You are a hammer, and everything else is a nail. More precisely, every Pakistani is infected with HIT-virus—full-blown disease is just a matter of time.

What is the point then? I cannot tell you anything that can change your mind. He is poor. *He is easily bought by Wahabi or Opium money.* He works hard for his meager food. *He will swallow whole the dialectic of revolution or of Khilafa.* He is traditional in his outlook, in his customs. *He is a fundamentalist and a sectarian.* He spent some time in the Gulf doing labor. *He was indoctrinated with Wahabi ideology.* He can recite Bulleh Shah or listen to the Heer for days. *He what?* He is a human being with a past, a present, a culture, a society, a vision of the good life, a sense of community, a method of belonging, a routine of daily practices, a collection of stories for his children, a corpus of songs for his friends, a set of possessions, a love for radio or TV, a daily grind, and an early night. *He is waiting to attack us in New York.*

You see his suffering through your security, your strategy, your politics. You don't see him as a human. Just as you don't see me as more than cattle. You don't know who he is, so he must be your worst nightmare. If you saw him as human, if you granted him agency, thought, you wouldn't be so afraid. You would want to help him. Not because he might become Taliban, but because he is your kind, and he needs your help.

Peccavistan[14]
October 31, 2010

I am currently rereading Salman Rushdie's *Shame*. Last time I read it, I was maybe 17 or 18. I remember liking parts of it and not understanding any of it. It is an insider novel, drowning in in-jokes, self-allusions, winks, and sad nods. I never realized how sad it is—Rushdie pokes into the narrative (in a rather laborious and "showing the seams" kind of way) and just laments those who made possible that country of shameless religiosity of which he writes. Several times, he mentions that it isn't Pakistan but a country set at an angle to it. Evoking the sin or shame in the apocryphal *Peccavi*, Rushdie tagged shame itself as the generative force at the heart of Pakistan. That conceit holds, for a while but falls apart in the middle of the novel, and it has fallen apart outside of it. I don't think shame or honor appears in public or private discourses, as the driving cultural forces in or about Pakistan. That *takalluf* (mannered) generation, which sparked Rushdie's imagination, is not around much these days.

The pun *Peccavi*—I have Sind/Sinned—works with an understanding of shame coupled with the acquisition of a particular piece of geography (of the state of Sindh that contains Karachi in current day Pakistan). This pun of conquest has long been attributed to Charles Napier, but, in fact, he never said it. Indeed, the notion of sin did not enter into the emotional registers that informed his actions. Charles Napier (1782–1853) was a hermit-turned-warrior, heady with the crusading spirit that afflicted some of the veterans of the European wars of the early 19th century. He was clear that the common people of Sindh (Hindus or Muslims) had to be "saved" from the despotic Muslim Mirs of Talpur. Whether there was just cause or not, Sindh had to be taken by the East India Company (EIC), and redemption—for him, as a great general, for the EIC, as a civilizing force, and for Sindh, as a country rendered anew in the faith—awaited.

I made up my mind that although war had not been declared (nor is it necessary to declare it), I would at once march upon Imangurh and prove to the whole Talpur family of both Khyrpor and Hyderabad that neither their deserts, nor their negotiations can protect them from the British troops. The Ameers will fly over the Indus, and we shall become masters of the left bank of the river from Mitenkote to the mouth; peace with civilization will then replace war and barbarism. My conscience will be light, for I see no wrong in so regulating a set of tyrants who are themselves invaders and have in sixty years nearly destroyed the country. The people hate them.[15]

In Napier's view, a particular violence and terror haunted the valleys of Sindh. It was the Muslim menace in power—the Mirs were the "greatest ruffians," "imbeciles," possessing "zenanas filled with young girls torn from their friends, and treated when in the hareem with revolting barbarity," and even prone to enjoying the occasional human "sacrifice." His civilizing mission, for which he invented a *casus belli*, was to counter this terror and violence. The EIC, and later the Raj, clung to this reading of the Sindh principality, declaring several "Wars On" dacoits, thugs, criminal tribes, and the like—the terrorism of Pir Pagaro's Hur being a late example portrayed in the former British administrator H. T. Lambrick's novel *The Terrorist* (1972).

This violence that was projected onto and into the Sindhis by the colonial voice masked, however, the colonial violence itself. The violence of breaking treaties established since 1801, of invasions, the killing and capturing of a principality on false pretenses (the Mirs were accused of seeking a conspiratorial connection with the Russians or the Afghanis against the EIC). The terror is clear in the dispatches of the Mirs—plaintively begging for some credence from the British for their legitimacy, for their rule. They know that they cannot do anything to stop the British troops, and their appeals to past treaties and past promises are all couched in the voice of honor, respect (and shame). "We" had a treaty, will you not honor it? The Mirs had already seen the violence.

To give just one example: In March 1839, British vessels *Wellesley* and *Algerine* under the command of Rear Admiral Frederick Lewis Maitland were approaching to dock at the harbor of Karachi. As the ships neared, a cannonball splashed into the water in front of the ship. It came from the garrison of the Manora fort. A welcoming blast. Maitland unleashed his 74 guns on the fort and the city of Karachi, reducing the fort to rubble and raining destruction on the civilians. The terror felt by the community from this bombardment is aptly captured in the memoir of Seth Naomul Hotchand. Afterward, the harbor and the city were promptly seized, and nothing more threatening than a few dozen sword-bearing dead troops were discovered at the fort. The port of Karachi became a permanent harbor for colonial ships, until 1947.

So even though Napier, who landed in Sindh in 1841, saw terror and violence everywhere, he failed to see it as his own violence. He believed that the Oriental despotism of the Mirs, in his view, could only come via such implementation of raw power. The Mirs had no such powers to exercise—they held a carefully negotiated shared political stage with various ethnic tribes, landed elites, and powerful Sufis in the 19th century. This is not to deny that there wasn't any "native" violence, but *that* violence—the one inflicted on peasants trapped in a feudal setting—was not the concern of someone like Napier. The violence and terror that played a rhetorical role in Napier's imagination of Sindh—he used it to construct a rationale for invading Sindh—was not the feudal violence: It was the wholly imagined atrocities (on "young girls"). More broadly, such hyperbolic invocations of local violence have played a substantive role in colonial imaginations of frontiers in general (hello, Africa). Now, it plays a rhetorical role in our present-day imagination of Pakistan.

Peccavi was a phrase that was never uttered about an event that never occurred. Rushdie's coinage of "Peccavistan" takes the myth and runs with it, using the notion of "sin" in the original Latin to resonate with his construction of Pakistan as a place dominated by the affective response of shame. He does so by invoking a class, a literary heritage, a particular politics, and a particular poetics. But, as we learn from the actual history of Napier's conquest of Sindh, at the root of the story lies not shame but something else—terror and violence—constructed with a rhetorical force to justify colonization and control. Peccavistan, with its rich history of misattribution and disjuncture, is a worthy banner to stake atop modern constructions of Pakistan. Nowadays, Peccavistan has become a bastion of terror and violence. Where Rushdie sees shame as an endemic value that clouds every interaction—social or political—I want to argue for Peccavistan as the phenomenon of observing Pakistan as endemically violent and terrorist. When Rushdie uses Peccavistan to argue for alternatives to history, to the way things could have been, I want to show that Peccavistan is perceived reality—the only way things make sense to a certain, shall we say, dominant perspective—an alternate emotional construct constituting discourse about the region.

This brings us to the terror and violence that permeates *Granta: Pakistan*—a special issue of the literary magazine covering the same geography that Rushdie and Napier did. Please see Lapata's thorough treatment at Bookslut, where she teases out the issue of translation and linguistic diversity. In my reading, the fiction quickly became a homogenous blob—female infanticide, honor killings, terrorist beheadings. The writing seemed monotonous, the violence peeking through exactly when I expected it to, terror permeating every interaction. Sure, there was truck art on the cover, some poems, and a few artists who did attempt to show other facets—but the conversation, the literal conversation, is dominated by Mohsin Hamid and Declan Walsh, each in their own, specific ways situating a primordial violence within Peccavistan. This was jarring, because I remember an avowed commitment, on the part of *Granta*'s publicity campaign, to show a different side of Pakistan.

The editor of *Granta*, John Freeman, was recently interviewed in *Herald*, an English monthly from Karachi:

> Q: There's a lot of militancy and fundamentalism and violence here. In fact, the only two prose pieces that don't include at least one of the above are located outside Pakistan.

Are we saying it's not possible to write about the country without writing about these things?

A: I was worried about making an issue that would fall into all the representational traps that Pakistanis feel and that you see in the media. On the other hand, when we ask people to write we don't always tell them what to write about, and in some ways I feel that's the way to get the truest representation of the country. And literature is not a direct representation of life or reality, it's a refraction. It magnifies the anxieties of people who live in a country beyond what they actually are, but it's a way of turning that into narrative and drama.

Also, the situation is deathly serious. And what's very exciting is that Pakistan now has a generation of writers up to the task of writing about that in a way that's interesting as literature, which makes for good short stories and novels and is not just politically or socially concerned. That's the big reason we did the issue. I found Mohsin's piece particularly powerful because it's about violence but also about his desire to avoid it, about what it means to write about it and the fear that it puts inside of him, what the costs of it are.

It's a catch-22 for many of them because it is in some ways what makes them marketable. I think they write about it because they're deeply concerned, but to be marketed based on something that's very close to your heart and very serious raises all sorts of questions. That's why we didn't want a cover with a Kalashnikov or a mullah. Because as much as this issue is addressing things that are of deep concern, it's also a chance to celebrate all this talent that's coming out of the country.[16]

Freeman's slippery response—and his rather risible equation of the "deathly serious" situation with "very exciting" possibilities—seems appropriate to me. Yes, Pakistan—as an object of consumption—is marketable only via its violence or its failure. Freeman, however, carrying the standard of *Granta* bestows a literary credibility to this particular selling that has evaded the editors of *Foreign Policy*. Note that the very reason Freeman wants to focus on Pakistan's artistic or literary voices is because (1) he is told but (2) he noticed the *New York Times Magazine* cover story on the country from 2009. A cover story that imagines Pakistan descriptively as "perilous, anarchic, broke, violent, splintering, corrupt, armed—governable?" Those were the parameters within which political Pakistan could be understood, and those were the parameters within which literary Peccavistan was to be sold.

What I found endearing was that some of the fiction contributors to the issue—Mohsin Hamid, Mohammed Hanif, Daniyal Mueenuddin, and Kamila Shamsie—decided to expose their own culpability by showcasing what they did so brilliantly in the issue. They released a co-written "How to Write About Pakistan" on the *Granta* website. Endearing, because theirs are among the only voices heard globally on Pakistan, so if any clichés exist, they are from them. Nadeem Aslam's "Where to Begin" is a more mature defense of violence in his short story but perhaps just as limiting as the paeans by mango farmers. Aslam does believe, inherently, in the embodied violence of the spaces he recreates in his work, but is that *all* those spaces can hold?

Let me be frank: Every individual author has perfect freedom to craft her voice as she wants and on whatever she damn well prefers. Clearly, Daniyal Mueenuddin or Kamila Shamsie's literary output has nothing distinctly about terrorism or militant Talibans. But insofar as they are allowed to make public statements about Pakistan, those metrics are predefined. The making of literary Peccavistan is, then, slightly different from an individual artist's output—it is about a collective conversation, an editing of a particular narrative on Pakistan that partakes profitably in the ways that the market has predetermined. Even that is, of course, inherently defensible. The problem, insofar as I am trying to locate a problem and not just providing a gloss, is that there is no counter, in public or political or literary discourse, to Peccavistan. There are no other histories, no other voices, there are no reflections on other constitutive qualities—hospitality, savvy, familial bonds, the cultural affinities. I say this not as an apologist or a nationalist but as a cultural historian who is all too aware of the power of framing discourses, which set up their own regimes of what is allowable and what is unmentionable and constrict all possibilities except those that have been prearticulated. I should add that, as a reader, it is disheartening to see the Pakistani English-sprache elite contribute so wholeheartedly to the construction of only *that* reality.

That this Peccavistan is constructed in a particular way is much clearer in the nonfiction inclusions in the issue. It is amazing to contemplate that John Freeman couldn't find a single Pakistani journalist who can write knowingly about her own country. Not a one. Declan Walsh and Jane Perlez must have been chafing from their constant appearances in the *Guardian* and the *New York Times* and needed the exposure. It seems to me that an editor with the avowed intent of finding the Pakistani voice may have noticed that the last 10 years have produced a veritable explosion of smart, young journalists—any of whom could have provided a long-form piece and benefited from the exposure. Why does it matter, you ask? Walsh and Perlez are remarkable journalists by all accounts—even if they don't have direct linguistic or social access to the communities they cover. It matters because the framing of the violence becomes all too distant. Take the matter of drones—the only times the subject of drone comes up in the nonfiction entries, it is uttered from the mouths of avowed terrorists. To the reader, there remains little doubt that there cannot be a debate on the drones, and their rhetorical usage are so much empty strategies of deceit employed by the evildoers. Yet little can be further from the truth. The violence and terror of drones is just as much as framing device for Pakistan's social pulse as the violence of Taliban or misogynist husbands. That Walsh or Perlez are not attuned to this is not surprising. And again, this is not a nativist argument. I am not criticizing Walsh or Perlez, because they are outsiders. The one piece that I thought was sensitive, nuanced, and a fine job of reporting was Lorraine Adams's reportage on Faisal Shahzad. (Strangely, though Ayesha Nasir is billed along with her, the piece contains no reporting from Pakistan. I am not sure what happened there.) What I am pointing out is that Walsh or Perlez, and their work, fit perfectly both the type of narrative the market wants to read about Pakistan and the type of persona best suited to bringing it to the market.

Peccavistan is just as real as Pakistan. *Granta: Pakistan* is a selling of Peccavistan. It is a bundling, an explaining, a framing, a means of demystification when the mystery is itself a reflection of paucity of sources not of intelligibility. Peccavistan sells because Peccavistan takes away complexity, it reduces our mental and emotional commitments to Pakistan. Pakistan, though 180 million strong, ravaged by floods and suicide bombers, continues to carry on. Apocryphally speaking.

Chapter Notes

1 This was the inaugural post on the *Chapati Mystery (CM)* blog. It is archived at http://www.chapatimystery.com/archives/homistan/basmati_rice.html. This URL has been shortened to http://bit.ly/gqhFeV. All the short texts in the book are taken from *CM* except where noted otherwise in the dateline. For all the short texts that follow, a Web-archived version of the original short text and all the sources and links therein can be accessed through the shortened URLs given at the footnote.

2 Archived at http://bit.ly/ej6szq.

3 National Commission on Terrorist Attacks on the United States, *The 9/11 Commission Report* (New York: W. W. Norton, 2004), 50.

4 Archived at http://bit.ly/f2Yo3l.

5 Archived at http://bit.ly/hfouxn.

6 Barack Obama, "The War We Need to Win," August 1, 2007, archived at http://bit.ly/mSDonD.

7 Archived at http://bit.ly/fcCsqd.

8 Jacques Derrida, *For Nelson Mandela* (New York: Seaver Press, 1987), 37.

9 Archived at http://bit.ly/fiYGsi.

10 "Transcript: Senate Confirmation Hearing: Hillary Clinton," *New York Times*, January 13, 2009, archived at http://nyti.ms/j0WgCj.

11 Ibid.

12 Archived at http://bit.ly/7Fa5mN.

13 Archived at http://bit.ly/9kLEAa.

14 Archived at http://bit.ly/c20alV.

15 William F. P. Napier, *The Life and Opinions of General Sir Charles James Napier,* vol. 2 (London: John Murray, 1857), 275.

16 Madiha Sattar, "Interview with John Freeman," *Herald,* October 2010, archived at http://bit.ly/jKwcDM.

2

Observe

Iraq looms large in our recent past and will loom large in our future—even if the conversation more recently has centered on Egypt, Tunisia, Libya, Bahrain, or Saudi Arabia. The fact remains that the legal, military, and cultural innovations (so to speak) of the Iraq War cast a long, long shadow within and outside the United States. As such, it was important to collect most of the worthwhile posts that deal with Iraq War—as a distant observer—at the front of the book. These posts are mostly commentary on the news as it came out every day, except in some posts—such as "Shadow of the Future"—where only a bit of discourse analysis happens.

Your Mother Was a Hamster and
Your Father Smelt of Elderberries[1]

April 17, 2004

Blasting loud rock (what, no Limp Bizkit?) and insults at the Fallujah uprisers is the current state of psychological operations in Iraq.

At night, a psychological operations unit attached to the Marine battalion here sends out messages from a loudspeaker mounted on an armored Humvee. On Thursday night, the crew and its Arabic-language interpreter taunted fighters, saying, "May all the ambulances in Fallujah have enough fuel to pick up the bodies of the mujahadeen!"

The message was specially timed for an attack moments later by an AC-130 gunship that pounded targets in the city. Later, the team blasted Jimi Hendrix and other rock music, and afterward some sound effects, such as babies crying, men screaming, a symphony of cats and barking dogs and piercing screeches. They were unable to draw any gunmen to fight and seemed disappointed.

As the insurgents very likely do not understand English and may, in fact, like classic rock, it seems a weird tactic designed to provoke more than prevent. But that seems to be the modus operandi in Iraq. There is no attempt at all to connect to the Iraqis as people with a proud heritage who have yet to achieve freedom. The tactics of war are good for just that: war. You cannot have a peace and reconstruction mission carried out by marines and soldiers. They are trained otherwise.

Fallujah is a fiercely tribal place that will answer only with aggression. Wiser heads than mine, one of them on Juan Cole's shoulders, have written on the need for temperance and restraint in Fallujah. Yet, here we have another account of a Briton in Baghdad pointing out the absurdity of peace-keeping with military tanks.

All this is, rather academic. Iraq has toppled into the chaos predicted before the war. Bush/Blair are leaving come July. Iraq belongs to the Iraqis. Afghanistan belongs to the Afghanis. We have done our job.

The Neocon Con[2]
April 28, 2004

Douglas Feith recently spoke here on campus. Chicago, home of Leo Strauss and Albert Wohlstetter, is an important place for Doug Feith to come and defend the assault on Iraq strategy of the administration—and, by extension, the neocon worldview.

Today's *New York Times* has an in-depth piece on the three-member crack team (and yes, crack) of Feith, Maloof, and Chalabi, who were responsible for coming up with lots of nice PowerPoint presentations on Iraq, WMDs, al-Qaida. There is an earlier *Washington Post* piece that covered most of this Shadow Squad. Both of these pieces show that post September 11, the neocons were ready to find the intelligence to support their gut feeling: that Saddam had to go, that the Empire had to return, that the World was a Dangerous Place. Of course, any kind of intelligence can easily be found if one culls over enough policy and analysis memos and, of course, calls a dissident insider who has all kinds of "neat" information. It is a pattern we have seen in every other public policy of this administration: Have a conclusion, find the reasons. And the reasons are all there in those books and memos. God forbid one has to leave the Regenstein.

What is fascinating to me is the way that the neocons have gone around defending themselves. Bernard Lewis, the doyen of Orientalists, was on *Charlie Rose* last night saying how wonderful a guy Chalabi is and how cruel the media have been to him. Oh yeah, the media are sooo bad to them.

The neocons *love* the spotlight. They do. Have you seen any tabletop lately that did not have Richard Perle perched on it? They know they were right, and they thought this was going to be the moment when sheepish intelligentsia would be lining up to shower them with flowers (ha). The fact that it did not happen in Iraq may have given them pause, but no. They want the accolades. They want to be proven right.

In the end, they are the quintessential Chicago students: Hungry for approval, utterly convinced of their rightness, and with immutable faith that the text will save us all.

Shame³
May 1, 2004

The Iraqi prisoner abuse story is extremely significant. It is a devastating blow to any notion of winning the hearts and minds of Arabs in or outside Iraq. Most newspapers are carrying stories on outrage in Cairo, the United Arab Emirates, Bahrain. The scandal has now spread to British soldiers as well.

What is the significance? In the Islamic world, home to dictatorships and police regimes, this is not newsworthy solely because it happened. Instead, it has immense symbolic power because the perpetrators are those who have had the rhetoric of "good" vs. evil. Those who claimed that it is civilization they bring to the people. And freedom, of course. Even more than that is the content of these pictures. If there is one thing valued higher than life, it is honor. The pictures of naked Iraqi prisoners in a pile or in sexual positions and being ridiculed by a white female soldier scream to the Arab and Muslim public that their honor has been stripped bare. Shame is in the unveiling.

A world that knows it has been militarily, economically, culturally, and politically dominated by the West now stares at pictures confirming their worst fears. The power of images need not be overly stressed, as such images as the little Vietnamese girl or the Tiananmen Square man, etc., are stark examples of visceral impact on the public mood. In the Arab psyche, the humility of 1967 was far greater than the military defeat of 1967. Similar was the symbolic shame of having non-Muslim troops in Saudi Arabia defending Mecca from Saddam for certain Muslims. These images have the potential to wreak the same havoc.

And no, I am not reading *too* much into it. And no, it is *not* worse than Saddam's "rape houses"—as our president is fond of saying. It is *not*.

I am talking about cultural memory and self-image. This war on terrah is a war for the hearts and minds, no? The uprising in Najaf, Fallujah, the attacks in Saudi Arabia, and this . . . the battle for Iraq may have been won, but the war on terrah is being lost.

Just got my hands on Seymour Hersh's piece in the *New Yorker*, "Torture at Abu Ghraib," that is chilling in its details.

The photographs tell it all. In one, Private Lynndie England, a cigarette dangling from her mouth, is giving a jaunty thumbs-up sign and pointing at the genitals of a young Iraqi, who is naked except for a sandbag over his head, as he masturbates. Three other hooded and naked Iraqi prisoners are shown, hands reflexively crossed over their genitals. A fifth prisoner has his hands at his sides. In another, England stands arm in arm with Specialist Charles Graner; both are grinning and giving the thumbs-up behind a cluster of perhaps seven naked Iraqis, knees bent, piled clumsily on top of each other in a pyramid. There is another photograph of a cluster of naked prisoners, again piled in a pyramid. Near them stands Graner, smiling, his arms crossed; a woman soldier stands in front of him, bending over, and she, too, is smiling. Then, there is another cluster of hooded bodies, with a female soldier standing in front, taking photographs. Yet another photograph shows a kneeling, naked, unhooded male prisoner, head momentarily turned away from the camera, posed to make it appear that he is performing oral sex on another male prisoner, who is naked and hooded.

Such dehumanization is unacceptable in any culture, but it is especially so in the Arab world. Homosexual acts are against Islamic law, and it is humiliating for men to be naked in front of other men, Bernard Haykel, a professor of Middle Eastern Studies at New York University, explained. "Being put on top of each other and forced to masturbate, being naked in front of each other, it's all a form of torture," Haykel said.

Chalabi Hits the Fan[4]
May 24, 2004

I am in the midst of reading *Charlie Wilson's War: The Extraordinary Story of the Largest Covert Operation in History*, by George Crile, which is blowing my mind away. As a historian, I am trained to eschew the individual-centered approach to history—to focus, instead, on processes and ideas. However, the book and the scandal swiveling around Ahmad Chalabi are keen reminders of the role played by individuals as both instruments of change and inertia.

Ahmad Chalabi is a '69 mathematics Ph.D. from the University of Chicago [where he studied with Albert Wohlstetter], a founder of Petra Bank in Jordan accused of swindling $200 million from the Jordanians [he escaped in the trunk of a palace limo], a man who sold Iraqi resistance to a wide-eyed Congress in 1998 and got hundreds of millions to fund it, and an installed president of the Iraqi Governing Council widely thought to be elected first president of Iraq [without any popular support]. And now on Paul Bremer's shit list.

So, how did Mr. Chalabi do all that? He was the right man at the right moment with the right pipe dream. To Paul Wolfowitz, Richard Perle, and Doug Feith, sweating the Dark Ages during the Clinton years, he was a former classmate who could deliver Iraq to them. So they latched on to him with a religious fervor, knowing that he would point to the WMDs. Sure that he had the inside scoop on Iraqi Freedom Fighters. In the postwar, they knew he could be trusted to lead Iraq as the First Democracy while remaining true to the First Empire. As Bernard Lewis, the current intellectual fountainhead for the neocons, wrote in a *Wall Street Journal* editorial in 2003, he is the only hope for Iraq.

Ahmad Chalabi is a Tinker, Tailor, Soldier, Spy for Iran, says the United States now. Surely, this "accusation" comes from Central Command. Is it a squeeze? Was he about to go public with some WMD after being shoved aside for UN envoy Lakhdar Brahimi? I am inclined to think that this is a preemptive strike to discredit him and cast his "revelations" as a disgruntled ex-employee.

The question is, When Will He Sing?

He is headed back to Washington to confront his "critics." He will have some words for Dick Cheney's ears. And, once he realizes that his con is truly up, he will start the endgame: a *60 Minutes Special.* . . .

Update: The Central Intelligence Agency is spreading the word that Chalabi was an Iranian agent who used the United States to bring Shia rule in Iraq. The Great Satan a tool? Bada bing! [thanks, Moacir]

Update 2: Oh, this will get pretty soon . . . from *Newsweek*:

> One Bush administration official said that in addition to harboring suspicions that Chalabi had been leaking sensitive U.S. information to Iran both before and after the U.S. invasion of Iraq, some U.S. officials also believe that Chalabi had collected and maintained files of potentially damaging information on U.S. officials with whom he had or was going to interact for the purpose of influencing them. Some officials said that when Iraqi authorities raided Chalabi's offices, one of the things American officials hoped they would look for was Chalabi's cache of information he had gathered on Americans.[5]

F Day[6]
June 28, 2004

Empires aren't supposed to beat a hastily arranged retreat, Niall Ferguson. What gives? Paul Bremer hands a blue folder to a confused older judge and a truly evil-looking Allawi, and the Empire has left the building.

The Bush administration's gamble here is pretty obvious. Paul Bremer boards the plane. Shia, Sunni, Kurds explode onto each other with Israel, Iran, and Turkey enabling participants. Who knows what it will look like when it all settles down, but no one will be calling the White House for explanations. Karl Rove will have a mark on his checklist [Liberated Iraq], and we are on to the races. I am afraid it doesn't work like that. Or as Colin Powell put it: You break it, you own it. The chaos in Iraq will remain front-page news, and the Bushies cannot dismiss it as an Iraqi problem. Iraqis are being granted the same freedom given to the Afghanis. A cobbled-up imported-elite rule, a country in chaos, and promises of freedom. And, just like the Afghanis, they are not buying it just yet.

Should this be Freedom Day for Iraq? Well, if you would like to define freedom as martial law:

> *Question:* Mr. President, Iraq's new prime minister has talked in recent days about the possibility of imposing martial law there as a way of restoring security. Is that something that you think a new, emerging government should do, and particularly with the use of U.S. forces, who would have to be instrumental in doing it?
>
> *Bush:* You know, Prime Minister Allawi has, you know, fought tyranny. He's a guy that stood up to Saddam Hussein. He's a patriot. And every conversation I've had with him has been one that recognizes human liberty, human rights. He's a man who's willing to risk his life for a democratic future for Iraq.
>
> Having said that, you know, he may take tough security measures to deal with Zarqawi. And he may have to. Zarqawi is a guy who beheads people on TV. He's a person that orders suiciders to kill women and children.
>
> And so, Prime Minister Allawi, as the head of the sovereign government, may decide he's going to have to take some tough measures to deal with a brutal, cold-blooded killer. And our job is to help the Iraqis stand up forces that are able to deal with these thugs.[7]

Right. Allawi's commitment to recognize human liberty must have been honed when his Iraqi National Accord was bombing women and children in Baghdad in the '90s. Do you really need martial law to deal with "one" killer? And while we wait to see if martial law becomes the rule, Bremer left behind 97 legal orders to keep things running smoothly [a traffic code that stipulates the use of a car horn in "emergency conditions only" and requires a driver to "hold the steering wheel with both hands"].

It is a different *F* word that comes to my mind.

Capturing Osama[8]
July 8, 2004

The Bush administration dropped mentioning Osama bin Laden around late 2002 (just from my recollection—if I was in the library I'd LexisNexis that) as the focus of the War on Terror moved towards Iraq. Actually, I just saw this great page, *Flip-*

Flopper-in-Chief, where you can read No. 14 yourself. Why was OBL dropped as Public Enemy No. 1? Because Bush wanted Saddam? Let's assume that the truth is more complex than that. The rhetoric from the Bush administration about the War on Terror has been that this is a "new" reality that has "fundamentally changed" the world. However, its actions belie that rhetoric.

Remember that the Bush thinkforce predominantly contains Cold War veterans and Soviet "experts." The reigning model for world conflict for the past 60 years has been aggression by the state, which will need a superior power to counteract or counterbalance. In winter 2001, that idea held on—there was a direct relationship between the Taliban (the State) and al-Qaida (the nonstate actor)—and Afghanistan was invaded.

Now, if the War on Terror was indeed a "new" mode of operation, the Bush administration would have shifted its focus to combating various terrorist organizations through economic, clandestine, and military-coop ways in various countries. Perhaps build a new coalition agency (like the International Criminal Police Organization) that could operate internationally and develop legislations in various countries to effectively combat terrorism.

The thinking should have been that these nonstate actors may take funds from certain states, they may even operate in those states, but they do not *represent* the interests of any given state. Their agenda is their own and unique, and it may dovetail here or there with a state, but that is coincidental not conspiratorial. But the Bush administration went on with the same old Cold War mentality. "Invade Iraq because they supported al-Qaida" is the latest iteration of that rationale. It remains just as false as the WMD claim, but that is not what I want to quibble with here.

According to the statist model, it makes sense that Osama is not a priority. What difference does it make whether he is captured or not? Unless, of course, the difference is between getting Mr. Bush reelected. The *New Republic* has a report entitled "July Surprise" that claims that the Bush administration has been pressuring Pakistan to deliver a high-value target (HVT) *before* November—in fact, during the Democratic National Convention:

> A third source, an official who works under ISI's director, Lieutenant General Ehsan ul-Haq, informed [the *New Republic*] that the Pakistanis "have been told at every level that apprehension or killing of HVTs before [the] election is [an] absolute must." What's more, this source claims that Bush administration officials have told their Pakistani counterparts they have a date in mind for announcing this achievement: "The last ten days of July deadline has been given repeatedly by visitors to Islamabad and during [ul-Haq's] meetings in Washington." Says [State Department spokesman Sean] McCormack: "I'm aware of no such comment." But according to this ISI official, a White House aide told ul-Haq last spring that "it would be best if the arrest or killing of [any] HVT were announced on" [July 26, 27, or 28]—the first three days of the Democratic National Convention in Boston.[9]

That Osama's capture will increase Bush's chance of reelection is a dubious claim. And from the way things have been going in Wana, Pakistan, it is highly debatable that Musharraf can deliver Osama on such a timetable. Regardless, the larger War on Terror remains mired in the Cold War context—looking for dark enemies in every nook and cranny (remember the Axis of Evil?). Can John Kerry promise a truly *new* way?

Operation Next[10]
December 13, 2004

Iraq is not over yet, but with the January 30 election approaching, the administration can bolt with a straight face. But where to go? I mean, we have half-a-million soldiers waiting to kick some ass, general.

Let us revisit the January 29, 2002, State of the Union address:

> Our second goal is to prevent regimes that sponsor terror from threatening America or our friends and allies with weapons of mass destruction. Some of these regimes have been pretty quiet since September 11. But we know their true nature. *North Korea* is a regime arming with missiles and weapons of mass destruction, while starving its citizens. *Iran* aggressively pursues these weapons and exports terror, while an unelected few repress the Iranian people's hope for freedom.
>
> *Iraq* continues to flaunt its hostility toward America and to support terror. The Iraqi regime has plotted to develop anthrax, and nerve gas, and nuclear weapons for over a decade. His is a regime that has already used poison gas to murder thousands of its own citizens—leaving the bodies of mothers huddled over their dead children. This is a regime that agreed to international inspections—then kicked out the inspectors. This is a regime that has something to hide from the civilized world.
>
> States like these, and their terrorist allies, constitute *an axis of evil*, arming to threaten the peace of the world. By seeking weapons of mass destruction, these regimes pose a grave and growing danger. They could provide these arms to terrorists, giving them the means to match their hatred. They could attack our allies or attempt to blackmail the United States. In any of these cases, the price of indifference would be catastrophic.[11]
> [*emphasis added*]

In May 2002, John Bolton, the undersecretary of state, added Cuba, Libya, and Syria to the Axis. Libya knocked itself off the list by proving, once and for all, its irrelevance. Cuba, with the election over, is worthless for the next 3 years.

I projected that Iran will be next in the crosshairs. If you remember a few months ago (in August/September), there was some talk of al-Qaida regrouping in Iran and that Iranians were sending massive aid to insurgents in Baghdad and were even hosting al-Qaida [forget the whole rabid anti-Shi'ism professed by OBL]. Ironically, Iran was also recently accused by King Abdullah of sending in a million voters to subvert the Iraqi elections [doesn't that prove that democracy has a foothold in Iran!]. Mansoor Ijaz, my favorite Terrorism Expert at Fox News, has been yelling "Osama is in Iran" for a long while.

Add the Chalabi factor—the *Mujahedin Khalq* (MEK). As Reza Aslan wrote in the *Los Angeles Times* a few days back:

> Ever since the invasion of Iraq, the MEK (and its Paris-based political front, the National Council of Resistance in Iran) has tried to establish itself as the Iranian equivalent of Ahmad Chalabi's "government in exile," the Iraqi National Congress, and not without success. Like the [Iraqi National Congress (INC)] before the war, the MEK has advocates in the highest levels of government. And like the INC, the MEK has been inundating the U.S. intelligence community with uncorroborated and, according to some intelligence officials, highly suspect information meant to encourage the White House to carry out the same policy of regime change in Iran that it did in Iraq. But the United States will probably discover that the MEK, just like the INC, can't be trusted.[12]

All this led me to conclude that Iran would indeed be the next target, and I have been teaching Persian cuss words to my draftable friends in preparation. But, a surprise development just threw off my prognostication powers.

The United States and Iraq have started mentioning Syria and the Ba'athists lately. Today, *Weekly Standard*'s Bill Kristol finally revealed Operation Next:

> By Bush Doctrine standards, Syria is a hostile regime. It is permitting and encouraging activities that are killing not just our Iraqi friends but also, and quite directly, American troops. So we have a real Syria problem.
>
> Of course we also have–the world also has–an Iran problem, and a Saudi problem, and lots of other problems. The Iran and Saudi problems may ultimately be more serious than the Syria problem. But the Syria problem is urgent: It is Bashar Assad's regime that seems to be doing more than any other, right now, to help Baathists and terrorists kill Americans in the central front of the war on terror. . . . We could bomb Syrian military facilities; we could go across the border in force to stop infiltration; we could occupy the town of Abu Kamal in eastern Syria, a few miles from the border, which seems to be the planning and organizing center for Syrian activities in Iraq, and in the broader Middle East.[13]

Here comes 2005.

Shadow of the Future[14]
January 19, 2005

Let's talk about wonderful phrases today. Just before the election there was a flurry of declarations on *reality-based* and *faith-based* worlds or somesuch. There is room at the table for another one, I think: future-based. As I was getting ready this morning, Barbara Boxer had Condoleezza Rice pinned on Iraq. Why couldn't you have dealt with Saddam as we dealt with Milosevic? Why did Rummy visit Saddam in the '80s when he was gassing Iranians? Why did you not tell that to the people when you claimed that we were taking Saddam out because he gassed Iranians? Why were there no WMDs? Why did you tell us the aluminium tubes were for building nukes when that was not the consensus? Rice didn't flinch. Let me transcribe her response clearly: ???? ? ??? ?? ???????? ??? ???? ??????????? Yeah. But she did say that we invaded Iraq because "the shadow of the future" dictated our actions.

The shadow of the future. What a beautiful, Tolkien-esque phrase. I have been rolling it around in my head all morning. The future, for millennia a sure peg to hang one's hopes and dreams on, now casts a dark, disturbing glance at the present, intimidating it, changing it, to ensure its own outcome. Or maybe it is more Borges-esque than Tolkien-esque: "Whosoever would undertake some atrocious enterprise should act as if it were already accomplished, should impose upon himself a future as irrevocable as the past."

And there is another beautiful formulation by Rice, *outposts of tyranny*, stated in her testimony yesterday, about which I am sure we will hear much more soon:

> To be sure, in our world, there remain outposts of tyranny, and America stands with oppressed people on every continent, in Cuba and Burma, and North Korea and Iran and Belarus and Zimbabwe. The world should really apply what Nathan Sharansky called the town square test. If a person cannot walk into the middle of the town square and express his or her views without fear of arrest, imprisonment and physical harm, then that person is living in a fear society. And we cannot rest until every person living in a fear society has finally won their freedom.[15]

Outposts, as contrasted with axis, give us a more spatially pronounced effect. It distances the threat, marginalizes it, and degrades it from pure evil to tyranny (anyone else thinking about *Pulp Fiction*?). There is more about those outposts in Sy Hersh's latest in the *New Yorker* called "The Coming Wars." Future as *fait accompli*:

> Rumsfeld will become even more important during the second term. In interviews with past and present intelligence and military officials, I was told that the agenda had been determined before the Presidential election, and much of it would be Rumsfeld's responsibility. The war on terrorism would be expanded, and effectively placed under

the Pentagon's control. The President has signed a series of findings and executive orders authorizing secret commando groups and other Special Forces units to conduct covert operations against suspected terrorist targets in as many as ten nations in the Middle East and South Asia.[16]

The Department of Defense responded: "By his own admission, Mr. Hersh evidently is working on an 'alternative history' novel. He is well along in that work, given the high quality of 'alternative present' that he has developed in several recent articles." *Alternative present*, another beautiful phrase that bifurcates our living reality into several frames. I never realized that bureaucrats were so poetic. Or inclined to fiction writing.

In this month's *Atlantic*, Richard Clarke writes a lecture delivered in 2011. Exhaustively footnoted, it contains the many missteps of this administration in the Web of Trust—some already taken and some destined to be taken. A series of suicide attacks on American casinos, malls, subways, railroads, and the Internets by al-Qaida of North America and Iranian Quds Force causes the arrest and detention of hundreds of thousands of Muslim-Americans, the creation of the draft, and the modern-day Minutemen.

A future waiting to be born imposes itself on the present to bear it. So the last phrase of the day—my least favorite—*the clash of cultures*. Which is marginally better than the Clash of Civilizations, but still off the mark. Me and Farangi are hard at work trying to figure all possible permutations of the Clash of . . . meme.

Aren't words fun?

The Gall[17]
November 30, 2005

My favorite bit in the newly unveiled National Strategy for Victory in Iraq, a.k.a. *Plan for Victory*, is not that it is 3 years too late; not that there is no Arabic translation of this plan available; not that the whole endeavor is regressive; not that there are cute checkmarks next to lines, such as "As the terrorists themselves recognize . . . "; not that the words "Islam," "Muslim," or "Rumsfeld" do not occur anywhere [or "Enemies of the legitimate Iraqi government"]; not that we learn that there are 3 million cell phones in Iraq today when a June 2004 Department of Commerce (DoC) report put the number at 315,000 [million, likely, but I nitpick]; not that there are *18* core assumptions ranging from the sappy "like people in all parts of the world, from all cultures and religions, when given the opportunity, the Iraqi people prefer to live in freedom rather than under tyranny" to the scary "regional meddling and infiltrations can be contained and/or neutralized"; no, my favorite bit lies among the quotes at the end of each Strategic Pillar:

> *Strategic Pillar Six: One of the most important ways to fight terrorism*
> *is to promote democracy, and one of the most important ways*
> *to promote democracy is the rule of law.*
>
> —Attorney General Alberto Gonzales, July 2005

That's rich, no?

Wrote David Denby at the end of his *Syriana* review in this week's *New Yorker*: "The taste of freedom has turned to wormwood and gall."

Path to Victory[18]
December 16, 2005

Say what we will about the adventures of The Chosen One in Iraq, yesterday was a memorable day for the future state of Iraq. Memorable because there will now be a parliament and, for better or worse, the last illusions of control over Iraq will slip away from the hands of the White House. I congratulate the Iraqi people for making it so far. And I hope that they continue to go to the polls in the future. The danger of a civil war remains; the danger of an Iran-fed theocracy clashing with the United States and other designs remains; and the mere fact that elections happened and that the Sunni participation was high does not mean any end to the hostilities. . . .

The first general elections in the history of Pakistan were held during December 1970. The resulting National Assembly was mandated to write a new constitution for the country in 120 days. The country, at the time, was divided geographically into East and West Pakistan. Even though the population tilted towards East Pakistan, the ruling elite, to that point, had all come from West Pakistan—whether military or civilian. The policies of General Ayub had created intense resentment in East Pakistan for their long standing marginalization and economic exploitation by West Pakistan–led military and civilian elite. The anemic response of the army to the massive cyclone of November 1970 gave further strength to the argument that the Bangla-speaking Pakistanis of East Pakistan were on their own. It was in this context that the election of 1970 gave an overwhelming victory to the local political party, Awami League, and its leader, Sheikh Mujibur Rahman, in East Pakistan. And with this victory, so they thought, a public mandate to implement their six-point plan [second point was that the federal government will be responsible only for defense and foreign affairs; the others argued for equal economic distribution and independent actions for the provinces]. In West Pakistan, Pakistan People's Party and Zulfiqar Ali Bhutto trumped Mawdudi and his Jama'at to claim premiership duties [did you know that Bhutto contested a seat against Javed Iqbal s/o of Allama?]. Neither party got anything in the other half of that fractured country.

And so it stood, that General Yahya [yes, there is always a general in charge in homistan], Sheikh Mujibur Rahman, and Bhutto started a fateful dance that would cast the country into civil war.

Awami League may or may not have been willing to negotiate on the Six Points, Bhutto certainly tried to argue that they weren't listening, and Yahya acted in the only way he knew—militarily. In the beginning of March, he declared curfew in Dhaka and installed General Tikka Khan, already known for his exploits in Baluchistan as the "Butcher of Baluchistan," as the martial law administrator. He was to live up to his moniker. All compromises between Bhutto, Mujib, and Yahya ended on March 25, 1970, when Yahya decided to gamble that military might would subdue East Pakistan, and the Pakistan army rolled into Dhaka. Awami League leaders who did not manage to escape were arrested or killed. Mujibur Rahman was charged with treason and sent to jail in West Pakistan. As the army laid seige to cities of their own country, the Bengali regiments disappeared and reemerged as the guerilla troops of Mukhti Bahni. Through November 1971, at least a million civilians had been killed at the hands of the West Pakistani Army, and the number of refugees into India was reaching the 10 million mark. Also, by November, the Indian Army had started military operations in East Pakistan, and on December 3, 1971, full-scale conflict erupted between the two nations. On December 15, West Pakistan's Army surrendered in Dhaka, and Bangladesh was born.

Whatever the dream of Pakistan had been in 1947, the creation of Bangladesh in 1971 was its death knell. One can even argue that both Pakistan and Bangladesh came into existence, simultaneously, in 1971. It will have to suffice for the day to state, rather broadly, that Islam and the neutron became the twin engines for the broken nation of Pakistan, which had no economy, a token state, and a mere dialectic as its sole raison d'être. For Bangladesh, on the other hand, the struggle to overcome the twin wounds of nationalism and nature was tremendous. Its tumultuous past since is once again rocking. It has been just as unlucky as Pakistan in being enslaved to families of civilian despots elected in recurring cycles of violence and voting.

The lesson of 1971 is important for the Iraq of 2006: There can be no good outcome when the tyranny of power seeks to rewrite the will of people. Kurdish nationalists, claimants of a Shia theocracy, "secular" voices, and the recalcitrant Sunnis will all win a seat at the Parliamentary table. Let's keep them *all* there.

Know Thy Enemy[19]
June 2, 2006

> The moon is a very important and complex symbol in Islamic culture.
> The horse is a very important symbol in both Arabic and Islamic culture.

There is perhaps no landscape in Islamic culture and tradition more evocative and recognizable than the desert.

Palm trees, particularly date palms, are inextricably linked to Mediterranean, Middle Eastern, and Islamic culture.

The lion is an important symbol in Islamic culture.

The camel has particular importance to Arab culture.

The horse is a very important symbol in both Arabic and Islamic culture.

The falcon is an important symbol in Islamic culture.

Women hold powerful symbolic value in Islamic culture.

There is a lot of symbology surrounding hand gestures in Islamic culture.

The element of blood is highly symbolic in Islamic culture.

The crescent moon is an important symbol of Islamic identity.

Weapons are symbolically important in Islamic culture.

Martyrs are a source of inspiration in Islamic culture.

The color black is a very significant color in the Islamic tradition.

The element of blood is highly symbolic in Islamic culture.

All this and more from the highly acclaimed West Point series, *The Islamic Imagery Project: Visual Motifs in Jihadi Internet Propaganda*,[20] a project that proudly proclaims that "each entry is grounded in a deep reading of Islamic history, culture, language and experience" and that "there is a certain timelessness to these motifs, which reflects the authors' desire to portray their extreme interpretation of Salafi thought as a logical refinement of traditional Islamic thought."

But wait. You ready for the punch line?

To die for one's faith is the most spiritual act in the Islamic tradition.

Well. There you have it.

Oh. Who, you ask, should we thank for this brilliant analysis? This rending of the veil? This violation of the inner sanctum of the harem? Why, it is Afshon Ostovar, who "wrote the analyses of the individual motifs" and who describes himself thusly on MySpace: Imagine a room full of women. Nubile, blonde, wet with desire, Schwartz. A harem, if you will. Me in leather. A harness, if you like. I am the object of this desire, and all eyes are on me as I speak. Ladies, I begin. I am the love god, Eros. I intoxicate you. My spunk is to you manna from heaven.[21]

And they say that the experts in "Islamic culture" are not helping in the War on Terror.

Dear Rumsfeld[22]
November 8, 2006

I hear they have a nice retirement colony in Cuba.

Chapter Notes

1 Archived at http://bit.ly/eyf4vB.
2 Archived at http://bit.ly/gO5zlj.
3 Archived at http://bit.ly/hdixm0.
4 Archived at http://bit.ly/ejPFQW.
5 Michael Isikoff, "Terror Watch: Tip of the Iceberg?" *Newsweek*, June 2, 2004, archived at http://bit.ly/iIOM4f.
6 Archived at http://bit.ly/e3wWMj.
7 Transcript of George W. Bush/Tony Blair briefing on transfer of power in Iraq, June 28, 2004, archived at http://bit.ly/kS5NvQ.
8 Archived at http://bit.ly/e9vohk.
9 John B. Judis, "July Surprise?" *New Republic*, July 19, 2004, archived at http://bit.ly/lrWFfe.
10 Archived at http://bit.ly/e1H5D4.
11 George W. Bush, "State of the Union Address," January 29, 2002, archived at http://bit.ly/dtduoh.
12 Reza Aslan, "A Cult Is Trying to Hijack Our Iran Policy," *Los Angeles Times*, December 10, 2004, archived at http://bit.ly/kKd6tW.
13 William Kristol, "Getting Serious About Syria," *Weekly Standard*, December 20, 2004, archived at http://bit.ly/jppeKD.
14 Archived at http://bit.ly/iinCcz.
15 "Transcript: Confirmation Hearing of Condoleezza Rice," *New York Times*, January 18, 2005, archived at http://nyti.ms/iyQ3o1.
16 Seymour M. Hersh, "The Coming Wars," *New Yorker*, January 24, 2005, archived at http://nyr.kr/HrYw1.
17 Archived at http://bit.ly/fiSvK5.
18 Archived at http://bit.ly/agrTHq.
19 Archived at http://bit.ly/e6O5Wq.
20 The Combating Terrorism Center, U.S. Military Academy, *The Islamic Imagery Project*, March 2006, archived at http://bit.ly/l0F5Pe.
21 This listing was accessed on MySpace in June 2006 but was subsequently taken off the site.
22 Archived at http://bit.ly/g2t2H0.

3
Resist

Speaking to the media, metaphorically speaking, is a particular obsession of CM. This is mostly a cathartic process, because little feedback loop is traditionally available to a casual reader. These entries represent the need to resist the overabundance of pablum, which newspapers and magazines (and state functionaries, such as Seth Jones) force onto the ill-informed and the misinformed.

Dear Robin[1]
May 16, 2004

You are a good journalist. You have been to the Middle East, to Iran, to all the other "hot spots." I usually agree with your articles, and you are one of the better talking heads on MSNBC. So, when I saw your piece in today's *Washington Post* entitled "Turning Points: Will the Modern Era Come Undone in Iraq?" I clicked on it immediately.

Girl. You need some happy pills.

The stakes in Iraq—for which the Abu Ghraib prison has tragically become the metaphor—are not just the future of a fragile oil-rich country or America's credibility in the world, even among close allies. The issues are not simply whether the Pentagon has systemic problems or whether Defense Secretary Donald H. Rumsfeld, the Pentagon brass or even the Bush administration can survive The Pictures. And the costs are not merely the billions from the U.S. Treasury to foot the Iraq bills today or the danger that Mideast oil becomes a political weapon during tumultuous days down the road.

The stakes are instead how the *final phase of the Modern Era plays out.*

That 500-year period, marked by the age of exploration, the creation of nations and the Enlightenment that unleashed ideologies designed to empower the individual, faces its last great challenge in the 50 disparate countries that constitute the Islamic world—ruled by the last bloc of authoritarian monarchs, dictators and leaders-for-life. The Iraq war was supposed to produce a new model for democratic transformation, a catalyst after which the United States and its allies could launch an ambitious initiative for regional change.

But now, whatever America's good intentions may have been, that historic moment may be lost for a long time to come.[2] [*emphasis added*]

Say what? End of Enlightenment? You think this will "also spur an intense clash of civilizations, a prospect I had until very recently rejected"? Wow. Not you, too!

The Iraq War was stupidly launched. The Iraq War was stupidly managed. The Iraq War will generate hundreds more terrorist wanna-be playas. I agree with all those wholeheartedly. But to say that the Project of Enlightenment itself will perish!? I have news for you, Ms. Wright. The Project of Enlightenment is gasping for breath in the United States itself. Your president talks to God. Your Congress fears Gay Union will end Civilization. Your country is holding hundreds of people without any recourse to legal aid and in extreme duress. It incarcerates more people than any other society on the planet. Racial or sexual equality is still a "goal" for the society. Your last election was stolen by a junta. I mean, I can go on here, but you get the picture. Don't start crying about this precious Enlightenment that launched the Modern Era and will perish because of some Arab tyrants. You want to save a clash of civilization? One clue: It's a self-fulfilling prophecy.

How about we try a whole new approach? How about we stop messing with the progress of the Modern Era by upholding dictators and commanding policy? How about we actually try to give Palestinians a homeland and aid to build a society after 60 years? How about we let Islamic governments be Islamic governments and not think that all theocracies are created equal? Because, the truth is, Robin, there are many Enlightenments and many Modern Eras. The one being exported by the barrel of a gun in Iraq is not gonna be the one the Iraqis live within 2 years or 5. They will construct their own.

So, please, be hopeful. Make your government answer to its people. Let the Iraqis answer to themselves.

Ararat[3]
July 19, 2004

Some nights ago, I watched *Ararat* at the local student theatre. Outside the screening, the Turkish Students Association had put a huge poster saying, "This Movie Is Not the Historical Truth." They were also passing out flyers that "disputed" the movie's claims and sought to "balance" the picture. For those in the dark, the movie deals with the genocide/holocaust of the Armenian population at the hands of the Ottoman Turks during World War I.

Atom Egoyan, of Armenian descent, chose to use his trademark screw-narra-tive-and-continuity-by-postmodernism-101 to tell this story. There are tangents enough to fill Euclid's nightmares. We get a movie-within-a-movie, and characters appear in both memory and reality as both characters and individuals. The author on whose work the movie is partially based appears as the author on whose work the movie-within-the movie is partially based (Charlie Kaufman is obviously a hack)—all that is good and well, and I expected as much.

More interesting to me was how he would treat the material. He allows one half-Turkish character to raise doubts about the overall scheme: "The genocide never happened. This was a war, and population get shifted during wars. The Armenians were allying with the Russians against the Ottomans, and they had to be moved." He is also the only character who says to the Armenian boy toy, "I was born here [Canada] and so were you. This is a new country. Let's forget what happened so long ago and come have a drink." To which the Armenian boy toy replies, "You know what Hitler told his commanders to convince them to carry out the Holocaust? He said, 'Who remembers the Armenian Genocide?'"

And that was the crux on which the movie rotates: memory—specifically, the demands of the Dead on the memory of the Living. What to remember? How to remember? And can one ever forget? The Armenians complained, in the movie and outside, that the Turkish government has never owned up to the genocide. That the Turks claim it never happened. Considering the fact that the present-day Turkish government has little to do with the Ottoman Empire, that accusation is ultimately directed at the Turkish people. They do not remember what they did to us. We were persecuted because of our religion (Christianity as opposed to Islam) and our society (Armenians were the traditional business class in the Ottoman Empire).

The Turkish students outside the theatre had a different memory. They claimed that the holocaust claimed Kurds, local Muslims, as well as Armenians. Let's remember all the people who died in that war and not the selected ones who desire to make their memories into political game play. Plus, Turks themselves have been victims of Armenian terrorism throughout the 20th century (numer-ous assassinations of Turkish diplomats were carried out by Armenians in the '50s–'80s).

Obviously, these are not the only silenced memories. The Gypsy holocaust at Auschwitz, the partition of India, civil wars in Sri Lanka, Rwanda, Congo, Hiroshima, Nagasaki, etc., etc., are all silent memories plaguing humanity. We chose not to pay attention, because no one is asking us to remember!

W. G. Sebald wrote recently on the absence of any memory of the destruction of German cities by Allied bombers at the end of the World War II; 600,000 lives, he said, have left no memory or trace on the inner life of the nation. When his book *On the Natural History of Destruction* was published earlier this year, there was a chorus of critiques that said either: (1) What about the bombings the Germans did of London or the Holocaust? or (2) it was war and that was the expected Allied reaction. These may be valid points but are hardly sympathetic to the civilians lost. According to Sebald, though, even the Germans want to forget. They quickly built over, and the episode was relegated to some "protohistory."

The memory of destruction, hence, becomes the memory of the present, whether the Turkish government, or the Holocaust deniers, must bear witness and admit to the memory. The memory of lives lost is subsumed under the politics of guilt and suppression.

The question I left the theater with was simple: Is it possible to remember a trauma of such immense proportion as a collective, social memory? That is, not counting those who lost family and friends to massacres, what memories do others who share ethnicity, religion, or nationality with the destroyed have?

I was raised in Pakistan with a very particular national memory of the partition. Lives lost, rapes, mass migration were part of a narrative that shared no culpability with the Hindus. But this memory was mine through the memory of the nation. I read the accounts left by those who were migrating away from Lahore. Only then it dawned on me that my collective memory had forgotten the one element around which this whole facade is built: the peasants who actually died. As a nation, we remembered what was convenient and permissible. The atrocities on that side of that blood-soaked border and not this.

The G.O.P. is holding the Republican Convention in New York as close to September 11 as possible. It is being held so late that many states will have to amend election laws to allow President Bush to appear on the slates. Only 2 years after, we are coming against the well of collective memory being used in political pulleys. Some who have said or written things contrary to this memory have already been silenced.

In the end, I think that there is little Atom Egoyan has to answer for. He is only trying his best to remember for his people. Could he have told the story of even one of those who lost their lives? Sure. But then it would not be the political statement that *Ararat* is. Who cares about people when memories live forever?

Dear Mr. Brooks[4]
August 25, 2005

In your August 25 column, "Divided They Stand," you conclude:

> But when you get Galbraith and Gerecht in the same mood, you know something important has happened. The U.S. has orchestrated a document that is organically Iraqi.
> It's their country, after all.[5]

However, in your entire piece, there is not a single quote from any actual Iraqi who may or may not have any opinion on the constitution. As I see it, you have demonstrated the myopia of the American enterprise in Iraq perfectly—American analysts talking about perceptions in the American media as counterspin in an American op-ed for American audience.

Since you couldn't find any "Iraqi" to tell you anything about what that Constitution means to him, I really fail to see your conclusion. I take your words of esteem for "Peter W. Galbraith, a former U.S. ambassador to Croatia, and smart Iraq analyst, Reuel Marc Gerecht, formerly of the C.I.A. and now at the American Enterprise Institute," but I doubt that they call Iraq their country.

If you would like to get the Baghdad street view of the Constitution, perhaps you can call someone who is (1) an Iraqi, (2) in Baghdad, and (3) involved in the Constitution-making process. *Then*, you can conclude whether the Iraqi Constitution is organic or not.

cheers,
m.

Dear Mr. Friedman[6]
September 28, 2005

In your September 28 column, "The Endgame in Iraq," you conclude:

> Maybe the cynical Europeans were right. Maybe this neighborhood is just beyond trans-formation. That will become clear in the next few months as we see just what kind of minority the Sunnis in Iraq intend to be. If they come around, a decent outcome in Iraq is still possible, and we should stay to help build it. If they won't, then we are wasting our time. We should arm the Shiites and Kurds and leave the Sunnis of Iraq to reap the wind. We must not throw more good American lives after good American lives for people who hate others more than they love their own children.[7]

You want to arm the Shiites and the Kurds to do exactly what? Oh! To let the Sunnis "reap the wind." I am sure that the TimeSelect barrier is not nearly enough for a *New York Times* columnist to advocate ethnic cleansing. But wait, you are way too smart for that, aren't you, Mr. Friedman? Because you have already accused the "minority" Sunnis of ethnic cleansing: *Do the Iraqi Sunnis understand their own interests, and does the Sunni world have any moral center? Up to now, the Sunni Arab world has stood mute while the Sunni Baathists and jihadists in Iraq have engaged in what can only be called "ethnic cleansing": murdering Shiite civilians in large numbers purely because they are Shiites in hopes of restoring a Sunni-dominated order in Iraq that is un-restorable.* Yes, the "jihadists" now represent the entirety of Sunnis—inside and outside Iraq [the actual count of Shia insurgents remains zero, according to a leading expert in Middle East asshatry, Tom Friedman]. The 80 percent Shia majority is being ethnically cleansed by the Sunnis—they pass out sect-identification cards before the car blows up, I am sure. Perhaps, only perhaps because I am not as astute as a *NYT* columnist, the jihadists are killing civilians to create unrest and panic regardless of sectarian affiliation? Hmm?

In any case, how should the Sunnis of Iraq feel about the bombs that kill their own—even if some of their own set them up? What should they do about the armies that enforce "evacuations"? So far, your army has decimated Fallujah, Tal Afar, and Qaim, among other Sunni "strongholds"—also known as cities. What is the proper response that you seek from this minority? To endorse the U.S.-designed "Constitution" that remains unavailable to be read by any Iraqi citizen to this day? That gives over control of Sunni areas to the majority (who, I am sure, are not at all pissed about the "brutaliz[ation] by an oil-backed Sunni minority regime," not to mention the more recent, "ethnic cleansing")? Yes, they should issue *fatwas* against the jihadists because that inscrutable Arab mind understands nothing more than a two-bit religious edict issuable by any GED-equivalency madrasa-diploma holder. And then suck it up. Right? The Sunnis that you want killed off already know that they are a target. Maybe some more Sunnis will raise arms and join the jihadists or *maybe*, just *maybe*, they will use other means. Maybe, before you have U.S. arms merchants sell U.S. weapons to the Kurds and the Shia to kill their fellow Iraqis and Muslims, you should listen to them:

> Imam Mu'ayad al-Adhami of the Abu Hanifa mosque in Baghdad also blames for-eign influence for the recent talk of rising sectarian tensions. "The Americans are using divide and conquer to try to split the Muslims of Iraq," he says softly, while gesturing with his large hands. "But Iraqi society is Muslim first and tribal second. That means Sunni and Shia are relatives, often in the same family with so many links and intermarriages. This is our society and anyone trying to divide us is blind to these facts."
>
> The sheik offered several examples of solidarity between the two sects. Last year, when his Shiite neighbors in the Khadamiya district just across the Tigris from Adhamiya were struck by a devastating suicide bomb attack during the Ashura holiday, his was the first mosque to ask people to donate blood.
>
> ...
>
> A visit to Baghdad University reinforces the sense that Iraqi nationalism and Islamic identity are more deeply felt than sectarian allegiances. Despite the fact that the university suffered looting in the aftermath of the invasion and much of it remains in disrepair, the campus, now home to more than 100 refugee families from Falluja, remains an island of normalcy for college students of both sects of

Islam. Most do not foresee sectarian differences necessitating civil war or the partition of their country.[8]

You, Mr. Friedman, are morally and ethically despicable.

cheers,
m.

Contra Niall[9]
January 15, 2006

Niall Ferguson, the über-historian, has one of those cute historian-of-the-future columns in the *Telegraph/Los Angeles Times*. Kinda like, what would your 40-year-old self say to your 14-year-old confused teenager, I suppose. So, in this back to the future column, the digitized Ferguson wonders whether it was the lack of balls of the "West" in 2006 that led to the Great Gulf War of 2007–2011, including a nuclear exchange between Tel Aviv and Tehran. See, if the leaders and people of America and London (that's all that counts as "West") had not deferred to internal politics and pressure, they would have invaded Iran and not caused the great war. Or something.

Since Ferguson loves contrafactuals, here is my random one:

With the world firmly behind them after the atrocious attack of 2001 and the routing of the Taliban in Afghanistan, the American state started a historically unprecedented effort to erase radicalization and terrorism throughout the world. By denying multinational companies the rights to do business with despots, cutting off all political and economical aid, and forcing a strict agenda of internal elections, the United States was able to lead by example a wellspring of democratic freedom from Lebanon to Pakistan. Working with the international agencies, it sunk billions of dollars in building up apparatus of civic and legal frameworks in societies that had hitherto only seen despots.

The efforts, which seemed like liberal pipedreams in the first decade of the 21st century, started to bear fruit when the United Kingdoms of Arabia swore in their first constitutionally elected federal government in 2011. Iran's efforts at market reforms and economic parity had already made it an important ally in the region, with the hard-line religious parties standing little chance unless they adapted the reform and integrate agendas. Or something.

The Break Dance[10]
June 26, 2006

In case you hadn't noticed, Iraq is kinda back in the news. The Chosen One is up 8 to 10 points in the polls. The Dems are finding every possible way to not think or act. In the annals of Iraq War, the following would get indexed as high comedy: Republicans say, "Stay the course"; Democrats say, "Cut and run"; the generals say, "Run through the course once, and then cut to the exit"; Iraqi prime minister says, "Excuse me!" Do you ever get the feeling that no one got the Pottery Barn memo? Every single party in D.C. has played and continues to play the Iraq War for domestic politics.

But what about our thinking heads? What are people who *aren't* running in elections saying about the future in Iraq? In a recent essay published in *Foreign Affairs*, "Seeing Baghdad, Thinking Saigon," Stephen Biddle argues that the United States has to stop with the Vietnamization of Iraq and instead: (a) "slow down the expansion of the Iraqi national military and police" and (b) "threaten to manipulate the military balance of power among Sunnis, Shiites, and Kurds to coerce them to negotiate." Clearly, Biddle is arguing for *Direct Rule* over Iraq—the stated policy of the British Empire after the Rising of 1857. The objective, then and now, is stability and the clear containment of local powers, whether military or political. Biddle may disagree with my characterization, but that is my conclusion when I read:

> Washington should also avoid setting any more arbitrary deadlines for democratization. . . . Democracy is the long-term goal in Iraq, of course, but getting there will require a near-term constitutional compromise whose key provision must be an agreement to limit the freedom of Iraqi voters to elect governments that concentrate ethnic and sectarian power. Resolving the country's communal security problems must take priority over bringing self-determination to the Iraqi people—or the democracy that many hope for will never emerge.[11]

To steal from *Spinal Tap*: "It's like, how much more colonialism could this be? And the answer is none. None more colonialism."

Foreign Affairs asked a group of policy heads and academics to respond to Biddle's article. Larry Diamond, James Dobbins, Chaim Kaufmann, and Leslie H. Gelb came back with their reading of Biddle as well as their suggestions on possible strategies in Iraq. Diamond argues that the United Nations and European Union should be asked to mediate in Iraq and get the communalism under control. Dobbins suggests that Iraq's neighbors have a vested interest in a stable Iraq and should be given that responsibility, along with a recommendation that the United States think along the lines of the "counterinsurgency campaigns of Central America in the 1980s, where U.S. military involvement was largely limited to advice and training." Paired, of course, with ~~a well-placed dictator~~, er, diplomacy. Kaufmann proclaims that Iraq is doomed to "develop internal communal borders with a few heavily guarded crossing points," and the best that the United States can do is minimize the ethnic cleansing. And finally Gelb also takes a page from the British Empire (the end of colonial India time, in his case) and states that "decentralization" is the only real option. A U.S. brokered partition with some attempt to "to assist those Iraqis who wish to relocate to safer terrain, temporarily or permanently."

Rather grim, no? What happened to the promised freedom? How did a country in 4 years develop sectarian and communal conflict so entrenched that one can only speak in terms like "ethnic cleansing" and "federated boundaries"? Is there any reading of Iraq's history in these assessments? Any reading of Iraq's present that is not informed wholly by U.S. media or state? Did they think of asking an Iraqi?

I have long maintained that the comparisons between the U.S. adventures in Iraq and the British Empire were short on facts and long on sentiments, but after reading these essays in the *Foreign Affairs*, I am of the mind that the facts are going to catch up to the sentiments, *real soon*.

Friedman, You Are a Racist Idiot[12]
December 23, 2006

I don't read Tom Friedman, or any other *New York Times* columnist, thanks (wholeheartedly) to TimeSelect. However, his column from December 20, "Mideast Rules to Live By,"[13] is so beyond the pale. The blog *Arabist* already has the fuller takedown, but short Friedman: Arabs are a tribe of lying, conniving, cheating, haters who are genetically unable to stop their lying, fighting, cheating, and hating—especially when it comes to Palestine. So, being a Great Power, we shouldn't have gotten involved with Small Tribes.

Oh, the burden of imperialism. Go ahead and substitute "Jew" for "Arab" in that column [hey, they are both Semitic people!], and let me know how that goes. That such racist pablum is published in our paper of record is indicative of how this country feels about Muslims and Arabs. Virgil Goode, have a Merry Christmas.

Say Wha? III[14]
October 4, 2007

> A specialist on Islam at the State Department nearly wept envisioning a "Danish-cartoons situation," Mr. Kiriakou said. An Afghan literature professor, he added, said Paramount was "willing to burn an already scorched nation for a fistful of dollars." The head of an Afghan political party said the movie would energize the Taliban. Nearly everyone Mr. Kiriakou met said that the boys had to be removed from Afghanistan for their safety. And a Hazara member of Parliament warned that Pashtun and Hazara "would be killing each other every night" in response to the film's depiction of them.[15]

The news piece, concerned as it is with the plight of the child actors from the movie *The Kite Runner*, sadly doesn't linger on that weeping Islam specialist at the State. (Are there other specialists who weep? For other injustices? Does that weeping cut into their "sober analysis time"?) And is much the poorer for it. Yet even in the rush to show us the topsy-turvy world of a Hollywood studio doing security-risk analysis and international diplomacy, it still manages to give us things to ponder:

> Though the book is admired in Afghanistan by many in the elite, its narrative remains unfamiliar to the broader population, for whom oral storytelling and rumor communication carry far greater weight.
>
> ...
>
> The film's director, Marc Forster, whose credits include *Finding Neverland* (2004), another film starring child actors, said he saw *The Kite Runner* as "giving a voice and a face to people who've been voiceless and faceless for the last 30 years."
>
> ...
>
> So on Sunday Rich Klein, a Middle East specialist at the consulting firm Kissinger McLarty Associates, flew to the United Arab Emirates to arrange visas, housing and schooling for the young actors and jobs for their guardians. (The United States is not an option, he said, because Afghans do not qualify for refugee status.)
>
> Those involved say that the studio doesn't want to be taken advantage of, but that it could accept responsibility for the boys' living expenses until they reach adulthood, a cost some estimated at up to $500,000. The families, of course, must first agree to the plan...

Nicholas Schmidle[16]
January 11, 2008

For crying out loud. *Hadh hoti hay.* Our mango republic, ran by the Dictator Formerly Known as the General, has lost its mind.

I have often highlighted the reports and writings of Nicholas Schmidle, a freelance journalist, reporting from Pakistan on numerous occasions. I have often exchanged emails with him. He was, contra majority, writing, researching, and engaging directly with the turmoil gripping that nation. Something that I admired and respected in him.

I say "was," because he was deported from the country by the government, Steve Clemons reported today. [Thanks, e.]

His sin, according to Clemons, may be that his recent piece in the *New York Times Magazine*, "Next-Gen Taliban,"[17] was deemed offensive.

I can, off the top of my head, list a thousand things more offensive in Pakistan at this moment.

Schmidle's piece doesn't make the list.

I am too angry to really pretend having that academic distance my gentle readers expect from me.

Once a Muslim[18]
May 12, 2008

For a while, the exemplar op-ed for ridiculousness and gross violation of logic, reason, history, and straw-men argumentation was Bernard Lewis's appearance on the *Wall Street Journal* pages declaring the End of Times. But, I think that standard has now been met, if not exceeded, by Edward Luttwak's incredibly offensive "President Apostate?"[19] Love that Question Mark. Oh, Luttwak, why the Question Mark? Tell us how you really know and understand the 1 billion Muslims and their burning hatreds.

To what purpose does the *New York Times* give space to such claptrap? I am sure there are many thousands of voices waiting for the ability to speak to the *NYT*'s global audience. And they chose this partisan hack?

Aaargh.

Update 1: It was heartening to see that all of the letters to the editors flayed Luttwak. Also, Juan Cole does the dutiful and takes on the theological argument in "Is Obama the Apostate, or Is Bush? A Reply to Luttwak."

Update 2: The public editor for the *NYT* has a note today, "Entitled to Their Opinions, Yes. But Their Facts?" Hoyt writes that he called up five experts of Islamic jurisprudence, and they all said Luttwak was wrong. And that the editors of the op-ed page never consulted any such experts, because they don't "customarily call experts to invite them to weigh in on the work of our contributors." Not only that, David Shipley, the editor of the op-ed page, does not "think the op-ed page was under any obligation to present an alternative view, beyond some letters to the editor."

Your liberal press in action.

Good God Man[20]
June 11, 2008

> I just had dinner at a Nile-side restaurant with two Egyptian officials and a businessman, and one of them quoted one of his children as asking: "Could something like this ever happen in Egypt?" And the answer from everyone at the table was, of course, "no." It couldn't happen anywhere in this region. Could a Copt become president of Egypt? Not a chance. Could a Shiite become the leader of Saudi Arabia? Not in a hundred years. A Bahai president of Iran? In your dreams. Here, the past always buries the future, not the other way around.[21]

Obama is not a Muslim!

If a Shiite cannot become the leader of Saudi Arabia, then a Muslim cannot lead the United States either. Okay? Do you have a functional brain??

Friedman's hilariously painful column "Obama on the Nile" is—as usual—full of inanities, but two points are worth yelling out aloud about: (1) American exceptionalism and (2) American exceptionalism.

Thanks to Lapata for telling me not to read today's Friedman.

Oh the Drudgery of Punditry . . . [22]
September 15, 2008

Christopher Hitchens, of much ill-repute, tries his hand at Pakistan in "Pakistan Is the Problem":

> The very name *Pakistan* inscribes the nature of the problem. It is not a real country or nation but an acronym devised in the 1930s by a Muslim propagandist for partition named Chaudhary Rahmat Ali. It stands for *Punjab, Afghania, Kashmir,* and *Indus-Sind.* The *stan* suffix merely means "land." In the Urdu language, the resulting acronym means "land of the pure." It can be easily seen that this very name expresses expansionist tendencies and also conceals discriminatory ones. Kashmir, for example, is

part of India. The Afghans are Muslim but not part of Pakistan. Most of Punjab is also in India. Interestingly, too, there is no B in this cobbled-together name, despite the fact that the country originally included the eastern part of Bengal (now Bangladesh, after fighting a war of independence against genocidal Pakistani repression) and still includes Baluchistan, a restive and neglected province that has been fighting a low-level secessionist struggle for decades. The P comes first only because Pakistan is essentially the property of the Punjabi military caste (which hated Benazir Bhutto, for example, because she came from Sind). As I once wrote, the country's name "might as easily be rendered as 'Akpistan' or 'Kapistan,' depending on whether the battle to take over Afghanistan or Kashmir is to the fore."[23]

Oh, so the *word* alone is enough! Who cares a whit about history, politics, culture, yada yada. Let's *divine* like oracles from Hafiz! Oh and quoting yourself? Priceless.

If I were a professor, and this were a freshman paper (about the level of analysis at display), I would have taken the paper to Jimmy's, invited all my friends, and read it aloud—karaoke style.

Simple Truths[24]
April 5, 2009

James Traub's cover story "Can Pakistan Be Governed?"[25] is actually fairly nuanced and one of the better things to have appeared in the *New York Times Magazine* recently.

More important is the cover image for the magazine. I like to compile short lists of reigning conventional wisdoms on Pakistan, and this cover is a beauty. Check it:

PERILOUS
ANARCHIC
BROKE
VIOLENT
SPLINTERING
CORRUPT
ARMED
GOVERNABLE?

The casual glance at this list confirms every fear in our secret liberal (or neocon) hearts even as the 8,000 words inside proffer a more complex world. But who has time for complexity? Or use?

Update 3: Anil gets the brownie for "Wordle'ing" the Traub article. Thanks, mate!

Fragile Rock[26]
November 12, 2009

In a (somewhat cringe-inducing) video report at the *New York Times*, Adam B. Ellick takes aim at some of the very popular Pakistani pop stars and their lack of attention to the Taliban.[27] (To be explicit, Ellick narrates this with more than a modicum of sneer as to why Pakistani rockers are singing of extraneous issues like "meddling America" or "torture at Gitmo" or "corruption or poverty" or "drone attacks" instead of, you know, "Taliban." Sure, the Noori kids are idiotic. But what exactly is his point in "Would you sing a song about Taliban blowing up schools?" or "the words don't even mention 'Taliban' or 'terrorism.'" Is this a reality that is somehow missing from Pakistan? Obviously not, since he does show news and views channels expressly against them.)

Not that we could tell much about U.S. campaigns in Afghanistan, Iraq, and Af-Pak since 2001 ("Courtesy of the Red, White, and Blue" anyone?) from U.S. population registers, it is still an illuminating look at what a "certain" segment of youth is consuming.

Mr. Ellick could look at a couple of recent anti-suicide bombing/Taliban songs. You may not understand the Punjabi/Urdu, but you can easily follow the visual story. Both of these singers are just as popular, if not more, than Ali Azmat or Shehzad Roy featured in the *NYT* report.

Abrar ul-Haq, *Awain Na Kar Zulm* (Do not do such tyranny).

What heaven after you blow up heaven? What heaven after you kill children? What are these lures of virgins? These are victims of conspiracies. Where will you hide from God?

And here is Rahat Fateh Ali Khan, the nephew of maestro Nusrat, *Khuda Zamin say giya nahin hai* (God has not left this world). This is the title song of a new PTV serial, which does shine forth in all patriotic glory. But still.

The Seth Jones Experience[28]
December 4, 2009

Seth G. Jones, the author of In the Graveyard of Empires: America's War in Afghanistan, *is a civilian adviser to the American military.*

One of the brains behind President Barack Obama's Afghanistan policy, Seth G. Jones, of RAND & McCrystal, has a particularly unhinged op-ed in today's *New York Times*: "Take the War to Pakistan":

> The United States and Pakistan must target Taliban leaders in Baluchistan. There are several ways to do it, and none requires military forces.
> The first is to conduct raids to capture Taliban leaders in Baluchistan. Most Taliban are in or near Baluchi cities like Quetta. These should be police and intelligence operations, much like American-Pakistani efforts to capture Khalid Shaikh Mohammed and other Qaeda operatives after 9/11. The second is to hit Taliban leaders with drone strikes, as the United States and Pakistan have done so effectively in the tribal areas.[29]

The moral bankruptcy apparent in the contrast between two sentences ("none requires military forces") and ("to hit the Taliban with drone strikes") is breathtaking. "Baluchi cities" like Quetta only have a million or so people, after all. Our precision strikes are surely only to singe a few curled mustaches. Right, Jones? But, yeah, I know. Crying about civilian casualties from nonmilitary force is a luxury that only the uninformed and uneducated can afford. There are hard choices to make for real wars to end. And harder sells to make, as Nathan Hodge demonstrates in regards to Jones's colleagues, the Kagans, in "How the Afghan Surge Was Sold."[30] In any case, Seth G. Jones is so much "civilian" cover for a war that has already spilled into Baluchistan. *And with only 20 casualties! Hallelujah.*

Since Jones has never shown a predilection to history. . . here be a crude lesson about what the United States is getting into in Baluchistan: an existing war since 2004.

Seth G. Jones comes from the University of Chicago's political science program and is an advisee of John Mearsheimer. His dissertation, "The Rise of Europe: Security Cooperation and the Balance of Power," deals with the European Union and intracountry security apparatus. He has no access to any relevant language or historical archive. All of which, of course, makes him the perfect man to construct and explain this.[31]

I am too tired even to complain.

Chapter Notes

1 Archived at http://bit.ly/hfergH.
2 Robin Wright, "Turning Points," *Washington Post*, May 16, 2004, archived at http://wapo.st/lofqVy.
3 Archived at http://bit.ly/fBfoku.
4 Archived at http://bit.ly/ftcBHS.

5 David Brooks, "Divided They Stand," *New York Times*, August 25, 2005, archived at http://nyti.ms/jfNJk5.

6 Archived at http://bit.ly/i9O11p.

7 Thomas L. Friedman, "The Endgame in Iraq," *New York Times*, September 28, 2005, archived at http://bit.ly/lmx7SD.

8 Dahr Jamail, "Sects and Solidarity in Iraq," *Nation*, March 22, 2005, archived at http://bit.ly/mMiWBc.

9 Archived at http://bit.ly/hqXFCG.

10 Archived at http://bit.ly/hVvq0b.

11 Stephen Biddle, "Seeing Baghdad, Thinking Saigon," *Foreign Affairs*, March/April 2006, archived at http://fam.ag/lxSTPc.

12 Archived at http://bit.ly/dSvllK.

13 Thomas L. Friedman, "Mideast Rules to Live By," *New York Times*, December 20, 2006, archived at http://bit.ly/k7JcfD.

14 Archived at http://bit.ly/fyxQtM.

15 David M. Halbfinger, "'The Kite Runner' Is Delayed to Protect Child Stars," *New York Times*, October 4, 2007, archived at http://nyti.ms/mQ5Szi.

16 Archived at http://bit.ly/fEU8Q0.

17 Nicholas Schmidle, "Next-Gen Taliban," *New York Times Magazine*, January 6, 2008, archived at http://nyti.ms/iOSlfN.

18 Archived at http://bit.ly/hXdlrs.

19 Edward N. Luttwak, "President Apostate?" *New York Times*, May 12, 2008, archived at http://nyti.ms/ioGwE8.

20 Archived at http://bit.ly/hN1hG0.

21 Thomas L. Friedman, "Obama on the Nile," *New York Times*, June 11, 2008, archived at http://nyti.ms/koYpwd.

22 Archived at http://bit.ly/htdsY5.

23 Christopher Hitchens, "Pakistan Is the Problem," *Slate.com*, September 15, 2008, archived at http://slate.me/bzlh6f.

24 Archived at http://bit.ly/erQBOp.

25 James Traub, "Can Pakistan Be Governed?" *New York Times Magazine*, March 31, 2009, archived at http://nyti.ms/3Fklbn.

26 Archived at http://bit.ly/3Gu01I.

27 Adam B. Ellick, "Pakistan Rock Rails Against the West, Not the Taliban," *New York Times*, November 11, 2009, archived at http://nyti.ms/226CKM.

28 Archived at http://bit.ly/5TbLtB.

29 Seth G. Jones, "Take the War to Pakistan," *New York Times*, December 3, 2009, archived at http://nyti.ms/6rzfsl.

30 Nathan Hodge, "How the Afghan Surge Was Sold," *Wired*, December 3, 2009, archived at http://bit.ly/530LQ1.

31 "This" refers to the document "Dynamic Planning for COIN in Afghanistan," archived at http://bit.ly/5iuHKp.

4
Debate

The question often raised since October 2001 is whether America has entered an imperial phase. This, I have maintained, is a horrid misreading of America's past, which was explicitly imperial and colonial from its very inception—certainly the long history of military expeditions on the American continent as well as beyond it are a clear testament to that. Yet the debate over the "empire-ness" of America seems never-ending, because it is a debate not over history but over representation. Early in the life of CM, I wrote a series of posts in an effort to engage with historian Bernard Porter's work on the British Empire. Those posts form the backbone of this chapter, but the last post—a review of Robert D. Kaplan's book Monsoon—*is really a summation of my own reading of America's past.*

Hiroshima[1]
August 6, 2004

Fifty-nine years ago, Colonel Tibbets and his crew flew the *Enola Gay* to Hiroshima and detonated Little Boy nearly 2,000 feet above the city. The crew knew at the moment of blast that the human future was now tied inextricably to its own means of destruction.

More than 200,000 people eventually perished in Hiroshima. About as many died from conventional B-29 bombing campaigns. It is not in numbering the dead that the true horror lies. It is in the power of instantaneity.

A plaque here on the University of Chicago campus reads:

Physicist Enrico Fermi and his colleagues established the first self-sustaining controlled nuclear reaction in makeshift laboratories constructed under the grandstands of Stagg Field Stadium on December 2, 1942. The success of this experiment ushered in the atomic age opening tremendous potential to modern science.

Was Hiroshima inevitable from that very day? In *On the Natural History of Destruction*, W. G. Sebald, writing about the Allied bombing of Germany in 1945, says:

> The construction of the strategy of air war in all its monstrous complexity . . . so much intelligence, capital and labour went into the planning of destruction that, under the pressure of all the accumulated potential, it *had* to happen in the end. . . .
>
> This is the history of industry as the open book of human thought and feeling—can materialistic epistemology or any other such theory be maintained in the face of such destruction? Is the destruction not, rather, irrefutable proof that the catastrophes which develop, so to speak, in our hands and seem to break out suddenly are a kind of experiment, anticipating the point at which we shall drop out of what we have thought for so long to be our autonomous history and back into the history of nature?[2]

Were Hiroshima and Nagasaki necessary to stop the war? Necessary to save American lives? Historians have debated these questions exhaustively. Read selections from Harry Truman's diary, about the Smithsonian controversy over the *Enola Gay*, and the history of destruction in "The Decision to Use the Atomic Bomb."[3]

Grand Gestures[4]
November 18, 2004

A couple of nights ago, at a gathering of friends, I did what most tree-hugging hippies do: imagine. I said, wouldn't it have been nice if, after Afghanistan, instead of invading Iraq, The Chosen One had made a grand gesture and said, "Here is $5 billion on the table. I will fund a school and a library in all major cities of the Gulf where anyone can have a free English medium education. And here is $1 billion to aid translation of texts (literature, history, art, etc.) from Arabic to English and back"? Wouldn't that have taken the wind out the sails of those insisting that America is the imperial Satan? Sure, the jihadis will be opposed, but the middle classes and the intelligentsia would have jumped at such a gesture. Just to break the status quo, the endless blame game, to start a new discussion, I said.

The next day, I read that such a gesture has indeed been made: by Manmohan Singh in Kashmir. He announced that he is going to reduce troops in Kashmir. Then, he recognized that the J&K civilians have suffered in the 15 years of turmoil and asked the troops to maintain ideal conduct. Then, he announced that the ban on hiring from J&K will be lifted and jobs will be provided for the youths. And then, he offered a $5.3 billion economic revival plan for the people of Kashmir.

He said, "The time has come to put forward a new blueprint, a fresh vision for Kashmir . . . free from the fear of war, want and exploitation."

Of course, the jihadis ain't buying it. Big surprise. Manmohan Singh just upped the ante for the hearts and minds of the people of Kashmir. A brilliant and timely move by someone I am really beginning to like. Who you gonna call, General Ji?

Empire Week I: The E Word[5]
June 2, 2005

I started Empire Week thinking it would be a cool showcase for talking about Bernard Porter's book, *The Absent-Minded Imperialist*, but I have gotten seriously sidetracked. Some stuff at work and other things have intruded rather rudely. So, today's entry is a tad late and also quite scattershot. Before the week is over, I would like to talk a bit about conceptions of empire in the Middle East and South Asia. I think there are rather interesting variations that can inform the way we look at empires in general. Let's hope I get that far.

From the Latin *imperium* came "empire" and "imperialism," often used interchangeably and, as Porter contends, with a bit of stigma attached. The Left loves throwing the E word around. Postcolonialists see one hidden in every Jane Austen novel. Also, there is American Neo-Imperialism, keeping them up at night. "Empire" is a now a dirty word, where once, and in living memory, it was a proud one.

While we are on the subject of words, let's list the *C* family: Civilization, Capitalism, and Colonialism. From this petri dish of ideas and agents—ancient, medieval, and modern—came the ascendancy of the West and the establishment of the greatest of modern empires: the British Empire.

The question before us is: What did it mean? What did the British Empire mean from the chartering of the British East India Company in 1600 to the British departure in 1947? What did it mean to the people at the center and to those in the colony? What did it mean to those with power and those subject to that power? Which particular worldviews and self-views were these various understandings of empire emerging?

According to the *Oxford English Dictionary*, an empire is "an extensive territory (*esp.* an aggregate of many separate states) under the sway of an emperor or supreme ruler; also, an aggregate of subject territories ruled over by a sovereign state" and refers, traditionally, to that *Imperium sine fine.*

In Britain's case, empire gave two related sets of beliefs to the citizens/believers. One was about the territoriality of the empire—a dominant "core" that ruled over a conquered "periphery." The other was the Emperor's right to create and execute laws universally (i.e., absolute sovereignty).

Empires cast their shadows in the future (e.g., Greeks to Romans, Byzantine and Sassanian to Umayyad, Abbasid to Mongol, Byzantine to Ottoman, Roman to British, British to American) as each of the latter explicitly construct their mythology in the light of the former. The British claim to Rome being rather obvious.

The rat race of conquest and colonialization between France and England had a lot to do with the ways Britain saw itself. At various points in the 17th century and early 18th century, we find England call its colonial administration the "Old Colonial System." By the 1690s, the term gets phased out, and specific references to "empire" crop up in maps, etc. It is not a complete process, nor an uncontested one. For example, Edward Littleton, one of the largest landowning planters in Barbados, wrote a pamphlet titled *The Groans of the Plantations* or *A True Account of Their Grievous and Extreme Sufferings by the Heavy Impositions upon Sugar, and Other Hardships Relating More Particularly to the Island of Barbados* (1689) in which we find one particular sales pitch for the British "Empire":

> To conclude, there needs no other Argument, That Empire may be raised sooner at Sea, than at Land, than by observing the Growth of the United Provinces. . . . But England seems the Properer Seat for such an Empire; . . . The Monarchy is both fitted for Trade and Empire . . . and if the Subjects increase, The ships, Excise and Customs, which are the Strength and Revenue of the Kingdom, will in Proportion increase, which may be so Great in a short time, not only to preserve its Ancient Soveraignty over the Narrow Seas, but to extend its Dominions over all the Great Ocean: An Empire, not less glorious, and of a much larger Extent than either Alexander's or Caesar's.

In earlier historiography, the period up to the American Revolution was called the First British Empire, its chief feature being that mercantile self-interests were tied to the power to enact laws in the colonies. This was followed by the high imperialism of the Second Empire [1776–1918]. During this period, we get the representations of imperialism as crass exploitation, and the empire with the belligerent civilization mission. By the late 19th century, things were also getting a tad introspective.

In 1880, at the height of the bombastic imperium, Cambridge historian J. R. Seeley's *The Expansion of England* quizzically proclaimed, "We seem, as it were, to have conquered and peopled half the world in a fit of absence of mind."

The anti-imperialists surface around the late 19th century as well. The Boer War had a lot to do with that. See, e.g., the Fabian Society or J. A. Hobson's *Imperialism: A Study.*

The 20th century dawned on a Britain internally and externally contested over its empire and its imperialism. I am fond of asserting that manifestations of colonialism in India were distinctly divergent from 1757 to 1956 and from Afghanistan to Bengal to Mysore. The other side of the equation is just as valid: "Empire" and "imperialism" were contested categories negotiated constantly within the metropole as much as within the colony.

What kind of historian would I be if I didn't endorse complexity?

Empire Week III: The Case of the Americans[6]
June 6, 2005

Benedict Anderson once wrote, "Nations (or, for our purposes, empires) loom from immemorial pasts and . . . glide into limitless futures." If Rome was, and continues to be, the template across which Western empires measured themselves, then Britain is the empire that looms over this American one. (It once was that we called Americans Neo-Imperialists, but now that we actually have a colony or two, we should probably reassess our "neo.")

Those who wanted to understand the nature and role of the British Empire in the 18th and 19th centuries looked to the Romans. In a similar vein, those seeking to understand the present state of "empire-itis" in America should look at the British.

There are the obvious places to compare Britain and America: their behaviors in their colonies, their administration of colonies, their rhetoric, their military spending, the economical benefits of colonization, etc. Even a cursory glance will tell the informed commentator that, while there are stark differences between the British and American models, they have much in common.

Americans invaded a country and installed indirect-rule colonial administrators, with Paul Bremer III as Viceroy and Iyad Allawi as the native elite. The colonial administrators sponsored a limited constitutive assembly and intend to maintain a military presence indefinitely; to sustain their colonial presence and to shore up the regime, they will *have* to expand military conflict outside the boundaries of the present colony.

As to the differences, the Americans will not call themselves an empire. They are quite averse to the E word. They have not claimed a civilizational or racial right to be in the colony (freedom being universal, according to The Chosen One). Naively, they want an early departure. But, if America claims it's not an empire, may we call it that?

As the motto of my dear high school asserted: *facta, non verba*. Whether politicians assert it publicly, America is an empire. It has had colonies in Haiti and the Philippines. It has one in Iraq. But the public demurral and debate remains important nonetheless.

It is the debate that shows how the empire will formulate itself and respond to its charges, and in some cases, how it will act. Comparisons are inherently tricky, but the greater danger lies in the urge to oversimplify and equate wrongly.

The British were not the Romans. The Americans are not British. I would shy away from making such explicit links, but there is one place where I would like to, at the very least, test the possibility of such a comparison: the domestic public and private spheres.

Benjamin Disraeli wrote in 1863:

> I am perfectly aware that there is a school of politicians—I don't believe they are rising politicians—who are hostile to the very principle of a British Empire. But I have yet to learn that the Majesty's Ministers have adopted the wild opinions which have been prevalent of late. Professors and rhetoricians find a system for every contingency and a principle for every chance; but you are not going, I hope, to leave the destinies of the British Empire to prigs and pedants. The statesmen who construct, and the warriors who achieve are only influenced by the instinct of power, and animated by the love of country. Those are the feelings and those the methods which form empire.

I'd like to imagine Donald Rumsfeld saying this under Jeb Bush's second presidency. However, such a quote would never come from the Bush White House.

Why not? Why isn't there wider discussion about empire in United States outside the prigs and pedants' circles? Niall Ferguson, author of *Empire: The Rise and Demise of the British World Order and the Lessons for Global Power* (2003), has sold a lot of books, but no one has actually read them. Why the aversion to the E word? In pop-psych terms, must Americans always root for the underdog? In historical terms, can't an America conceived in anti-colonial struggle fathom becoming one itself? In sociological terms, is it because America itself is a cultural and racial heterogeny? Maybe it is all of the above. To the average American—and I tested this in an impromptu poll on a Chicago street—there is no empire.

Bernard Porter's *Absent-Minded Imperialists: What the British Really Thought about Empire* caught my attention a while ago. I snarked over it. Yet, a more mature, polished sepoy has some thoughts on the book, including about what Porter says empire meant to a subject in the metropole and what it all can possibly mean today.

Empire Week IV: Absent-Minded Imperialists and the Doughnut Effect[7]
June 8, 2005

Maps and tables show empires most clearly. In 1884, a tabulation of the British Empire[8] found the following: It controlled nearly 10 million square miles of territory with 305 million inhabitants, of which only 35 million lived in Britain. The empire generated yearly revenues of £203 million sterling, with one-quarter of that coming from direct taxation. The Imperial Army fielded almost a million soldiers, of which a third came from "the dark races and the remainder . . . of the fair and dominant race." It had 30,000 merchant navy ships manned by 270,000 sailors, thus having 49 percent of the world's carrying power. It exported £241 million sterling worth of British produce, £65 million sterling worth of colonial produce and imported £413 million sterling in produce. Forty-six percent of the world's rails ran British trains. The empire boasted 20 percent of the world's telegraph lines, carrying 31 million messages per year. Policed by 210,000 officers (147,000 of which patrolled India), the British held 145,000 prisoners, of which 103,000 were Indian. In the last 100 years, 8.5 million of its subjects had emigrated, of them, almost all to America. Britain's schools taught 2.5 million kids, one of every three units of world currency passed through British banks, and, at 39 percent, Britain held not most of the world's capital but the most capital in any one nation. The empire's cumulative value, including "land, cattle, railways, public works, houses and furniture, merchandise, bullion, shipping, and sundries," amounted to £1.2 trillion sterling, rending it the wealthiest agglomeration of nations on Earth, by far.

It was this empire, Bernard Porter claims provocatively in *Absent-Minded Imperialists*, that was "marginal" for most British people living inside Britain. Porter's book is a direct response (and a much more effective one than Cannadine's) to Edward Said and the generation of "code-breakers" looking for "hidden imperial signals" in Victorian society. I am a historian, Porter seems to say, and not a cultural theorist, so I will look at the archives and see what it is one can actually prove and not make assumptions. In doing so, he seeks to render complex, what are for him, the two central categories of this discourse: Imperialism and the British.

Power, it appears to me, has always been in the hands of the elite. Policy, it follows, always got dictated by the royal edict or Parliament. Masses, whether Indian or British, have never had a chance to play on the historical playground outside an occasional game of "Off With Their Heads." Cultures are diverse, belief systems are diverse, motivations differ, saturation of ideas vary, implementations of programs diverge. All these are self-evident declarations.

In balance, a historian always makes a case for one narrative over another to render any given past. The question here is: Were the British an imperial society, *in general* assuming given definitions of "British," "imperial," and "society" apply? Sure, says Potter: "Of course they could all be said to be imperialists in a sense. Every one of them was complicit in the empire (as indeed were the workers). They tolerated it. There were no significant movements of protest at this time [late 19th to early 20th century] against imperialism generally."

So what's the new here?

The study of imperialism since Edward Said, Porter believes, has become fashionable and trendy, but it suffers from vague and overgeneralized definitions of "empire," "colonialism," and "imperialism," all operating on the unhistorical assumption that there was a "national culture" in 19th- and early-20th-century Britain.

The first step, in his methodological framework, is to cut away all ancillary systems (exploration, translations, map making, curry eating, or Dr. Watson's adventures in Afghanistan) and concentrate on the central idea of imperialism: "control or domination" over the dominion. Next, one has to take into account the range of "controls" exerted over a diverse geography by a specific "class" of people. The key argument of the book is the demonstration that the British society was stratified along class lines, leaving little or nothing to do about the empire to anyone outside a thin segment of the upper-middle class. Porter sees no national culture to speak of during this time period, but rather "cultures" distributed along classes. Lower classes *did* have knowledge of, and conception of, the empire, but these were different *kinds* of understandings and not the "domineering imperialism" Porter studies. Thusly, imperial conceptions cannot be assumed to have existed within greater British society.

Porter seeks the rehabilitation not just of empire studies, but the British themselves. He is tired of the broad-stroke maligning of the British people. "One whole country does not rule another whole country," he says. "Each . . . contains its share of imperial masters and subjects." As a "white, English, middle-class male, and with rather old-fashioned left-wing proclivities" who grew up with "relative nonawareness of the empire," he cannot identify with the Pom-bashing prevalent in the academy. By segmenting the knowledge of, engagement with, and control of the empire to a particularly powerful subclass, Porter argues for the lack of culpability among the rest.

Because—let's not beat around the bush any longer—what we are really talking about here is "culpability," exemplified by his tiff with Ferguson in the *London Review of Books*.[9] He does not dispute that the empire was a reality or that the empire did terrible things (maybe, some good things?), but he asks us to reconsider whether this was because British society was sexist, racist, jingoist, missionary, and imperial.

Postcolonial scholarship loves to lay into the Victorian mind for being all of those things. But, it also taints current British society: "This in fact may well be the empire's major domestic legacy to post-imperial Britain, overshadowing all others: the reaction against it, the resultant constant apologizing for it, and the blaming it for everything."[10]

Porter does not want to apologize for the empire, because the empire was never *there* for the majority of the population in late-18th- to late-19th-century Britain. What about the atrocities? Porter disarmingly admits to all, yet suggests careful historians should not be so indiscriminate in laying blame. The majority of British people had no involvement. If racism, sexism, religious zeal existed, it does not necessarily follow that imperialism was the root cause. In any case, it was all a "ruling-class imperialism." And if the picture appears differently to those outside the colony, don't despair, because everyone got played equally:

> For them [foreign observors], Britain was defended by her empire, and by the power, arrogance, and sometimes atrocious behaviour they associated with it. This was because the face Britain presented to them, as foreigners, was her imperial one. All the while, however, she was presenting an entirely different self-image to most of her own people: of a free, moderate, and peaceful nation, marked off from other nations by those qualities, and by the domestic "progress" that had formed the main motif of her history for 400 years. . . . There may be a parallel here with the contrast between the [way] Americans are regarded today by foreigners, based on their governments' and corporations' external policies, and the way they regard themselves: all that "shining city on the hill" stuff. Each is a half-truth.[11]

Absent-Minded Imperialists is, in effect, a historiographical critique of empire studies and an engagement with the public and private consumption of knowledge, or lack of it, in any case, about the empire created by the British state and the academy. The bulk of his argument, in this regard, rests on the curriculum of public and private schools and the work of historians during the Second Empire. He finds that, contrary to belief, there was no history or geography taught in British public schools prior to 1880. The curricula were drawn entirely from Greek and Roman classics.

From the 1880s to 1960s, he finds little evidence of imperial studies in schools or universities (this, despite the lament of J. R. Seeley). Textbooks did pick up discussions about the empire after 1880 but did so with a particularly *anti-imperial* outlook—hardly one suitable to train generations of imperialists. The trend held across class lines. The working classes did not get the inculcation of patriotism one expects to find. Instead they got examples of private virtue and dedication from history.

It was only after 1900 that history became a routine subject, led largely due to public efforts of imperial propagandists like the *League of Empire*. These were the early-20th-century history texts that created the genealogies of empire for popular memorialization. The inter-war period saw a new historiography of the empire emerge that whitewashed, ahem, Britain's past. This historiography becomes problematic both for the British academy and the postcolonial one. There is much to appreciate in Porter's handling of this historiography; while I do not agree with his contention that the citizen, or subject, is trained solely in the classroom, I think that this history has not received the attention due to it.

My main objections concern Porter's restrictive definition of "imperialism" and his overemphasis of "class" to the detriment of "religion" or "race" or "civilizational" factors. He acknowledges these areas would be problematic to some and is willing to advance his argument. My complaint is Porter ventures into the other extreme in his efforts to offer a corrective to Saidian-influenced cultural theorists. Where they see the hidden hand of imperialism in every Jane Austen line, he refuses to see it unless it comes under a bullet-pointed subheading labeled "imperialism": Whoever thought of the subcontinent, for example, in connection with 'India Pale Ale'?" he asks.[12]

Perhaps, I respond, anyone who read the word "India" in the title?

"The mere fact that Britain ruled a particular market as a colony did not necessarily mean that she had only traded with it because it was a colony."

I am racking my brain but I cannot really come up with the scenario wherein Britain would *not* trade with a colony.

He writes:

> The "Jingo Song" implies imperialism—it refers to Britain's "Road unto the East" as a reason for resisting the "Russian Bear"; as do, for example, Fat Albert's "We Mean to Keep Our Empire in East" and Henry Rickard's "Hats Off to the Empire" from the same period, 1876–8. But such messages only appear at times of diplomatic excitement and crisis, and the "imperialism" in them is clearly secondary to simple "John Bull" boastfulness and Russophobia.[13]

Did people stop singing the songs in times of diplomatic boredom and status quo? Did these songs disappear? How are John Bull boastfulness and Russophobia not imperialism? Are they untied from nationalist jingoism? Doesn't Porter use the lack of that as his argument against imperialism?

He writes:

> *Crusoe* is perhaps the likeliest soil for empire-diggers, even that is ambivalent on the question . . . . Contemporaries also could have inferred other morals from Crusoe, especially when presented to them in cheap, condensed and sensationalised "chapbook" forms: the woodcut image of a naked Friday cowering before an imperious Crusoe that appeared on the covers of many of the latter might well have negated any more subtle messages.[14]

Well, right. There you go.

> Most working class newspapers content themselves with only token references to events in the colonies. How these struck their subscribers is difficult to say. A clue may be given by a later reader of working-class origins: "these were remote from our little sphere, and only affected us like stories in books."[15]

Stories being quite effective, in their own rights.

In essence, I am unpersuaded Porter can separate racism or jingoism or exploration or translation so easily from imperialism. As one can see from these almost random quotes, Porter has to do some strenuous juggling. I can appreciate an asterisk next to the word, but I cannot, and we should not, restrict "imperialism" to Porter's definition.

I will leave class aside for now. As to the question of race: Porter acknowledges that he neglects it in large measure, but states the motivating factors behind racism did not necessarily need to be imperialism. Point taken, but the application of racist ideology *was* imperialist. Latent or not, racism played an integral part in the formation of the empire narrative and however much of that narrative trickled down the class flue, it brought racism with it. I *could* agree with Porter that an Earl *would* look at a Nawab with some amount of equality, but I *cannot* agree that a London street sweeper would look at a Bombay street vendor with any amount of equality. The language of poverty and dispossession is not quite universal. Porter is largely silent in the matter of religion, since he deems it outside the scope of his defined "imperialism"—along with the curiously discarded "map making" (I am at a loss for a snide comment here about Cyril Radcliffe and his "map making," alas).

Porter discards as much evidence as he accuses others of ignoring. He justifies his methodology by focusing on the semantics of "imperialism," but that is three-card monte: "Everywhere we look we see the same phenomenon: the working classes sucking the sugar, then *probably* spitting the pill of imperial propoganda out."

A lot of probables, indeed.

Porter's imperialism is akin to a doughnut: hollow in the middle, crushing the littoral colonies with fried, white, sugar-coated dough.

Empire Week VI: Back to the Colony[16]
June 10, 2005

It's been fun doing this empire thing. I should have called it "Empire Days." Why do clever things always occur to me *post facto*? I have a lot more to say, but this isn't my field, which makes all I have to say suspect from the beginning. But there will be other times for reflections on discipline-creep.

Let's wrap this up, shall we?

My concern really is to engage the discourse of empire about America. I am pretty comfortable calling America an imperial formation. I know within and without the academy that is an intensely disputed claim; however, that is exactly why Porter's work is valuable. The one lesson to take from Porter is that imperialism, however one defines it, manifests itself differently from political policy to cultural practice to belief systems. It varies as well through the levels within which citizen-subjects are engaged with the state. It varies even among the social hierarchies operating within the society.

There is no need to make a checklist of "empire" and see if America 2005 fits the bill or not. Just as futile is the facile comparison with the British one. While I call the Americans an imperium, I do not think that they are merely the latest reincarnation of the British one.

For those that noticed, Britain and the United States made an announcement today to give relief to African nations. By the overall reticence in the White House, I see the aid package as a reward for Tony Blair's dedication to the Chosen One. It is primarily a project championed by Gordon Brown and Tony Blair. Brown, looking to succeed Blair, remarked to the Tanzanians while signing a £1.87-billion aid package:

"I think the days of Britain having to apologize for its colonial history are over," said Brown, who is the chancellor of the exchequer. "I think we should move forward. I think we should celebrate much of our past rather than apologize for it. I think in particular that we should talk, rightly so, about British values. If we look at the whole span of history, then it's time to emphasize then that's at the core of British history, that's at the core of what people think most of when they think of Britishness. And that's such a powerful potential influence on our future, then I think we should be talking about it more, not less."

It is not a simply an effort to move beyond apologetics for the old regime. It is not simply one man talking, either. In 2002, Robert Cooper, Blair's foreign policy advisor, published an essay in *Re-Ordering the World: The Long-Term Implications of September 11th* called "The Post-Modern State." In it, he declared, "Imperialism in the traditional sense is dead, at least among the Western Powers." And more:

What form should intervention take? The most logical way to deal with chaos, and the one most often employed in the past, is colonisation. But colonisation is unacceptable to postmodern states (and, as it happens, to some modern states too). It is precisely because of the death of imperialism that we are seeing the emergence of the pre-modern world. Empire and imperialism are words that have become terms of abuse in the postmodern world. Today, there are no colonial powers willing to take on the job, though the opportunities, perhaps even the need, for colonisation is as great as it ever was in the 19th century. Those left out of the global economy risk falling into a vicious circle. Weak government means disorder and that means falling investment. In the 1950s, South Korea had a lower GNP per head than Zambia; one has since achieved membership of the global economy, the other has not. All the conditions for imperialism are there, but both the supply and demand for imperialism have dried up. And yet the weak still need the strong and the strong still need an orderly world. A world in which the efficient and well-governed export stability and liberty, and which is open for investment and growth—all of this seems eminently desirable.

What is needed, then, is a new kind of imperialism: one acceptable to a world concerned with human rights and cosmopolitan values. [17]

This new kind of imperialism is not the lone-nation imperialism. It has to be multistate. It is governed, akin to the First Empire, by the desires of global markets, but, like the later empires, it states as its noblesse oblige security, democracy, and the uplift of mankind. The unwelcomed agreement for Africa from the G8 meeting will come with a renewed program of development as outlined in the "Commission for Africa Report." It doesn't take a genius to read the summaries of buzzwords— "Public and private sector working together to identify the obstacles to a favorable investment climate, together with outside support to fund the necessary actions," or "removing trade barriers in developed and other developing-country markets that frustrate the fulfillment of Africa's trade potential"—for the sham of corporate greed and external intervention that they are. Uncoded, they remain the words of goodwill and self-help. The discourse of the new imperium has to be doubly complex. They have all read Fanon.

My contention is we have an Amero-British empire of the present. Not only are the colonies split by oceans but the metropoli as well. What unites this empire— indeed, *makes it so*—are tenets of ideology and the free market (just like before, but version 2.0s) coupled with the American demand for security (remember that African nations like Somalia, Kenya, and Nigeria are considered hot-spots for al-Qaida). It is clear the two nations have unified in ways none thought possible prior to 9/11.

Consider, for a moment, Iraq. The United States could never have launched war without Blair. Consider, the Africa aid. Blair and Gordon cannot do this without the White House. It is a partnership of a shared global vision, one that recognizes the "burden" of spreading wealth, prosperity, freedom, and democracy. It does not want direct rule, because it is corporations that rule, manpower and technology courtesy of Halliburton or Aegis or Bechtel. It does not want indirect rule, because it is the global consortiums like International Monetary Fund and the World Bank who will oversee the process. It merely wants to set the path and the roadmap for the progress—a *particular* type of progress—for the world that lags so sadly behind and threatens to bring it down. There is no choice but to begin the "new imperium" and return to the colony.

It is Friday. I must stop. I promise that there will be no more on empires from me for the next week. I won't see my readership dwindle day by day. I wish you a good weekend, gentle readers.

Recall America's Imperial Past, Understand Its Present[18]
Published in the *National* (Abu Dhabi), December 16, 2010

Deliberate forgetting, like deliberate remembering (in museums, in monuments, in public commemorations), is an integral part of political memory and, indeed, in our everyday lives. It is human nature to omit parts of our past or to relegate them behind carefully constructed narrative frameworks that avoid excessive scrutiny.

The imperial and colonial past of the United States of America is one such example of this institutional amnesia and would explain Donald Rumsfeld's petulant declaration in April 2003 that "we don't seek empires . . . we're not imperialistic, we never have been." Rumsfeld was not particularly in conversation with history when he made his statement. He was responding, perhaps, to the long list of journalists, academics, public-policy thinkers, and government employees who argued America should embrace its already present empire. An early, and forceful voice, was Niall Ferguson, an economic historian, who penned in October 31, 2001, an opinion piece entitled "Welcome the new imperialism," which urged a similar burden onto the United States. The "new," however, is rather galling.

Starting from the Declaration of Independence in 1776, the continental spread of America toward the Pacific is deemed neither colonial nor particularly imperialistic. It is the conflicts with European powers—France, Spain, and England—that frame that particular version of the past. Manifest Destiny ("to overspread the continent allotted by Providence for the free development of our yearly multiplying millions" as described in 1845), once specifically articulated in the 1840s, was abundantly realized in the annexations of Texas, Kansas, and California. Expansion, commerce, and some notion of "popular sovereignty principle" were clearly marked in the opening up of the seas beyond the continent.

Furthermore, the 1856 Guano Islands Act claimed for the United States any "unclaimed" island with sufficient supplies of bird waste (to be used as fertilizer by American farmers) by any American entrepreneur, and this annexation would be defended by the U.S. Navy. The list of island territories annexed, claimed or contested—Cuba, Puerto Rico, Guam, Hawaii, the Philippines, and so on—is long and scattered around the globe.

The last of these, the Philippines and the Spanish-American War in 1898 are two particularly glaring omissions in American historical memory. It was to mark, and urge towards, a global colonial strategy for the United States that the "old India hand" Rudyard Kipling penned his *The White Man's Burden: United States and the Philippine Islands* (1899) and sent it directly to Theodore Roosevelt, then the governor of New York.

The "silent, sullen peoples"—who await salvation from bondage, freedom from the iron rule of kings—watch with trepidation and with hope the march of the American imperial might ("The ports ye shall not enter / the roads ye shall not tread / Go, make them with your living / And mark them with your dead"). The Kipling invocation to do empire better has lived on in other inheritors of that particular worldview, such as Ferguson. But Kipling himself, as a model of a citizen-journalist, firmly attuned to the greater glory and greater hubris of his own state, and committed to a deep knowledge of the charges of his empire, is now forgotten. Kipling, born and employed in British India, was about to embark on a trip to the United States and possibly meant his poem to be his calling card. As a reporter for the *Civil and Military Gazette* in Lahore and *Pioneer* in Allahabad, he urged that his critiques of the failures of imperial strategies were based on his intimate knowledge of India: "I met a hundred men on the road to Delhi and they were all my brothers" was the epigraph he chose for *Life's Handicap*.

His many short stories, reportage, travelogues were genuinely multilingual, multivocal, and strove to present all the corruptions and contradictions of his imperial age. Yet, he managed to always convey a singular vision of greater good—achievable only via a united empire—for the populations he called family and territories he called home, which were far away from London. That need to argue for a better strategy for empire meant, for Kipling, a deep involvement for those to whom the empire dictated.

In *Letters of Marque* (1887), he contrasts the travelling "King of Loafers" who has an "unholy knowledge" of the natives via his life lived among them with the "Globe Trotters" who claim expertise by staying in hotels and who produce nothing but banal observations: "With rare and sparkling originality he remarked that India was a 'big place,' and that there were many things to buy."

Robert D. Kaplan is an eminent globetrotter. His list of previous publications puts him in Central Asia, Eastern Europe, South America, West Africa, North Africa, South Asia, and Southeast Asia. He is also an eminent articulator for the need to do empire better.

"Where's the American empire when we need it?" he asked in a long essay in the *Washington Post* on December 3. A heartfelt plea to not go gently into that good night ("The American empire has always been more structural than spiritual"), Kaplan locates American imperial power as a magnetic pole—which attracts certain configurations and repels others. In his previous works such as *Balkan Ghosts: A Journey Through History* (1993), *The Ends of the Earth: A Journey to the Frontiers of Anarchy* (1996) and the most recent *Monsoon: The Indian Ocean and the Future of American Power* (2010), the U.S. Empire exists mainly to thwart other anarchic forces—political, such as the Soviets, and maybe the Chinese, but mainly the historical, the geographical, and ethnic.

Kaplan argues for a new cartography of empire—one that takes as its centre the Indian Ocean world. This configuration, which he holds was the key to the European colonial hegemony, has fallen out of America's strategic sights during the last half of the 20th century and the first decade of the new century.

While America has focused on the Middle East or Central Asia, a new world order is emerging in the port sites of Oman, Yemen, Pakistan, India, Bangladesh, Myanmar, Sri Lanka, Somalia, and Zanzibar. This world order, which is a revival of medieval and early modern trade networks, is being financed by the Chinese, in a blatant effort to project soft power throughout the Indian Ocean (to become a "two-ocean" empire).

India is the only contender in this space, and as both of these emergent world powers divide up the ports, the supply routes, the fuel and tank depots, America will lurk uneasily in the background, despite having both aerial and naval superiority. In this network, lies for Kaplan, the emergence of a new global class of African and Asian merchants and consumers who are key to both military and civilizational domination. Kaplan argues that the struggle is not for military hegemony between China and America, but a co-existence that emulates patterns of habitations that have been centuries in the making. To buttress his claim, Kaplan travels to ports and cities that feed into the Indian Ocean trade and presents an uneasy mixture of academic analysis and first-person narrative.

Kaplan's central thesis, of an Indian Ocean *oikoumene* comes largely from the work of historian Janet L Abu-Lughod—whose *Before European Hegemony: The World System AD 1250–1350* is cited numerous times and provides Kaplan with the bulwark of an Arab-Asian trading network across the Indian Ocean—and from the anthropologist Clifford Geertz—from whose nuanced *Islam Observed: Religious Development in Morocco and Indonesia* (1968) Kaplan emerges with the highly problematic dialectic "Desert Islam" versus "Tropical Islam." Between these central texts, Kaplan reproduces in a prose both clunky and confused a wide array of secondary academic scholarship, academic talks, academics who talk to him, and policy and position papers.

The various contradictions and examples of ill-digested scholarship that mark Kaplan's pages cannot truly be appreciated without reproducing entire chunks of pages. To this reader, they appear not to be contradictions or confusions in Kaplan's thought but simply the efforts of a studious neophyte, eager to marshal everything he has read—and he has read everything—into the narrative. This makes for headache inducing; historical fact after political factoid after cultural stereotype constantly clashing on the page.

A more fruitful exercise would be to deal specifically with two intertwined thematic underpinnings of *Monsoon*: geography and civilization. As Kaplan writes: "Geography rules," "Geography encompasses," we remain at the "mercy of geography." Geography also guides, dictates, and determines. It is impersonal, but "politics must follow geography," as does culture. Geography determines "national character." The desert is one such manifestation of an overdetermining geography. The desert is dry, "unforgiving," "violent," "constricting," gives its people "extremities of thought," "chaotic." As such, the desert not only contains such anthropomorphic qualities, it formulates them in those who come near it, or live in it—to provide a one-sentence summary: "Indeed, the deeper and broader the desert, potentially the more unstable and violent the state." It is in this cradle that Islam is born.

He contrasts this with the world of the ocean. The ocean is wet, "encompassing," "stimulating," "a global agglomeration," "culturally sophisticated. "It is when Islam comes into contact with this geographical force that it develops from "Desert Islam" to "Tropical Islam"—representing precisely the qualities which Kaplan imbues in the respective geographical features. In its essentializing of diversity, and diversification of essentially material realities, Kaplan's dichotomy—yes, the two Islams are at war with each other—beggars belief. Not to mention, it beggars geography. How exactly will he explain Egypt, one wonders.

He is misreading not only Geertz's careful ethnographies of agrarian practices in Morocco and Indonesia, he is contradicting his own deeply held beliefs. Because, for Kaplan, geography isn't really all that powerful. It must bow before the will of man. Now, granted in Kaplan's reading only a handful of men—historically speaking—have been capable enough to stand up to geography's predestination. These men, and the regimes they built, are fulsomely praised by Kaplan. These men have much in common: They are brutal, in thought and in acts, men of action and few words, men who make the right decision even at the cost of righteous moral claims.

These are men like Alfonso d'Albuquerque, the 16th-century Portuguese conqueror of the Indian Ocean; Robert Clive, the 18th-century governor of the East India Company and the conqueror of Bengal; the current Sultan Qaboos of Oman; the current President Mahinda Rajapaksa of Sri Lanka; as well as the faceless men who run China. Kaplan finds that such men, carved new destinies out of blood and sweat (mostly blood) for their historically afflicted regions and are to be praised, even emulated. After describing the horrors inflicted by the Portuguese in their conquest of India, Kaplan concludes: "Indeed, there is much the United States can learn from the positive side of the Portuguese national character, with many Catholic converts and the persistence of the Portuguese language in places like Sri Lanka and the Maluccas."

The most glaring lack, in Kaplan's imagination for the empire, is ultimately his inability actually to know. The languages, the customs, the rhythms, the cultures of places he visits, from Oman to Gwadar, to Kolkata, to Dhaka, to Zanzibar remain out of his purview. He makes a valiant effort to let historical writing, act as a substitute for his incomprehensibility of the present: "Here, along a coast so empty that you can almost hear the echo of the camel hooves of Alexander's army, you lose yourself in geology." He is often surprised ("Miniature donkeys emerging from the sea!"), often overwhelmed (by the poverty on display in Dhaka and in Zanzibar) and always dependent on others to explain to him the significance of what he observes. The significance of what he does observe, and what he argues for in *Monsoon* is what is at stake for most readers of his book. Kaplan is, after all like Kipling, offering prescriptives to the American Empire, whether he considers America an empire per se.

Kaplan forgets that America and Americans remain intimately intertwined with lives in the Indian Ocean world. In its long-storied past, Elihu Yale—who founded Yale University, the birthplace of American Indology—was a governor of the East India Company. The opium trade network, which sustained the East India Company coffers in the mid-19th century by supplying Bengal-raised opium to China, was also remitted through American cotton. And in its tumultuous present, the drones that fly over Afghanistan and Pakistan dispensing justice reportedly use bases in Balochistan.

Neither those American mercantile interests nor the drones receive any mention from Kaplan. He also forgets that his argument for American engagement is suspiciously similar to his argument for supporting the Iraq War. The after-effects of Iraq linger throughout his pages but are explicitly commented on only once and in relation to the conditions in Pakistan: "Because Pakistan and its stability had figured so prominently in Bush's foreign policy, the lack of improvement here constituted an indictment of his strategy, and an indictment of the diversion of resources to Iraq, a war I had supported early on." The significance of what he observes, and what he argues for in *Monsoon*, cannot be unmoored from this compromised position as a herald of a false dawn of democracy in Iraq. The only lesson he has learnt is to temper his claims for democracy—he praises military rule in Bangladesh as a viable option—and to add a note of caution to American power.

Hence, this is a text with a vague unease with an unqualified notion of American Empire—and to clarify here, not an unease with empire itself. This unease is perhaps the dominant factor in the largely conciliatory gesture Kaplan maintains toward China (a state whose economy and military are not at par with the United States but that has shown an intellectual awareness that outsmarts the US). He argues that China can easily be considered a "partner" that can be counted on to maintain a precarious balance of power in the Indian Ocean. This balance is necessary to reintegrate places like Yemen, Pakistan, Bangladesh, and Zanzibar into the global commercial classes and to bring closer the two faces of Islam.

The policy readers of this book will find it sober reading. The empire, which does listen to Robert Kaplan, will surely invite him to speak to groups with shiny brass and shinier domes. The historians reading this book will have less cause to be charitable. The now-standard collapse of lived history from "Alexander the Great" to "us" would be laughable if it wasn't so tragic.

Again and again, centuries disappear from Kaplan's narrative as routinely elaborated customs and practices are relegated to either geographic determinism or something called "Desert Islam." Those inhabitants of the climes in which Kaplan locates his narrative will have more than ample reason to be offended by his caricatures or by his invocations to the healing power of violence—be it Robert Clive or Sultan Qaboos. In this, however, Kaplan is neither unique nor exemplary in a pantheon of great American commentators, which stretches from Thomas L. Friedman to Fareed Zakaria. The empire requires a particular kind of information alone.

What is more glaringly at stake is that nearly 8 years after the invasion of Iraq and under a new administration in the White House, the "debate" of the global war on terror remains stuck in the same analytical framework as it did in 2001. Contrasting Robert Kaplan in 2010 with Niall Ferguson from 2001 is an exercise akin to examining a patient suffering from a fugue state: the amnesia is stark and starkly present.

Chapter Notes

1 Archived at http://bit.ly/fuMHzn.
2 W. G. Sebald, *On the Natural History of Destruction* (New York: Random House, 2004), 65–67.
3 Archived at http://bit.ly/2hMum.
4 Archived at http://bit.ly/fp904i.
5 Archived at http://bit.ly/fO2N1A.
6 Archived at http://bit.ly/haZjUX.
7 Archived at http://bit.ly/geDVCl.
8 Richard Temple, "The General Statistics of the British Empire," *Journal of the Statistical Society of London* 47, no. 3 (1884): 468–484.
9 Bernard Porter, "How Did They Get away with It?" *London Review of Books* 27, no. 5 (2005): 3–6, archived at http://bit.ly/bHzNh4.
10 Bernard Porter, *Absent-Minded Imperialists: What the British Really Thought about Empire* (New York: Oxford University Press, 2004), 299.
11 Ibid., 306.
12 Ibid., 35.
13 Ibid., 152.
14 Ibid., 158.
15 Ibid., 127.
16 Archived at http://bit.ly/e3fbn8.
17 Robert Cooper, "The New Liberal Imperialism," *Guardian*, April 7, 2002, archived at http://bit.ly/a1Nr48.
18 Archived at http://bit.ly/dYjoYS.

5
Support

Since the freedom agenda became a central tenet of U.S. foreign policy, we have supported the oppressive regimes in the following places (in the Muslim world) against the will of their own people: Pakistan, Egypt, Jordan, Saudi Arabia, Libya, Bahrain, Yemen. Collectively, that is a near majority of the Muslim population. This support is militaristic (sale or grant of hardware or technology) and political (rhetorical, diplomatic). Pakistan, the key ally in the war on terror, was already a state under a military coup by the time of September 11, 2001. This state of being has been de rigueur for Pakistan for a very long time—Field Marshall Ayub Khan (ruled from 1958–1969), General Zia-ul-Haq (ruled from 1977–1988), and General Pervez Musharraf (in power from 1999–2008). And all of them were supported explicitly and openly by the governments of Eisenhower, Kennedy, Johnson, Nixon, Reagan, and George W. Bush. That this support was detrimental to even the geopolitical interests of United States has always been clear and yet. . . . This chapter is a collection of posts dealing with the support the Bush White House showed to Pervez Musharraf and the antidemocratic agenda in Pakistan. Of particular interest should be "To Dream a Man" as well as the "Round-Up" series, which tried to document the protests against Musharraf's rule as they unfolded in 2007 and 2008.

Paths to Democracy[1]
May 7, 2004

I remember reading Lawrence Ziring's *Pakistan: At the Crosscurrent of History* and realizing that the discussions on Pakistan in the academy are completely divorced from the political spheres and the blogosphere. In fact, that is what gave me the idea to start *CM* in the first place. Hence, I am glad to find that Patrick Belton, of *Oxblog*, has just concluded a three-part series on "Democracy in Pakistan" at *Winds of Change.net*, which provides excellent points to start a discussion. It is refreshingly candid and intellectually stimulating. I suggest you go over and give it a gander. My main quibble with it is that it sticks to some dated realities (ISI-religious party alliances) and ignores some of the drastic changes brought about by 9/11 and Musharraf's dictatorship.

There is something unique about this new military regime from previous ones. The standard triptych of power in Pakistan—*Military + Civil Bureaucracy + Landed/Industrial Elite*—has historically managed to keep other claimants to mass power out. The Jama'at-i Islami, under Maududi, tried to ally itself with one or the other but failed to resonate with the public. Zia, notoriously, used and discarded the Jama'at during his Islamization process.

Musharraf has destroyed that [quasi]-balance. First, his policies of reassigning civil bureaucrats and judges and installing military overseers have crippled the influence of the bureaucracy (remember: the District Commissioner has been king in Pakistan since the British Raj as the most immediate holder of all municipal and civil authority). Second, he has managed to cut the knees off the ISI (simply look at the mass resignation of upper cadres of the army in the last 3 years from brigadiers to generals). Third, and most importantly, he has promoted economic business reforms that have empowered a new entrepreneurial class to emerge (the booming software and tech houses in Lahore and Karachi are clear examples). The impact of this particular step is the fostering of a new business class that will look towards the links with the global economy and internal stability as prime objectives. The old business class, which was a subsection of the industrial and landed elite, will get waylaid. Yes, I am being overly simplistic, but stick with me for a second.

The impact of all these policies is the emergence of the military as a *civil* bureaucracy (where do you think those retired colonels and brigadiers are going?) along with an *immense* power vacuum. For now, Musharraf fills that power vacuum, but, for the first time in Pakistani history, the Islamist organizations have a chance to glean some of that power. The victory of Mutahida Majlis-e Amal (MMA) points to that, as does the rise of various overtly religious figures in Pakistan Muslim League and Pakistan People's Party (PPP), etc.

Now, the claim to power of these faith-based parties is still not Islamization but anti-American rhetoric. That will either fade away with the Iraq hand-off and a Bush ouster or it will metastasize with continuing bungling in Iraq and any further neocon adventures in Arabian nights. Regardless, the path to victory itself will change these parties. One need only look at the rhetoric of the Bharat Janata Party (BJP) in India in 1992 and in 2004. Extreme politics gets you noticed, but if you fight your way to power, you *must* adapt.

As for Dictator Musharraf, he has both supporters and detractors. I am ambivalent. Anything that upends the status quo is good news to me. Yet, I am utterly convinced that there is only one way to get to democracy: Practice, Practice, Practice. Any blip on that road is bad news for Pakistan. The argument that

Pakistanis don't know how to handle democracy is elitist and bogus. Democracy must return to Pakistan.

Overall, I think Pakistan has an excellent chance of promoting systematic reform in its key areas—economic, social, political—in the coming years. For that to happen, it will have to continue to enjoy the lavish (and rich) attention of the United States, it will have to continue to participate in the global (by global, I mean Asian) economies, and it will have to continue to develop a civil society around the excellent work done by nongovernmental organizations (which are finally starting to pull some political weight).

Lastly, I want to mention one key thing that never enters any discussion of Pakistani future (no, *Islam* is not it!). That is, the role played by the return of the millions who left Pakistan for the Gulf in '70s and '80s. This population is ill-fitted in the fabric of the society (I know, my father is one of them), and the first political or governmental group that touches its core issues (education, civic law, and business) will harvest a mass following just as great as Bhutto with his cry of *Roti, Kapra aur Makan* (Bread, Cloth, and House) in the '70s.

Exile Left[2]
May 12, 2004

A weird game of chicken happened in Lahore this past week. Shahbaz Sharif, brother of twice-and-former Prime Minister Nawaz Sharif, told his party loyalists that he was coming back to Lahore. The government stated its firm opposition and, when his plane landed in Lahore, shipped him right back. Bit of background: When Musharraf gained power, he exiled the Sharif family to Saudi Arabia for 10 years under an "agreement" instead of having them stand trial for corruption or murder. Musharraf knew his history and knew not to do as Zia did unto Bhutto (i.e., have him executed after a farce trial). Now Shahbaz Sharif, who was the chief minister of Punjab, has said, "I am coming home." The government responded in a very subdued and sober manner—by putting up roadblocks around Lahore one week in advance, rounding up all the leaders under some obscure Martial Law Ordinance and putting them under house arrests, and arresting hundreds of low-level Pakistan Muslim League-Nawaz (PML-N) operators. Then, it stopped TV channels from broadcasting an interview with Mr. Sharif in London and barricaded the office of the CNN in Lahore lest it show Mr. Sharif emerging from the Lahore airport surrounded by supporters. Nice subdued response.

And the funny thing is that Shahbaz was a nobody before this. Now, he is Nelson Mandela. Maybe the government remembers the magic that was the return of Benazir Bhutto to Pakistan under Zia. I remember that. She was a rock star. Her parade was endless. The flowers reached the clouds. Perhaps, they were scared that Shahbaz Sharif would get that reception and galvanize the Alliance for Restoration of Democracy (ARD) movement. Instead, they made fools out of themselves by trampling on every citizen's right and may well galvanize the anti-Musharraf movements.

Human Rights 2004[3]
May 25, 2004

Finally got around to reading the State Department's annual Human Rights Report on Pakistan. Some highlights [please check irony at the door—in fact, this report was delayed due to the Iraqi prison scandal]:

> Government: The government's human rights record remained poor; although there were some improvements in a few areas, serious problems remained. On October 29, opposition leader and member of Parliament, Javed Hashmi, was arrested for releasing an anonymous letter allegedly written by army officers that was critical of President Musharraf's leadership. Hashmi was charged with conspiracy, forgery, and inciting the armed forces against the government. The Government has sought to hold all court proceedings before a panel of judges inside the prison where Hashmi was held. The incitement charge carries a maximum penalty of life imprisonment. Authorities refused family access and legal counsel for the first several weeks of his incarceration. Hashmi remained in detention at year's end. The Government does not respect the right to privacy. The Anti-Terrorist Act allowed police or military personnel acting as police to enter and to search homes and offices without search warrants and to confiscate property or arms likely to be used in an alleged terrorist act (which is defined very broadly).
>
> Police: Killings between rival political factions and sectarian groups continued to be a problem. Police abused and raped citizens. Prison conditions remained extremely poor and life threatening, and police arbitrarily arrested and detained citizens. Several political leaders remained in detention or exile abroad at year's end. Case backlogs led to long delays in trials, and lengthy pretrial detention was common. In the absence of a warrant, a policeman is subject to charges of criminal trespass. However, police seldom were punished for illegal entry.
>
> Women: Domestic violence against women, rape, and abuse of children remained serious problems. The government publicly criticized the practice of "honor killings," but such killings continued. Discrimination against women was widespread, and traditional social and legal constraints generally kept women in a subordinate position in society. Human Rights organizations estimated that at least 631 women and girls were killed by family members in so-called honor killings; however, many more women are believed to be affected by this crime. According to UNICEF, about half the honor killing

deaths took place in Sindh, and it is believed that many more cases go unreported in Baluchistan and the North West Frontier Province (NWFP). Approximately 102 honor killings took place in Punjab according to the HRCP. The problem was believed to be even more extensive in rural Sindh and Baluchistan, where "karo/kari" killings were common. Tribal custom among the Baluch and the Pathans sanctions such killings.

Minority rights: During the year, the number of cases filed under the blasphemy laws continued to be significant. A local NGO estimated that 157 persons had been incarcerated for violations of the blasphemy law during the year. For example, in July, Munawar Mohsin, an editor at the Frontier Post newspaper, was convicted of publishing a blasphemous letter and sentenced to life imprisonment (see Section 2a.).

The General in His Labyrinth[4]
September 24, 2004

The General spoke to the UN General Assembly two days ago and met with Our Fearless Leader (George W. Bush) before that and with Sardar Ji (Manmohan Singh) today. He weaved democracy, terrorism, hope, conviction, and CBMs (confidence-building measures, not continental ballistic missiles). There is some talk about the "disappointment" of The General remaining the general. But, honestly people, I ask you: What is a general without his *vardi* [uniform]? Nothing. Absolutely worthless. Just a run-of-the-mill civilian with some expensive dogs and nice cigars. The pattern is so familiar. The United States will support a military dictator, because he is fighting a proxy war for the United States. And, in the end, The General will fall in battle and the Pakistanis will be left holding the check—a country held hostage.

Let's start with the assembly address published in the *Pakistan Times*. Filled with the usual homilies. Although, The General did seem to give a bit on the Kashmiri issue by mentioning the "the people of Kashmir." One would not be amiss in thinking that Kashmir was uninhabited if one went by [usual] political discourse in Pakistan. Still, on Pakistan:

> In Pakistan, we are well on the way to transforming our country into a modern, progressive, tolerant, democratic, Islamic state, reflecting the vision of our founding father, the Quaid-e-Azam. Democracy has been restored in Pakistan. The people have been empowered through a revolutionary Local Government System. Our women have been empowered.

One thing that is *not* happening in Pakistan is any "transformation." Dictators come, and they go (only via Opus Dei). Pakistani democracies are akin to Iraqi WMDs . . . lots of talk about them but no sign on the grounds. The more he insists on democracy flourishing in Pakistan, the bigger the disconnect gets.

The General, earlier, met with Bush, and they talked about a host of issues. Most news reports described that Bush "nudged" Musharraf into being "democratic." But more significant discussion took place between the two leaders:

> Senior administration official: The interesting thing that both Prime Minister Singh and President Musharraf pointed out to the President is that the Prime Minister of India was born in what is now Pakistan, and President Musharraf was born in what is now India.
>
> ...
>
> Q: Does President Musharraf have a take on the situation in Iraq? Any counsel or thoughts for President Bush?
>
> Senior administration official: No, not in any detail. Actually, they spent much of the time talking about President Musharraf's concept of what he calls "enlightened moderation." He has—he's written in the Washington Post, actually, he published an article I guess about two months ago on this concept, and it's something that Pakistan, working with other secular enlightened Muslim states, like Malaysia, for example, or Turkey, have brought into the Organization of Islamic Conferences—and the notion, what they're after is trying to have enlightened scholars interpret Islam, because Islam is a religion that should be timeless, that should be adopted to the times. And the problem with the extremists is that many of these more extreme mullahs are trying to return to the fourth caliphate, you know, trying to move time, the clock back two centuries. So he talked a bit about that. And in that context, the two leaders also talked about—and the president talked about his interest in Pakistan's efforts at domestic reform of the economy, moving forward with democratic institutions and the democratic process as part of this overall concept of enlightened moderation and development.
>
> Q: Did Bush lean on Musharraf to relinquish his military title by the end of the year?
>
> Senior administration official: No, they had a more general discussion about the importance of enlightened moderation and the president's support for the process of reform and democracy in Pakistan as part of that.[5]

I am sure the facts about Musharraf's and Singh's birthplaces blew the lid off Bush's mind. *Whoo!* Dangbit Dat! I do like that the term "enlightened" Muslims (I picture some glowing beards, maybe?) is creeping into the political lexicon. It gives me hope, because I have a few terms of my own that I am pushing lately: "empowered" Muslims, "democratized" Muslims, "not-living-under-a-dictatorship-or-kingship-sponsored-by-U.S.-money-and-military-power" Muslims. Just around the corner, these terms.

Still, here was the gem in the briefing:

Q: Was there any mention at all of either the Afghan elections or the U.S. elections?

Senior administration official: Yes. The Afghan elections, again, President Musharraf has helped with out of country voting so that Afghan citizens in Pakistan can vote and can participate in the election, which was logistically, you know, a big step, but very important for the success of the election. And President Musharraf reiterated that.

I'm going to pass on our election. These leaders are always interested in how it's going, but—you know what the Hatch Act is? [Laughter.]

Q: But the Hatch Act does not—it only affects your political activities, it does not affect your ability to answer a question about the discussion—

Senior administration official: Wow, you—

Q: I do know a little bit about the Hatch Act. [Laughter.]

Senior administration official: All the leaders, frankly—from Singh to Koizumi to Musharraf—they're all curious how it's going.

Q: So they would all raise it in a general sense with the president?

Senior administration official: Right. Right. But I'm going to leave it at that. They're all politicians. They're all politicians, and at one time or another they all have their own elections, or their own congresses or their own parliaments. And it's something that, you know, when these heads of state get together, it's one thing—whether they're English speaking, or Japanese speaking, Christian, Muslim—it's one thing they all have in common, is that they have to deal with elections and parliaments, and they always, in my experience, talk about it.

Clash of civilization, my posterior. We can *always* have the politicians connect.

I did like the [imagine a snooty voice now] *"you know what the Hatch Act is?"* Takedown.

Today, Sardar Ji and The General met. I hope they did hatch some secret plan, because we know the Pakistani press will undoubtedly assert that The General made a secret plan to sell out the Kashmiri mujahideen. And I hope that Sardar Ji threw his teacup and punched his pillow, because the Indian press will undoubtedly assert that he was not assertive enough. Politics as usual, everywhere.

Watans, Wickets, and Walis[6]
April 17, 2005

Pakistan's Military Dictator-cum-President Pervez Musharraf is in India this weekend, in what is being hailed on both sides of the border (India, Pakistan, and even in vilayat) as another successful round of cricket diplomacy (the first being Zia's surprise trip to meet Rajiv Gandhi in Rajasthan in 1987). This cricket match, played in the Firuz Shah Kotla area of Delhi, is the latest in the 2004–2005 series of home and home contests in India and Pakistan. Many are a bit more skeptical, and justifiably so, about the possibilities of cricket diplomacy, especially over at the Acorn blog, where the extension of an Indian invitation to The General in the first place is roundly condemned.

I have no love whatsoever for Musharraf and his role in continuing the long, sordid history of military rule in Pakistan, but I think it does little good to Indo-Pak relations to renew the "Butcher of Kargil" rhetoric and refuse to negotiate. (I do not want to get into the blame game of Kargil, but in the final analysis, two were tangoing, as it were.) Musharraf is clearly and unambiguously running the show now, and a snub to the man will not get us any closer to a resolution of the Kashmir conflict, nor will it bring Pakistanis nearer to going to the polls. Pakistan may well have a bit to learn from India's reasonably robust democracy. On the other hand, India's self-appointed role of watchdog over the entirety of the subcontinent is decidedly not helping the democratization process across the border.

The building and maintenance of stable participatory democratic institutions is something that cannot be externally compelled. Military occupation is especially poorly suited to this cause, the most recent examples being the mockery of democracy that U.S.-run elections have wrought in Afghanistan and Iraq (perhaps soon Pakistan too if Benazir's unalloyed praise of the Bush doctrine bears political fruit). Likewise, I doubt diplomatic intransigence by India is going to help matters in Pakistan. On the contrary, giving Musharraf the international relations equivalent of a tight slap as some seem to advocate would provide a fair amount more leeway to anti-democracy forces in Pakistan (The General himself included), just as the recent refusal of the United States to grant Narendra Modi a visa will without question be converted into political capital by the BJP.

Certainly, there is great potential for human contact in border-hopping with the subcontinent's pastime, as evidenced by Anand's touching tale of camaraderie, romance, and cricket visas. As for "real" politics, I hold out scant hope for much substantive progress being made in negotiations between Manmohan and Musharraf in Delhi (it certainly does not bode well that Basmati [Rice] is dropping by in hopes of getting all involved to do her bidding). I do think both Pakistan and India stand to benefit from negotiations not restricted to the question of Kashmir. The two nations collaborating to create conditions for people to trade, fish, and ride buses or trains across the border is important, and I, for one, would like to see this trend continue.

On another note entirely, Musharraf made a point of stopping by in Ajmer for a visit to the famous Dargah of Khwajah Muinuddin Chishti, the major 12th- and 13th-century Sufi Pir. This gestures to more positive shared histories of the people of India and Pakistan, ones invisible from the perspective of debates over democracy, authoritarianism, and military conflict. Sufi shrines, Gurdwaras, and other pilgrimage sites across South Asia serve as major nodes of transnational contact, and the flow of people across political boundaries has been severely limited (but not stopped) by the partition of the subcontinent. While political movements and states in both Pakistan and India have attempted to link the control over these spiritually invested and often economically productive sites to discourses of religious nationalism (mandir-mosque conflicts in India, state control or restriction of Sufi shrine veneration in Pakistan), the Dargah at Ajmer remains a site patronized by people of all creeds.

While one sometimes encounters exclusivist visions of political community coming from Sufis in South Asia at various points in history, the Chishtiyya tariqa and their interpretation of Sufism has since medieval times represented an idiom for the integration of Islam and local religious traditions. This process took place in the political sphere as well. If we follow the argument of Muzaffar Alam in his latest book, *The Languages of Political Islam*, the "Sufi Intervention" encouraged a pluralistic trend in Mughal governance.

One wonders to what extent a Sufi imagining of politics can be extended into the contemporary South Asian scenario. It would certainly be a stretch to suggest that Musharraf's visit to Ajmer and generous patronage of the Dargah will have visible political effects in either India or Pakistan (after all, the instigator of the intolerant and misogynistic so-called Islamization of law and society in Pakistan, General Zia, also made a stop in Ajmer on his cricket diplomacy mission almost two decades ago). Still, it is heartening somehow to see politicians bringing arenas of shared South Asian culture and history like Muinuddin Chishti's shrine into the public eye for at least a moment.

Softer Side of Freedom[7]
May 18, 2005

Freedom, as they say, is growing in leaps and bounds. And one of the places it is leaping right over is Pakistan. In an announcement leaked to the press, and surprising only to the South Asia Desk at State, The General has decided to "stand for elections after his current term expires in 2007." Of course, this is for the better of all concerned. Right?

I am going to come off as a broken record by now. Here is what they say: *The General is good for Pakistan. He can keep the jihadists in check. He is good for the United States. He can hunt for United Bank Limited (UBL). He is good for the economy. He is good for peace with India. He is a good guy. He means well. He promises Enlightened Moderation. He shoots straight from the hip.* Here is what I say: *Bullshit.* Give the Pakistani people what they deserve: democracy.

One must remember, though, that there is no problem that a sycophantic press and a media consultant can't fix. Democracy included. The truth is that this

General is not my father's General or my grandfather's General. This General "can talk politics with Manmohan Singh and entertainment with Shahrukh Khan and Rani Mukerjee. Democracy, the Legal Framework Order (LFO), and coup d'états aside, the President, to put it in a nutshell, is 'cool.'" *Cool*, I say. Take that, Mugabe. Take that, Lil' Kim.

In a puff piece that will shame Jeff Gannon, the *News International* visits The General to find him delighting to some Pakistani pop on his Bang and Olufsen system, "which is one of the best sound systems you can buy"; ruminating on Urdu, "Even Indian songs are in Urdu"; on the gentler side of Pakistan, "Extremists held sway, and they pushed the soft face; the art face of Pakistan into the background calling it un-Islamic whereas it is not"; on Art, "Islamic art has been embraced and adopted by many in the world. It is known as Islamic art. It is Islamic, and we should be very proud of it." Right you are, Mr. President.

To show the world the "soft face" of Pakistan, The General has hired a media advisor: One Mahreen Khan. I wish *India Shining* on the lot of them. I also breathlessly await the next press briefing from the State Department to see what they have to say about freedom in Pakistan.

Autumn of the Patriarch[8]
October 3, 2005

There is little that I have left to say on The General—besides my daily pot shots. . . . However, the summer is over, and we should bring ourselves up to date on this little-country-that-can't and the one who leads it.

This General is a bit different from other dictators. For one, he is hyperaware of himself and his role in international media. Ergo, his biggest setbacks are of the public relations variety and not tactical blunders. To be fair, it is hard to become a military dictator in Pakistan and not labor under the long shadows of General Ayub or General Zia, who perfected the spin of international relations.

Our glorious General Fathers not only had the élan of a Jefferson or a Roosevelt, but they also had great 'staches, which intimidated and seduced to equal degrees. What they did not have was any sense that they ruled people who deserved freedom to make their choices—good and bad. The legacy of the General Fathers is one of "benevolent" dictatorship—the patriarch who stoops down and picks up the little child and carries her over the hill; the wise guide who patiently awaits the moment of maturity; the patient taskmaster who know what is best. That is the mantle inherited by The General, and he has taken a shine to it. His *Enlightened Moderation* and his repeated criticisms of journalists and NGOs who speak against him as "doing the work of the enemies of Pakistan" are hallmarks of such an approach. There is nothing "there"—no policies, no laws, no results. But there is a marked attention to what the world can and should know about Pakistan. Just listen to the audio of the now-famous *Washington Post* interview in which he made the remark about getting raped for a Canadian visa. Listen carefully, because you can actually hear his tortured psyche, and you will hear his fear of these NGOs and the media, which runs with the bad news about Pakistan alone. It is all a matter of spin, he sincerely believes, because *every* country is just as bad as the other.

The spin, though, is unspinning. He is surrounded by, and to a large extent a hostage of, forces that appear to be on a marked path to their realization. Islamism, whether understood as a general sense of religiosity in the society or in the more extreme case of Talibanization, is growing. Kashmir, the fountain of army's youth since 1947, is fast approaching the point of bilateral resolution—between Kashmir and India. Baluchistan and Waziristan remain unresolved and continue to ferment. A. Q. Khan doesn't want to leave the newsstands. And, oh, the biggest bombshell, the aforementioned interview with *WaPo* and the resultant backlash. As I argued earlier, the best effect of Mukhtar Mai's case was the international attention. Kristoff led the case in the *New York Times*, but it is Musharraf himself who has begun the irreversible process of alienating the Washington wallahs.

So, what now for The General? The blogger Raven at *Reality Café* says that he is an insensitive jerk. I concur. More important, I think he is in serious trouble. The opposition is rallying. The Chosen One is in heaps of trouble internally to pay attention to Pakistan. The greatest sin the world community committed on Pakistan was the sin of neglect. Thanks to Osama bin Laden, A. Q. Khan, the plight of various women and the forces of Islamism, that sin will not get repeated. The calls for justice, for democracy, aren't gonna get any easier. The Congress still has lots of money to approve for Pakistan, and they may look askance (you know, Katrina and all) at funding Pakistan with no strings attached. The only respite is if The General can produce the ace up his sleeve: Osama himself. The problem is, once he plays that card, he will have none left, and the game is far from being over.

On Daily Show[9]
September 26, 2006

In an amazing display of cultural hipness, The General will be appearing on *The Daily Show with Jon Stewart* tonight. As Stewart quipped last night, "I have no idea why." Ostensibly, The General is out promoting his memoirs, *In the Line of Fire* [currently No. 3 on Amazon! Check out the nonpartisan reviews; also, when did Amazon start comments on reviews?].

The memoir is hot, especially for this bit of non-news: After 9/11, Dick Armitage told The General that Pakistan would be "bombed back to the Stone Age if it failed to help Washington," which is not a meaningless threat, especially if you've seen Dick Armitage.

Armitage claims that it is a classic case either of "selling wares" or "lost in translation." According to accounts, Mahmoud Ahmad told The General over the phone from Washington, "*Wo hamari einth sey einth baja dey gain*" (a beautiful bit of colloquialism meaning, "They will dismantle us.") It is this news that is all over the Internets and interwaves of Homistan (though there are other bits of interesting info). Obviously, it plays nicely with a crowd that has about had it with The General. The recent ham-handed killing of Bugti, the "pact" with the Taliban in Waziristan, and more bombshells (literally) of A. Q. Khan, and it is evident that The General needs good P.R.

I should note that there was another general who wrote his memoir while in office—General Ayub Khan (ruler dictator of Pakistan 1958–1969). His book, *Friends Not Masters, a Political Autobiography*, was published in 1967.

The writing, as they say, was on the wall.

Now, *live-bloggin' the show*:

[Jon Stewart (JS)] offers The General tea! Jasmine tea! Mush is wearing a Pakistani pin—looking relaxed and casual. Nice suit.
- JS sets up a softball. "How has it been to hold it together?" "It" being the shite show of Pakistani domestic and foreign policy.
- Dick Armitage. Mush says he wanted to make sure Pakistan's national interest was upheld.
- "We did take into consideration a confrontationist approach"!
- Defends his agreement in Waziristan with the Taliban factions. Gives an ethnicity lesson. Studio audience asleep.
- "We have eliminated them from our cities" Them = al-Qaida.
- Break. Okay. I think pretty softball all around. JS being super deferential. Mush is a superstar when it comes to dealing with the Western press.
- "It has led certainly to more extremism and terrorism around the world." The "it" is Iraq. Man, Bush is not sending any Xmas gifts to Mush.
- "Who would win a popularity vote between George W. Bush and Osama Bin Laden in Pakistan?" "They will both lose miserably."
- Over. The Iraq bit is nice news. I bet it gets picked up by *Daily Kos* bloggers, what with all the NIE chatter.
- P.S. Colbert is so good.

No One Writes to The General[10]
March 27, 2007

In the *New York Times* today is "Pakistan's Silent Majority Is Not to Be Feared," an op-ed by the author Mohsin Hamid on Musharraf and the rising tide of discontent with his dictatorial ways. He begins by admitting that he was an early supporter of Musharraf and cites some of the economic booms during the last 7 years. However, in sympathy to the growing unrest against Musharraf, he has rethought his position:

> General Musharraf now appears to be more concerned with perpetuating his rule than with furthering the cause of "enlightened moderation" that he had claimed to champion. He has never been particularly popular, but he is now estranging the liberals who previously supported his progressive ends if not his autocratic means. People like me are realizing that the short-term gains from even a well-intentioned dictator's policies can be easily reversed.
>
> This Devil's bargain has been a consistent part of the popular psyche that has supported dictatorial rule in Pakistan since the 1950s. My parent's generation praised Ayub for bringing industrialization and development and Zia for trying to harmonize Islam in Pakistan. And in 1999, I heard the same appeasements coming from the intellectuals— Musharraf will bring democracy or will train us to appreciate democracy. I consider this line of argument entirely specious:
>
> [The argument is that . . .] Pakistanis are forever stuck in the "not yet" time—lacking education or training or a civil society to elect governments to represent themselves. The masses are uncouth and uncivilized. "Mature" democracies such as the United States do not have mass rallies and tire burning after a child is killed in a road accident. "Mature" democracies elect their leaders after impassioned and logical thought as the best representing the ideals of the collective society. Pakistan has to be trained and Condi Rice is completely devoted to the "steps towards democratization" that The General is undertaking. The pendulum of metaphors swings from "time" to "distance."[11]

On this one, I am squarely with the Subalternists. The filthy masses of Pakistan *are* political agents, and they *are* ready for democracy. And they even have leaders. But the unsurprising reality is that the system is set to prohibit any populist challenge to the regime. The two-legged bar stool of Pakistani dictatorship is firmly situated at this moment.

But now, this blunder by The General has swung the momentum toward that populist challenge. Until now, Musharraf had been coasting on U.S./World Bank support, good economic news, and a shrugging acceptance of status quo— that has now ended. There is no way for him to deescalate without giving in on several key issues: uniform, presidency, participation of all political parties in the election. This particular agitation by the lawyers follows closely the pattern after student unrest on campuses across the nation, which gave birth to the Movement for Restoration of Democracy (MRD) during Zia, which, in turn, resulted in the elections of 1985.

Question is, will the United States support The General or back the calls for democracy? Will the president support the Black Revolution sweeping Pakistan?

In that, I join Mohsin Hamid's concluding paragraph:

> An exaggerated fear of Pakistan's people must not prevent America from realizing that Pakistanis are turning away from General Musharraf. By prolonging his rule, the general risks taking Pakistan backward and undermining much of the considerable good that he has been able to achieve. The time has come for him to begin thinking of a transition, and for Americans to realize that, scare stories notwithstanding, a more democratic Pakistan might be better not just for Pakistanis but for Americans as well.

To Dream a Man[12]
June 6, 2007

> *He wanted to dream a man; he wanted to dream him*
> *in minute entirety and impose him on reality.*
> —*The Circular Ruins*, Jorge Luis Borges

Rawalpindi, Pakistan, September 8, 1970

1. During Ambassador's conversation with President Yahya here September 8, Yahya said he had been greatly upset by need for his decision to postpone general elections from October 5 until December 7. He said a number of factors had led to his decision. He mentioned specifically the inability of existing bureaucratic machinery to cope simultaneously with flood relief requirements and election preparations in East Pakistan. Yayha noted that Paks were completely out of practice on election procedures.

2. Yahya said he hoped no one would get the idea he was wavering in any way in his determination to restore civilian government and get back to barracks.

3. Yahya went on to voice disappointment over the course of the political campaign to date. He said he was appalled at the lack of leadership and programs offered by the politicians, many of whom were acting like spoiled kids. He had failed to see emergence of any statesmen-like leadership. When he became discouraged, Yahya said, he had to remind himself here had been no democracy in Pakistan, and the politicians had little conception of rules and requirements.

> —Telegram reporting President Yahya's views on Pakistan's
> political situation, U.S. Department of State.[13]

Washington, D.C., June 21, 2001

We are very concerned that Pakistan has taken a turn away from, rather than toward, democracy. And I think General Musharraf's actions to dissolve the elected assemblies and appoint himself president severely undermine Pakistan's constitutional order and clearly cast Pakistan as a country ruled by decree rather than by a democratic process.

—Phillip T. Reeker, Deputy Spokesman

Washington, D.C., August 22, 2002

Question: If President Musharraf does not change his mind about these measures and Pakistan becomes just another dictatorship, what effect would that have on its relations with the United States and your cooperation in the so-called war on terrorism?

Mr. Reeker: I think, again, the hypotheticals there, Jonathan, are something I'm just not going to pursue. We've made clear what our goals are, what we think is important, what we believe President Musharraf wants in terms of developing strong democratic institutions.

—Philip T. Reeker, Deputy Spokesman

Camp David, June 24, 2003

Question: You mentioned that you would like to see a movement toward democracy in Pakistan. What would you like to see happen? There's a report that he might dissolve the parliament there.

President Bush: Well, the president and I talked about the reforms that he's putting in place, and the democracy to which he is committed. One of the things that he has done that is most impressive for the long-term stability of Pakistan is to address education reform. A good education system is one that is going to mean more likely for any country, including ourselves, to be a freer country, and a more democratic country.

And he is—he's taking on the issue in a way that is a visionary and strong. He's dealing with the madrasas in a way that is productive and constructive. He is working on a national curriculum that will focus on basic education. I'll let him describe his vision. But this country is committed to democracy, and we're committed to freedom. We're also committed to working with our partner to fight off the influences of terrorism. And we've had no better partner in our fight on terror than President Musharraf.

President Musharraf: Thank you, Mr. President. I would like to say a word on the previous question, also, and before I address your—answer your question. . . .

Coming to your question, sir, about democracy, let me assure you it may sound rather odd that I, being a military man, am talking of democracy. But let me assure you that I am extremely concerned about introducing sustainable democracy in Pakistan.

Over the last 50 years, five decades, we have had dysfunctional democracy in Pakistan. And what I am doing, really, is to introduce sustainable democracy. Let me assure you, all the constitution changes, all the political restructuring that we have done is in line with ensuring sustainable democracy in Pakistan. We will continue with this process, to ensure that democracy is never derailed in Pakistan. This is my assurance.

—President George W. Bush and President Musharraf of Pakistan

Islamabad, Pakistan, March 4, 2006

Question: Some critics say that Pakistan is not moving quickly enough on democratic reforms. And moves toward democracy have been one of the hallmarks of your administration. How do you respond to critics who say you are holding back on pressing President Musharraf on moves toward democracy because of its help in the war on terrorism? And I would also ask—

President Bush: Well, we discussed—we spent a lot of time talking about democracy in Pakistan, and I believe democracy is Pakistan's future. And we share a strong commitment to democracy. I just mentioned in my opening address the idea of making sure the elections go forward in 2007, and I discussed that with the president. President Musharraf has made clear that he intends to hold elections—I'll let him speak for himself on this issue, but democracy has been definitely a part of our agenda here, as it should be.

Second, one of the things that the president is constantly talking about is the ways to defeat extremism. We're talking about making sure that we work closely to bring the terrorists to justice, but in the long run he understands that extremism can be defeated by freedom and democracy and prosperity and better education. And we spent a lot of time strategizing on that subject today.

I'll let you speak for yourself on the subject, though, Mr. President.

President Musharraf: Unfortunately, we are accused a lot on not moving forward on democracy. But as I understand democracy, we are a—may I venture to tell you what we've done in line with democracy to introduce sustainable democracy in Pakistan? The first ingredient of democracy, I believe, is the empowerment of the people. We have empowered the people of Pakistan now—they were never empowered before—by introducing a local government system where we have given the destiny of their areas for development, for welfare, for progress in their own hands through financial, political and administrative involvement.

Also democracy also means empowerment of women. It is the first time that we have empowered the women of Pakistan, by giving them a say in the political milieu of Pakistan. Today, there are over 30,000 women in the political hierarchy of Pakistan. We have empowered the minorities of Pakistan for the first time. They have got a joint election system, where previously they had a separate election system. Therefore, they have been mainstreamed in that every person standing for elections has to go to the minorities to ask for their votes now. Therefore, they feel more a part of the Pakistani culture and Pakistan society.

Then we have empowered also—we have liberated the media and the press. If you see this press today sitting around here, and the media, previously there was only one Pakistan television. Today there are dozens of channels. All these people sitting around are the result of my democratization of Pakistan, opening the Pakistan society of the media—the print media and the electronic media, both. And they're totally liberated.

And then, finally—obviously, this is to do with freedom of speech and freedom of expression. And then finally is the issue of their having the right to work and elect their own people. And that is what we do. Today the senate, the national assembly, the provincial assemblies and the—of the local government is there. And they've been voted through absolute—franchise in a free and fair manner.

So, therefore, may I say that we have introduced the essence of democracy now in Pakistan. It has been done now. It never—all these things never existed before. What maybe you are talking of is merely the label which probably you are inferring on to my uniform. Indeed, and without saying that you are inferring to it, yes, indeed, that is an issue which needs to be addressed. And I will follow constitutional norms. Even now I am following constitutional norms where I have been allowed to wear this uniform until 2007—being in uniform as the President of Pakistan. Beyond 2007, yes, indeed, this is an issue which has to be addressed and it has to be addressed according to the constitution of Pakistan. And I will never violate the constitution of Pakistan.

So let me assure you that democracy will prevail. Sustainable democracy has been introduced in Pakistan and will prevail in Pakistan, especially beyond 2007.

Long answer.

President Bush: Yes—important answer.

President Musharraf: Thank you very much.

President Bush: Very good job. Thank you again, sir.

—President George W. Bush and President Musharraf of Pakistan

Washington, D.C., March 16, 2007

Question: You say that having a free press is important in developing a democracy and that Musharraf is serving in the interest of the Pakistani people. How do those things go together when you've got evidence of them moving against the media to keep them from reporting on this?

Mr. McCormack: Well, it's interesting you brought that up and I looked into this. And this is with respect to police action against Geo TV, an independent—as I understand it, an independent TV station in Pakistan. And President Musharraf himself has spoken to the issue, and he has said that those actions should not have taken place and that the journalists and TV media should be able to be free to report on events that are transpiring in their country.

—Sean McCormack, spokesman

Washington, D.C., June 5, 2007

Question: Yes. And it seems that the response so far to the apparent crackdown on the media has been somewhat circumspect in comparison to other countries like say, Venezuela. How would you respond to that?

Mr. McCormack: Well, we're watching very closely the events in Pakistan. I know this is a very sensitive issue for Pakistanis; how to resolve this judicial case within the bounds of Pakistani law. I know that President Musharraf's decision within Pakistan, if you read the media accounts, has been quite controversial. Obviously, you've seen that with a number of demonstrations.

So the Pakistani people are going to have to resolve this issue for themselves. They are going to have to decide for themselves whether or not rule of law has been followed, whether or not proper procedures have been followed. It's not something that we can dictate nor want to dictate to the Pakistani people.

There have been advances in bringing greater freedoms, including greater freedom of the press in Pakistan over the years under President Musharraf's government. There has been—there have been some openings in that regard. Certainly, nobody would want to see those openings reversed. And I know that the decree was issued, and I'm not sure—at least to my knowledge—that there had been any media outlets that have been closed down as a result of the decree, certainly that would be a step that we would watch very closely.

And we would just encourage our friends in Pakistan to look at the role of a free media in a society as one that ultimately strengthens a society. It's a critically important function that the media serve all around the globe. And they have certain responsibilities, obviously, that come along with a free media: to report accurately and objectively.

So as of right now, it's a situation, I think, that we're watching closely. But we are right there with Pakistan as they make these political and economic reforms that are ultimately going to result in a different kind of Pakistan. That's what everybody wants to see: a more politically stable, more open, a more economically prosperous Pakistan. And that's—that is the program that President Musharraf's government has laid out. And we support that, we encourage that. There's a lot at stake, certainly. Pakistan is an important country in a very important region that has not known a lot of stability, if you look back over the past 40 or 50 years. If you look back, you know, over the recent history, that area has been constituted in what some have referred to as a crescent of crisis.

So the steps that the Pakistani Government are—have taken over the past several years, we believe are generally in the right direction and we want to encourage them. But it's also important to remember that even though a situation may be somewhat difficult and that there is some turmoil in the system, over the long term, it is important not to roll back any of the advances that have been made over recent years.

—Sean McCormack

Round-Up[14]

November 4, 2007

★ Protests are being planned—most notably in New York/Karachi/Lahore and on November 7 in London/Paris/Lahore/etc. Of course, it goes without saying that those walking in the streets in Lahore or Karachi will most likely risk their immediate safety and freedom. I wish I could walk with them.

New York City:
2 p.m., Monday, November 5, 2007
Pakistani Embassy, New York
12 East 65th Street, New York, NY 10021

★ And a word from Habib Jalib:

Jackbooted State

If the Watchman had not helped the Dacoit
Today our feet wouldn't be in chains, our victory not defeat
Wrap your turbans around your neck, crawl on your bellies
Once on top, it is hard to bring down, the jackbooted state.

★ The code of conduct for media has finally been issued by The General. Highlights:

The media can

(j)   not broadcast video footage of suicide bombers, terrorists, bodies of victims of terrorism, statements and pronouncements of militants and extremist elements, and any other act that may, in any way, promote, aid, or abet terrorists' activities or terrorism

(k)   ensure that no anchor person, moderator, or host propagates any opinion or acts in any manner prejudicial to the ideology of Pakistan or sovereignty, integrity, or security of Pakistan

(l)   not broadcast any program inciting violence or hatred or any action prejudicial to maintenance of law and order

(m) not broadcast anything that defames or brings into ridicule the Head of State, members of the armed forces, or executive, legislative, or judicial organs of the state

Basically, it comes down to a "don't-mock-me" law. This is probably okay, though. Most of the media is still blacked out.

Round-Up II[15]
November 6, 2007

★ An email from students at Lahore University of Management Sciences (LUMS) regarding their upcoming protests:

Things to keep in mind for upcoming protests:

- Keep a wet cloth handy to cover your mouth, nose, and eyes during possible tear gassing.
- Salt for your throat, under the same eventuality.
- Be careful of what you discuss on the phone, telephone lines, and the Internet.
- Make sure you leave your contact information with someone responsible to check on you in case something happens.
- Girls are specially advised to wear shalwaar kameez.
- Do not carry expensive items with you.
- Do not travel in large groups without sufficient organization, because you could arouse needless scrutiny.
- And, of course, a pair of good running shoes.

Declaration I:

"We the students of Ghulam Ishaq Khan Institute, Topi, Distt. Swabi, Pakistan, strongly protest the imposed emergency in Pakistan. Many of our students have expressed their protest by wearing black clothes and armbands. We will support the protests all around Pakistan and the world in every possible way we can."

Declaration II:

Our voice echoes the popular desires of the nation—the resolution of the crisis that has unveiled itself to our nation and its people—and, in attempting to echo these considerations we call upon the state to:

- Lift the "Martial Law" immediately.
- Retract the new Provisional Constitutional Order (PCO).
- Restore the Judiciary to its pre–Martial Law state.
- Demarcate a method to return the military to the barracks for good.
- Provide the assurance of the right to life to each citizen of Pakistan.
- Restore legitimacy to the government by the exercise of the right of voting to the citizens.

Therefore, we call for an immediate declaration of the election schedule.

★ News:

- The General is now arresting *opposition party leaders and key workers.* They started with Jama'at-i Islami (JI) workers/leaders after Qazi Hussain Ahmed called him a traitor and arrested more than 400 JI workers and their families. Now, they are also out to arrest Muslim League leaders. The sole exception seems to be the Pakistan People's Party, aka Benazir Bhutto's party. The police and the Rangers (equivalent to our National Guard) are the primary forces acting for The General—however, reports are that *plainclothes army personnel are involved in the crackdown, arresting protestors across the country.*

- On the other hand: The government released 25 of Mr. Mehsud's militants in exchange for 213 army soldiers captured by Mr. Mehsud's forces in August. The army also agreed to withdraw soldiers from the area inhabited by Mr. Mehsud's tribe in South Waziristan and allow members of the Frontier Corps, a lightly armed paramilitary force, to patrol the area instead.
- He fights them here so he doesn't have to fight them there.
- The General has reduced the Supreme Court from a bench of 17 judges to 12. They still haven't been able to fill the bench.
- The private broadcast channels have been shut now for 72 hours. The Press Clubs in Karachi, Lahore, Multan, and Islamabad were raided by the police, journalists were arrested, and some dailies were prohibited from publication.
- The Karachi Stock Exchange fell 636 index points—the worst day in its history.
- There was a complete boycott of judicial cases across the country, as lawyers declared a "Black Day." Thousands have been arrested and beaten.

★ And finally, a small section from a report of a fellow graduate student doing fieldwork in Karachi:

[T]he massive disconnect between the problems that plague the country and the solutions proposed by Musharraf leaves one aghast. The rise of armed extremism and brazen confrontations between security forces and militants was already a serious issue when it was confined to tribal regions and the north of the country. Now that suicide attacks and bomb blasts are happening on a routine basis across Pakistani cities, it's an even more urgent threat. This kind of everyday violence and uncertainty is new here (regardless of certain Western perspectives that see Pakistan as just another unstable Muslim country, no different from contemporary Iraq, Afghanistan or Palestinian territories). Of course these incidences of violence and the 'war on terror' cropped up in the President's list of justifications for imposing an emergency. Yet the measures actually undertaken under the Provisional Constitutional Order (PCO) do little to strengthen the state's ability to tackle this security crisis or help restore any legitimacy or morale to the badly weakened armed forces. The wholesale purge of the judiciary and the gagging of the media are as unlikely to help as are the crackdown and arrests of secular civil society members or the postponement of elections. The rhetoric of saving the nation cloaks the Musharraf regime's attempts at self-preservation, which have the tragic consequence of aligning both radical right-wing and moderate liberal sections of society against it.

Today is Tuesday, and so far we are still not clear just how long this state of constitutional suspension is going to last and when/if the political process is coming back on track.

Round-Up III[16]
November 7, 2007

★ The United States gives Musharraf's government about $200 million annually and his military $100 million monthly in the form of direct cash transfers. That's just how we roll!

★ Via Bill Swersey comes the news that Asia Society will be having an Emergency Town Hall meeting on Thursday, November 8, at 8:30 a.m. EST. Asma Jahangir, head of Human Rights Commission of Pakistan; Awaz Amir, columnist with DAWN; and others will join a New York City crew via teleconference. You can watch the live webcast on their website.

★ Two private channels, CNBC-Pakistan and Business Plus, are back on the air. The rest are still being blocked. Folks inside Pakistan should take a look at TVU Networks to bypass the restrictions.

★ My father reports from Lahore: "Things are as usual. No one even knows what is going on. It's only the lawyers. We have had four martial laws and nine emergencies. What is so special about this one?" I think Nicholas Schmidle talked to my father, because he files a similar report from Islamabad. I agree with both of them, and I disagree with both of them. The onus of a "common people" uprising is not really a realistic criterion. (Are the lawyers and students not common, btw?) Why should we discount that the supporting bulwarks of any political system—the lawyers, the bureaucrats, the educated middle class—do not constitute mass politics? I see them as essential both as legitimization of mass unrest and a viable alternative to the status quo.

★ There is now a wiki to coordinate the many activities.

★ The *New York Times* has not one but two op-eds. First up is Benazir Bhutto, who seeks to create a coalition of moderation. I am unclear as to what that means, but good for her to try and make this all about herself: "My party would most likely have swept parliamentary elections." *Right.* Is that why you cut a deal, Bibi? The other op-ed is by Muhammad Hanif, who has a forthcoming novel, *A Case of Exploding Mangoes.* The less we linger on that one, the better.

Our Cute Little Dictators[17]
November 7, 2007

> Question: *Dana, does the White House believe that Musharraf is now a dictator?*
> Ms. Perino: *Look, I think that that is—it's premature to say that. This is a president—*

The glorious founding fathers of this nation really did us a bad. They kicked out the king, banned all pomp and circumstance, and made us seek manifestations of our glory in bald eagles and giant cracked bells. Political Power, that most pompous and most glorious of all sports, became the dominion of dour grey suits, subdued haircuts, and sober visages (despite some recent divergences, aside).

What to do, then, about our yearning desires to see the bright plumage of our ruling kings and queens? How do we fill our fantasies of unilateral and benevolent power personified? If we are God's own nation and this is the City on the Hill and that is our Manifest Destiny, then where, oh where, can we observe righteous Leadership in action? Sure, we can transpose some of those desires to the celebrities and give Oscars to anyone who makes any movie about the British queens—dead or dying. But . . . it just doesn't cut it, you know?

Hence, we outsource our plumage needs. There are many a people who have the ability to produce a variety of genus *homo dictatorus*—with a little support and guidance from us. This species comes with their own funny hats, chests filled with medals and bars, a posse of killing hardware, and a determination to "put things right." We like that. We support their nascent abilities to lead their people. We put their glamorous, glittering visages on our papers and our screens—hungrily following them from "crisis" to "crisis." There is so much more substance in their turbulent lives than in our Lindsey Lohan, after all. Now and then, we remind ourselves that our support for these dictators is not "permanent" and that one day soon, they should bring "democracy" to their people.

But, come on. We are smart people here. We know how it is. Democracy is *way* complicated. Electoral colleges and votes and quorums and, oh, those hanging chads! We know that these people have no idea how to keep the poor from clogging up the mainstream with their opinions successfully or even how a black-robed junta can strike an election toward the candidate who lost. Those are skills that take centuries to learn. Still, we ask of these inveterate performers to keep an eye on the road ahead—to tell us that you are working very, very hard in training the people in democracy. We ask them to believe that freedom is the birthright of every human on this planet. They have the freedom to enslave their people. We have the freedom to fund that march for freedom.

To those among us, dour on the inside and out, who make loud pronouncements about repression and oppression and all that. *Please.* This is a completely harmless species. They bark. But they do not bite. And they are necessary. For their people. And also, for us.

Round-Up IV[18]
November 10, 2007

★ Benazir Bhutto was put under house arrest and then released. I think the *Boston Globe* has it about right:

> This is a political shadow play. Many Pakistanis know that Bhutto's family and entourage presided over egregiously corrupt and incompetent governments, and that Musharraf's military cronies have been placed in key business sinecures from which they control a large swath of Pakistan's economy.
>
> Amid all this intrigue, the current prime minister, the apolitical former Citibank executive Shaukat Aziz, has fostered stunning economic growth in the last few years, without the corruption of his predecessors. His stewardship comes much closer to the

ideals of competence, transparency, and accountability than to Bhutto's penchant for feudal privilege or Musharraf's for Napoleonic authoritarianism. Whatever the outcome of the Bhutto-Musharraf shadow play, Pakistan needs the kind of good governance it has had from Aziz.[19]

★ Joseph Biden starts making sense:

> A drastic increase in non-security aid, guaranteed for a long period, would help persuade Pakistan's people that America is an all-weather friend—and Pakistan's leaders that America is a reliable ally. Pakistanis suspect our support is purely tactical. They point to the aid cut-off that followed the fall of the Soviet Union to our refusal to deliver or refund purchased jets in the 1990s and to our blossoming relationship with rival India. Many Pakistanis believe that the moment Osama bin Laden is gone, U.S. interest will go with him.
>
> When U.S. aid makes a real difference in people's lives, the results are powerful. In October 2005, after a devastating earthquake, American military helicopters delivering relief did far more to improve relations than any amount of arms sales or debt rescheduling. And the Mobile Army Surgery Hospital we left behind is a daily reminder that America cares.
>
> To have a real impact on a nation of 165 million, we'll have to raise our spending dramatically. A baseline of $1.5 billion annually, for a decade, is a reasonable place to start. That might sound like a lot—but it's about what we spend every week in Iraq. Conditioning security aid—now about three-quarters of our package—would help push the Pakistani military to finally crush al-Qaida and the Taliban.
>
> Aid to the Pakistani people should be unconditioned—that is, not subject to the ups and downs of a particular government in Islamabad or Washington. But aid to the Pakistani military and intelligence service should be closely conditioned—that is, carefully calibrated to results. Like it or not, the Pakistani security services will remain vital players—and our best shot at finding bin Laden and shutting down the Taliban. Their performance has been decidedly mixed: we've caught more terrorists in Pakistan than in any other country—but $10 billion later, Pakistan remains the central base of al-Qaida operations. We must strike a much better bargain.[20]

★ *Getting Away with Farce* by Ayaz Amir: *This* is unsustainable and cannot last. You can't mock the heavens and think there will be nothing to pay for it. These are the acts of desperate men who know that their moment in the sun is up, from whose fingers power is slipping but who want to stave off the inevitable.

★ Happy Diwali, to all my gentle readers. Go light some firecrackers, but not in Southern California, please.

Round-Up V[21]
November 13, 2007

The high school kids in Islamabad got lathi-charged right after a peaceful demonstration in Islamabad. The youth, the numbers, and the "spirited" response by the police—your tax dollars at work.

Things to keep in mind: Thursday, November 15, is officially the end of Musharraf's current term as president. Which means The General has to take the new oath—which he is prohibited to do by the house-arrested Supreme Court—and he has to do it as a civilian. The General wants a new election for the dissolved assemblies by January 9. My bet is that Musharraf keeps that army uniform on for a while, and maybe we will have another "crisis." Yeah?

Benazir Bhutto is getting tons of press. Our intrepid reporters should note that, unlike virtually every other opposition leader, Benazir Bhutto seems to have direct access to all international and state media—including holding gloriously orchestrated press conferences. Still, she has been ratcheting up her rhetoric—declaring now that, "I will not serve as prime minister as long as Musharraf is president." Of course, she follows that with the clear-eyed assessment that, "Even if I wanted to work with him, I would not have the public support." Ah, the machinations of freedom's glorious march across the Muslim world.

I say what I said before, these protests are fulfilling a crucial role: They are making sure that things do not return to status quo, that the vacuum persists, and that back-channel deals are forced into the public. In that regard, the role of Internet-based distribution of information cannot be stressed highly enough. Benazir may have landed in Pakistan with deals, but the democratic forces—those lawyers and college kids—are forcing her to play by new rules. And I say "forcing," because, trust me, she is no Aung San Suu Kyi.

Which isn't to say that there is no other "viable" leadership in Pakistan (a common refrain from the likes of "realists" like Fareed Zakaria and Zakaria-lites). The *New York Times* has a great profile of Aitzaz Ahsan—a stalwart of opposition in many a regime. He is currently in jail.

Perhaps feeling the inevitable Buyer's Remorse, The General has been out of sight, but he makes a brilliant comeback in a press conference. First off, he is mad at being called our sonofabitch, and so he kicks out the *Telegraph* reporters. Then, the interview, which promises to be just scads of fun with some amazing quotes from the *NYT* write-up:

> About Benazir Bhutto, speaking as a dejected suitor promised a scented garden: "You come here on supposedly on a reconciliatory mode, and right before you land, you're on a confrontationist mode. I am afraid this is producing negative vibes, negative optics."
>
> . . .
>
> And next speaking as a truly enlightened man of the 21st century:
>
> He called Ms. Jehangir, the leading human rights advocate in Pakistan and one of the first women lawyers, "quite an unbalanced character."
>
> General Musharraf criticized Ms. Jehangir for being too ambitious in her agenda on how to achieve better rights for women.
>
> Pakistani women deserved more opportunities, and he cited his own legislation that amended the laws to protect women against accusations of rape and adultery.
>
> But Ms. Jehangir, he said, wanted to go too fast, and would therefore fail.[22]

[Thanks, Sunit.]

And this, from Stephen Zunes, "Pakistan's Dictatorships and the United States," *Foreign Policy in Focus Report* (Washington, D.C.: Foreign Policy in Focus, November 11, 2007):

> Given the unwillingness of both the Republican administration and the Democratic-controlled Congress to stop U.S. military support for the current Pakistani dictatorship, it may be time once again for concerned citizens to engage in similar nonviolent actions to end U.S. support for the oppression. For those at risk as a result of U.S. policy are no longer just those currently oppressed by the Pakistani regime. Someday, as a result of a possible blowback from this policy, it could be Americans as well.[23]

I discussed all of these matters, in great depth, at a recent luncheon with Benazir and Ahmadinejad (The General was kept begging in the background). We failed to reach any consensus except that the avocado salad was delicious.

Finally, below the fold is a letter from Dr. Pervaiz Hasan, a lawyer and member of LUMS who was arrested on November 5:

> They herded lawyers in the police, about 35 of us. We knew nothing about where we were being taken after our arrest at the Lahore High Court on [November 5, 2007]. Speculation mounted in discussions in the bus but it was soon overtaken by the rumor/news received on some mobile telephones with the lawyers that General Musharraf had been removed and placed under house arrest. The hatred for Musharraf seemed so intense that this appeared the best news of the day although with the reported take over by General Kiani, it was sadly a case of "from the fire into the frying pan."
>
> The first thing when we arrived at the Sabzazar Police Station (further out of Lahore near Allama Iqbal Town) was that we were unlocked out of the police bus and searched. All mobile phones were confiscated. I do not use, have or carry a mobile phone and by this time the expectation, subtly fed to us, was that we would be taken from Sabzazar to jails in Bahawalpur, Sahiwal or Mianwali. I am a heart patient: I had a heart attack in 2004, and doctors at the Punjab Institute of Cardiology in Lahore then operated [on] me to place three stents in my heart blood vessels. I have been regimented since to taking several medicines, morning and evening. Some of these are important for the thinning of the blood to prevent strokes. When I saw the prospect of being held incommunicado without information to my family, I wanted desperately to reach out for my medicines.
>
> Courtesy [of] a colleague on the bus, I hurriedly used his mobile before getting out of the bus to be searched in the police station to inform my Secretary in the office

about the Sabzazar Police Station minutes before the mobile was confiscated by the Police Station. Otherwise, no one could have found out where we were being held. The only redeeming thing for the whole day turned out to be that the Police Station allowed the medicines to be delivered to me in the cell when my son, Omar, rushed to bring these to Sabzazar.

The cell in Sabzazar was an unclean, filthy room with a toilet and tap in the middle with a 4-foot wall around it. The 35 of us were all jam-packed, once again, into this room which was actually meant for fewer people. Having been a political activist with the Tehrik-i-Istiqlal and, later, with the Tehrik-e-Insaf as its first Secretary General, I well know and have been exposed to the conditions of our police stations and jails. In criticizing the conditions for the detainees, one is not asking for 5-star comfort, but what I am suggesting is that 60 years after our independence, the conditions in our police stations and jails have not matched the worldwide developments toward the dignity of human beings increasingly recognized through international Magna Cartas such as the United Nation's Universal Declaration of Human Rights, 1948, and the International Covenants on Human Rights, 1966 and the human rights provisions in our own national Constitution. It is a measure of our national shame that even enemy prisoners of war receive better treatment under the Geneva Conventions than do our detainees in our police stations and jails.

We slept on the hard dirty floor in our court dresses without access to any cover of blankets in the cool and mosquito-infested night. The space was so over-crowded that when I got up from a brief nap, I found a young lawyer using my legs as a pillow.

But the mood was optimistic and the spirits high. We soon went into telling jokes and reciting poetry and found a Master of Ceremonies who directed the order of our presentations. Much of the humor, mostly obscene was in respect of General Pervez Musharraf and if there were any (spy) bugs in the room, many of the 35 lawyers could easily be hauled up under anti-obscenity statutes!

The most eloquent and, for me, the most moving presentation was from a young lawyer who proudly declared that 5 November 2007 was the most important day of his life because he had decided, on this date, that he would never appear before a PCO Judge. He was equally proud to announce that, acting on this resolve, he had only that morning returned a (huge) fee of Rs. 4,000 to a client whose case he would no longer handle. This was the most humbling experience for me. That morning, I too had acted on the same resolve to return the professional fee of over Rs. one (1) crore paid to me by clients whose cases I would no longer argue because of the PCO Judges. But I felt that my gesture after 37 years of a busy professional life did not match the sacrifice of this young struggling lawyer. I wish all other lawyers see similar light on the start of their careers.

My bonding with the 35 colleagues at Sabzazar came to an end early on 6 November 2007 when because of the dedicated and worried efforts of my architect son, Omar, and nephew, Jawad, I was released from Sabzazar Police Station on grounds of age (66) and a medical condition duly certified by the country's leading cardiologist, Dr. Shaharyar

Sheikh. I should also acknowledge the humane response to my medical problems by the efficient SHO of the Sabzazar Police Station, Qamar Abbas, and his deputy, Atif.

—Dr. Pervaiz Hasan

Round-Up VI²⁴
November 14, 2007

★ Following last week's military crackdown in Pakistan and the detention of hundreds of lawyers, the Harvard Law School Association has decided to award Pakistani Chief Justice Iftikhar Chaudhry its highest honor: The Harvard Law School Medal of Freedom.

★ "Mentally and in my heart, I am not a dictator. In my heart, I have introduced democracy," appeals The General during a recent sit-down with *Sky News*. The proof? He was not a dictator when he was commanding the army. The mind boggles at the logical contradiction buried in there. (Try imagining a democratic army.) But, I am giving him too much credit if I say he is contradicting himself. He is lying. There is news that he has arrested key members of the leadership of Pakistan People's Party in Punjab, including Abida Hussain, Pakistan's former ambassador to Washington. Democratic, no?

★ I went to the sneak preview of *Persepolis*—based on Marjane Satrapi's comic book. It is a poignant film—amazing two-dimensional illustrations, perhaps some of the best music I have heard in a movie recently, and lots of "applicability to our current situations" (as I heard one sage describe it on the way out). The story takes place immediately before the 1979 Islamic Revolution in Iran and follows Marjane through the early '90s. Especially notable is the nuanced portrayal of a child growing up and learning what it means to know who she is and how to live with integrity. History and memory weigh heavy on Satrapi, though I am sure she will flick her burning cigarette into my eye for such academic l33t speech. I also know that Satrapi did not write this to "explain" the Islamic Revolution or life under the Mullahs in Iran to the United States at the moment we are actively contemplating "liberating" that nation from its suicidal regime. But that is how the U.S. media will see this movie. I predict lots of reviews about how factual or authentic the description of life under Islamic regime is; how she is an apologist for the mullahs or handmaiden to the Great Satan, etc., etc. There is no denying that this movie is grist for the hard news-wallah's mill.

★ Nicholas Schmidle, reporting in the *New Republic*, compares Musharraf and the Shah in Iran—with the backdrop of U.S. support of a dictator. The comparison is mostly facile, and the fear is not a new one. General Zia-ul-Haq thought as much in the immediate aftermath and went on to inject his Sunnification policies into the Pakistani bloodstream (often mislabeled "Islamization"). The Iranian example does provide one crucial point to ponder: the role of the cultural intelligentsia and their ability to know and predict what is going on in their own country. We are focused on the middle class and the youth, but we need to gauge where the country's overall mood is tilting toward. Let us not get carried away and forget that two of the biggest states in Pakistan are effectively ungovernable by the federal regime, that an incredibly ruthless adversary is currently operating in Swat, that the people of Baluchistan have long awaited justice, and that the Pakistani people are just as scared and helpless to control the direction of their country as we have been in this country. I am hopeful that Musharraf and his uniform and his throne will part soon enough, but we need to know what happens next.

In the meantime, we can take heart from Schmidle. After all, it did take two years of hanging out with nastiest Islamists around before he got spooked from anti-Americanism:

> At least, not yet. After living in Pakistan for almost two years and traveling to all parts of the country meeting some of the nastiest Islamists around, I had my first encounter with visceral anti-Americanism on Saturday night, an hour after the State of Emergency was declared. I was walking from one side of a police cordon, back into a crowd of anti-Musharraf protesters, when a tall man with a long beard called out from 15 feet away, berating me and accusing me of being a CIA agent. "America is destroying a nation of [160] million people to save one person!" he yelled.
>
> I looked back at the line of riot police and wondered if they were going to come to my rescue. But I didn't fault the man with the beard; even though the White House has criticized Musharraf in the last few days, they have spent the past six years telling Musharraf that he could do no wrong. I just wondered how many American journalists faced a similar barrage in the months before the Shah fled Iran.[25]

★ In some earlier post, I mentioned Zakaria and his particular brand of "realism." He now demands our attention with Pakistan's Pinstripe Revolution. Pinstripe? The analysis is so off base that it screams for a proper fisking—for which I have no energy. Can I just say that when so-called liberal pundits are proclaiming "Periods of transition are never placid" à la Donald Rumsfeld, then we really need to reassess the meaning of the word "liberal." The meaning of the word "pundit" thankfully should remain what it is.

★ Imran Khan finally came out—went to Punjab University—and was tossed unceremoniously into the hands of the police by the members of the IJT (student wing of the Jama'at-i Islami, the hardline mullahs). Imran Khan needs to be released, now. He has justifiable fears for his safety.

Round-Up VII[26]
November 17, 2007

★ Bowing to The General's pressure, the United Arab Emirates has shut down Geo TV transmissions from Dubai. Even though it was shut from cable, Pakistanis could catch Geo over satellite or the Internet. Not anymore. Before November 3, the people in Pakistan could enjoy news and analysis from Dawn News, Aaj, Geo, Ary One World, as well as BBC World, CNN, and *Al-Jazeera*. They now have PTV—the state channel. The White House says they are "bothered."

It is shameful that such a "progressive" and "capitalist-friendly" nation, such as the United Arab Emirates, has succumbed to the pressure from the Pakistan State. I can wager, though, that they didn't need too much convincing. The role of media (TV and the Internets) in the upheaval against the dictatorial regime in Pakistan cannot be stressed highly enough. It is not simply the fact that these channels have carried live footage of riots and police brutality since February 2007 into the living rooms of millions of Pakistanis. More pointedly, it is the sharply delineated public space that has emerged in news-analysis and commentary pieces since 2004. *Al-Jazeera* deserves tremendous credit for changing the face of media, and one of the seismic changes was in Pakistan. Sitting in the United States, with a TV media that is as fiercely scripted by market and ideological forces as anything the politburo could have imagined, it is hard to conceive of government officials, opposition folks, intellectuals, and live call-ins mingling on the same stage. Often vehemently. The United Arab Emirates is protecting its own royal future.

Watch this broadcast on the attack on the Geo office in Islamabad on March 16, 2007.[27] The anchor Kamran Khan is speaking on the phone with the Minister (at 2:12): *What are you doing? What are you doing, Mr. Minister? What is your government doing? These scenes are not just being seen in Pakistan but across the world, Mr. Muhammad Ali Durrani. You have spent your life in this country, have you ever seen such a spectacle? You are the minister of information and broadcasting, what will you do? Stay there and protect our workers.*

Or just watch this, broadcast on AAJ TV on the program *Bolta Pakistan* (*Pakistan Speaking*).[28]

I could never imagine even a portion of such critiques leveled at the politicians of this country on our TV channels.

★ Nawaz Sharif has an op-ed in the *Washington Post*, "Pakistan's One-Man Calamity."[29] Very Hemingway-esque. I would like to see Mian Ji back in Pakistan and contesting with Bibi. Bhutto's niece, Fatima Bhutto, had a piece in the *Los Angeles Times*, "Aunt Benazir's False Promises,"[30] which is more Dorothy Parker than Hemingway. (Fatima Bhutto sadly failed to introduce "Auntie" to the American audience. Auntie Benazir. Not Aunt Benazir.)

★ No word yet on what Negroponte really said to The General.

Sab Theek Hai[31]
November 20, 2007

The General's crackdown on media involves the key "code of conduct," which prohibits making fun of His Enlightened Excellency. It is a healthy decree—no society can survive if its Elders Are Targeted by Base Humor. Perhaps it was after his trip to *The Daily Show with Jon Stewart*, where he was treated with deference and respect, that He Who Is Pakistan decided that the Pakistanis need to grow up.

Sadly, kids at *4 Man Show* have not learned their lesson. In the guise of exaggerated humility and compliance, they continue to mock him. Ruthlessly. ("*Sab Theek Hai.* Everything is fine in Pakistan. I saw with my own eyes, the lion and the lamb drinking water from the pond outside. All is just fine in Pakistan. Diamonds are being sold on the street like peas.")

Round-Up VIII[32]
November 22, 2007

Bush has called The General an all-around great guy; the Supreme Court in Pakistan has cleared The General for takeoff; a Baluchistan Liberation Army leader was killed somewhere in Afghanistan; Imran Khan is out of jail; they kicked Pakistan out of the commonwealth. More later.

Missing in Pakistan[33]
November 25, 2007

Missing in Pakistan is a short documentary written and directed by Ziad Zafar, an independent journalist and filmmaker. It was shot in February and March 2007 and highlights one of the key causes of the judicial and political crisis in Musharraf's Pakistan: the extralegal disappearances of ordinary citizens at the hands of military intelligence. It reveals, as well, that the average Pakistani citizen can easily draw a stark connection between U.S. ideals and policy with the realities in Pakistan. It is time we did the same here.

The documentary was to be screened at FAST-NU in Lahore. The screening was halted by the administration of the university at the behest of the government.

Two Letters and a Temper Tantrum[34]
December 14, 2007

Two letters in today's *Dawn* need your attention.

"Guilty as Charged": Farhat Haq, a professor of political science in Illinois, tells us how the emergency came to her: "A warrant has been issued for my arrest, despite the fact that I am thousands of miles away from the trouble. I accept this warrant proudly. In a way, it is no mistake. If it is criminal for a daughter of Pakistan to long for freedom and justice, then I plead guilty."

"Relevance of Bulleh Shah": Ayesha Siddiqa, author of *Military, Inc.*, attends a play on the life of a 17th-century mystic: "It is important to know if the ruling elite thought beyond the message of secularism of folk religion and looked into the deeper issue of how woeful is the life of the common man, and it is this that must be changed. The elite shy away from creating institutional mechanisms to ameliorate the problems of the poor."

Seeking the personal and the literary in the current crisis in Pakistan is quite easy. Bulleh Shah, Habib Jalib, and Faiz Ahmed Faiz are on everyone's lips and in every political communiqué. Similarly, the crisis manifests as individual struggles writ large—the travails of Justices Munir Malik and Iftikhar Chaudhry or Aitzaz Ahsan and Asma Jahangir are the lightning rods for immense energy and focus among the protestors.

What is remarkable about those two letters—even as they are individual stories—is that they highlight the pervasive oppression by the Pakistani state in every aspect of society. The people are not fighting solely for electoral politics or freedoms for one or two . . . it is this Leviathan they want to eliminate.

Also, not to be missed . . . President Pervez Musharraf unveils his softer side:

Q: Will the judges be restored to their prior positions?

A: No, not at all. What judges? Why should they be restored? New judges are there. They will never be restored.

Q: People in the West will have a hard time understanding that.

A: Let them not understand. They should come to Pakistan and understand Pakistan.

. . .

Q: Then, why are you now clamping down on the media? You seem far more angry now than ever before.

A: I think you are right. [*Laughs.*] Why don't you understand? Am I a madman? Have I suddenly changed? Am I a Dr. Jekyll and Mr. Hyde?

. . .

Q: And you feel you could work with her?

A: I think so. I am not such an unpleasant person.

Q: Some say that you want the prime minister to come from your own party.

A: We are going to have fair and transparent elections.

Q: Is that really true?

A: Why do you think it is untrue?[35]

New Prisons for Old[36]
April 14, 2008

There was a news item in a Lahore daily, a few days ago. In the *Daily Waqt*, the unnamed reporter sought to highlight destruction and disappearance of the Lal Qila dungeons in Lahore. These dungeons, the article stated, had housed political prisoners and criminals for centuries—Lodhi to Akbar to Shah Jahan to the British and down, most recently to Zia-ul-Haq (who put them to good use in the mass arrests in '84–'85). It had some renown as a "torture cell" and "hanging depot" among the locals. Barring a few noted prisoners, these dungeons had remained shuttered and ignored during Pervez Musharraf's tenure and can now only be considered relics of the past. Will no one, asked *Daily Waqt*, think of our Mughal history?

Since there has been no lack of prisoners—political or otherwise—in Pakistan during the last ten years, it is a good question: What did happen? Where are the political prisoners in Pakistan? The first response is surely: vanished. The second response needs a broader view of what has happened in Pakistan. I would argue that the state of extraconstitutional constitutionality that has existed in the United States since early 2002 has had a frank implementation in Pakistan under Musharraf. There has been a "new" language of security and safety—subtly undercutting the language of rights and eschewing usual channels (legal or otherwise)—that the state claims supersedes all else. The dungeons under Lahore Fort may be an extreme case, but the "prison" has had a long and noted history for those daring to speak up against tyranny. One need only think of a Faiz stewing in prison and writing letters and poems to see that discursive power. The state in Pakistan, following the United States, sought to declaim such memories for the current generations of Aitzaz Ahsans and Iftikhar Chaudhries.

I say post-2002 United States deliberately and precisely. The recent revelations of John Yoo's memos arguing suspension of the Geneva Convention, authorizing torture, suspending the Fourth Amendment for domestic military operations; the state's admission of wide snooping powers over U.S. citizens; the gulag at Gitmo; the "state" media, which unquestionably led us into the Iraq War, were all efforts that unfurled in early and mid-2002, and it was these practices that provided explicit and implicit templates to the likes of Pervez Musharraf.

It is perhaps the penultimate nail in irony's coffin that, in his address, Musharraf quoted Lincoln as his ideologue while contemplating emergency. The ultimate nail being that Musharraf found an inspirational quote from Lincoln in none other than Richard M. Nixon's 1980 bestseller *Leaders: Profiles and Reminiscences of Men Who Have Shaped the World*—Musharraf's self-proclaimed favorite book of all time. But that was all show and tell for the American audience. The real inspiration was George W. Bush's America, not Lincoln's.

Just as the United States declared a new category of "enemy combatants" for prisoners taken during a war who are not prisoners of war and sought to incarcerate them on "non-U.S." U.S. territory, Musharraf called into being a new category of "enemies of the state"—a designation for whoever sought to criticize or work for the removal of this dictator. The enemies of the state being, simply, the "enemies" of Musharraf. (A biological necessity since he embodied the country: "This country lives in my heart. This country lives in my blood. And it lives in my soul.") And for this special category of prisoners, the prison cell couldn't be the prison that housed Gandhi, Nehru, Bhagat Singh, and Zulfiqar Ali Bhutto. The prison compound about which Faiz wrote: *Sahn-e Zindan kay be-Watan Ashjar / Sar nigoun mahv hain bananay mein/Daman-e Asman pe Naksh-o Nigar* (the homeless trees of the prison's courtyard / with heads bent, are busy tracing / patterns across the sky).

That prison compound, Musharraf knew, would be used as a platform to build ever greater public support against his anarchy. Hence, his regime operated under the "vanished" scenario, wherein Military Intelligence simply erased a suspect from legal and geographical space. Such, though, couldn't be the fate of Chief Justice Iftikhar Chaudhry or Aitzaz Ahsan.

For our "new" political prisoners, the idea of House Arrest was enshrined as state practice. The houses were surrounded by military and police, the phones were audibly tapped, and all ingress and egress rigidly controlled. In effect, the Pakistani state was able to create hundreds of miniature Guantanamo Bays wherein undesirables could be sequestered for the *longue durée*.

Sadly, Musharraf didn't count on the power of "new" technologies to influence mass politics. SMS/TXT messages, viral cell phone videos, compiled and transmitted from within the houses of the CJ or Asma Jahangir, spread to possibly every cell phone in the country, onto *YouTube*, and across the diaspora. The state efforts to curtail these modern-day chapatis also failed: the ban on cell phones had to be lifted for the sake of global capital; the ban on *YouTube* and *BlogSpot* had to be lifted for creating even worse publicity.

The language of liberal democracy and republic, which enshrines basic rights and protects minorities, is the very language that Musharraf used in his destruction of Pakistan's Constitution. Similar is the case in India, where Dr. Binayak Sen continues to languish in prison for almost a year—claimed a terrorist by the same state that uses terror against its own people. In essence, a shared, global history of terror has been written around us, since 2002. Its public manifestations are policies that govern our lives here and elsewhere. The global politics of Washington and Islamabad are the politics of unrestrained freedom of action—in the name of security and security, alone. These global politics need our firmest critiques and sustained analysis. These dungeons need some sunlight.

Agency[37]
August 18, 2008

Two possible beginnings:

Pakistan is in dire straits. It is a nation at a crossroads. Extremism is around the corner. The politicians are corrupt. The nukes could end up in the hands of bin Laden. We need a strong ally at the helm, a strong military man.

Pakistan is in dire straits. Its people demand accountability. Those who claim to protect it and make it prosperous seem busy keeping themselves in power. There is no hope for change since the people have no power. They are stuck under a dictator. If the citizens of Pakistan are to be real agents of change, they need a way forward. They need democracy.

In March of 2007, when lawyers came out on the streets, there were only two available narratives. Those who held a results-based approach argued that Musharraf's dictatorial regime was the best-case scenario, the lesser of the two evils. The evil being, of course, justice, accountability, and democracy. They raised the specter of rampant jihadism spreading through the populations. They pointed towards the economic development that had occurred on Musharraf's watch. They warned that Pakistan had some amazingly corrupt politicians. And that the United States needed a stable ally, a dependable ally, in our war against terror(ism).

Then, there were those of us who trusted the people of Pakistan. We knew that jihadism is not some airborne virus that people can contract by simply inhaling. We knew that it wasn't Musharraf who had brought about economic development, but the people themselves. We knew that politicians are corrupt everywhere—including the United States—so why the exception of dictator for Pakistan? We knew that a partnership can only be among equals. And the will of the people needed to be heard.

Ah. But this so-called Lawyer's Movement was a big sham, we were told. These are just elites. Where are the "people"? Why can't the lawyers bring out the masses?

Why do they insist on democracy and justice when the people are more concerned with food and security?

Well. Pakistan just had a slow-burning, people-powered, secular revolution, and they forced a sitting dictator—who had the complete confidence and support of the only superpower in the world—out. Peacefully. Without any bloodshed. Without any crazy *mullah* grabbing the nukes and blowing up the world. Without inflation hitting 10,000,000 percent. Without any riots. With suicide bombings in Lahore. With two regions embroiled in near civil war. With the same corrupt politicians in charge. With the unshakeable faith, the belief, that they deserved justice. That they deserved the right to have the power to act. That they were citizens of their country, not keeps.

This is unprecedented. This is historic. This is a momentous time in the history of this nation. It has successfully forced accountability—through peaceful and legal means—on its leaders. The people of Pakistan—lawyers and all—have exercised their agency.

And like every other such exercise—be it the election of 2000 or the upcoming election of 2008 in the United States—the outcome is up in the air. And hence, the hope is not in the fate of this particular dictator, it is in the accountability to the Pakistani publics, of their representative. If we really want a secure ally in Pakistan, we would do our best to strengthen the people of Pakistan.

Chapter Notes

1 Archived at http://bit.ly/hhBtXm.

2 Archived at http://bit.ly/hVqkad.

3 Archived at http://bit.ly/ehx3sN.

4 Archived at http://bit.ly/fKpBEy.

5 "Senior Administration Official Holds a Background Briefing," September 22, 2004, archived at http://bit.ly/dPbVS1.

6 Archived at http://bit.ly/ehEfdv.

7 Archived at http://bit.ly/hcvwPW.

8 Archived at http://bit.ly/fHYpwC.

9 Archived at http://bit.ly/gVpHQh.

10 Archived at http://bit.ly/dJYeZF.

11 Mohsin Hamid, "Pakistan's Silent Majority Is Not to Be Feared," *New York Times*, March 27, 2007, archived at http://nyti.ms/lRrziu.

12 Archived at http://bit.ly/ggrMmU.

13 *Foreign Relations of the United States, 1969–1976, Vol. XI, South Asia Crisis, 1971*, ed. Louis J. Smith (Washington, DC: GPO), archived at http://bit.ly/fpkhcB.

14 Archived at http://bit.ly/fMvb5L.

15 Archived at http://bit.ly/hhxtim. The photos reproduced over the following eight pages are all photos that circulated widely on the Internet in November 2007 and since, and are assumed to be in the public domain.

16 Archived at http://bit.ly/eGKvPr.

17 Archived at http://bit.ly/eMA0vY.

18 Archived at http://bit.ly/g5msv1.

19 "Pakistani Make-Believe," *Boston Globe*, November 10, 2007, archived at http://bo.st/m9THwN.

20 Joe Biden, "A New Approach to Pakistan," *Huffington Post*, November 8, 2007, archived at http://huff.to/lzbORd.

21 Archived at http://bit.ly/dKRqJ6.

22 Carlotta Gall, David Rohde, and Jane Perlez, "Rebuffing U.S., Musharraf Calls Crackdown Crucial to a Fair Vote," *New York Times*, November 14, 2007, archived at http://nyti.ms/hIr5s1.

23 Archived at http://bit.ly/l3hV1e.

24 Archived at http://bit.ly/eV5Wlv.

25 Nicholas Schmidle, "Pak It In," *New Republic*, November 12, 2007, archived at http://bit.ly/fAT4Wu.

26 Archived at http://bit.ly/dOTDTY.

27 "GEO TV Attacked by Police," *YouTube.com*, archived at http://bit.ly/eqWWoL.

28 "Best of *Bolta Pakistan*," *YouTube.com*, archived at http://bit.ly/eRGLmi.

29 Nawaz Sharif, "Pakistan's One-Man Calamity," *Washington Post*, November 17, 2007, archived at http://wapo.st/mcEqbG.

30 Fatima Bhutto, "Aunt Benazir's False Promises," *Los Angeles Times*, November 14, 2007, archived at http://lat.ms/lgnMco.

31 Archived at http://bit.ly/e7YFes.

32 Archived at http://bit.ly/hcDtcE.

33 Archived at http://bit.ly/fSzNzQ.

34 Archived at http://bit.ly/fwdf0i.

35 Lally Weymouth, "A Conversation with Pervez Musharraf," *Washington Post*, December 16, 2007, archived at http://wapo.st/iYrt2V.

36 Archived at http://bit.ly/eQnJKs.

37 Archived at http://bit.ly/hfF3Qz.

6
Deny

In April 2007, I began the "Tick Tock" series, which was a countdown to the ouster of the President Musharraf. I won't claim that I foresaw the end before others—but if you insist, I will take credit for at least documenting events as they unfolded. As the events spiraled out of U.S. control, the administration continued to deny that they had any idea what was going on in Pakistan.

Tick Tock[1]
April 6, 2007

Formally announcing the establishment of a parallel judicial system, the pro-Taliban Lal Masjid administration on Friday vowed to enforce Islamic laws in the federal capital and threatened to unleash a wave of suicide bombers if the government took any action to counter it.

The Justice[2]
May 6, 2007

It had taken the chief justice 25 hours rather than the usual 4 to reach Lahore, which is considered Pakistan's cultural capital and an important political center.

He left Islamabad, the capital, at 7:30 a.m. on Saturday. But his caravan moved at a snail's pace. Hundreds of vehicles followed Mr. Chaudhry as he traveled through various cities of Punjab, the most populous province. Thousands of people stood by the road as the caravan passed by, making victory signs and shouting that General Musharraf should leave office.

Mr. Chaudhry's vehicle was showered with rose petals at every stop, and people pushed close to get a glimpse of him.[3]

Karachi Is Burning[4]
May 12, 2007

In a showdown that was seen coming, at least 33 people were killed and scores injured in Karachi today in clashes set off by the arrival of the chief justice of Pakistan's Supreme Court.

Troubles[5]
May 15, 2007

"Karachi is smelling quite similar to the early '90s." My dear friend, who lives and works in Karachi, responded thusly to my query about his safety. For everyone's sake, I pray not.

I saw this ad in *Daily Jang* the day after the massacres. In a sanctimonious tone, it decries the spilling of blood in Karachi and says, "Why is politics being played in the name of justice?" and "These martyrs are not martyrs for justice but for individual egos." I don't know who sponsored it—but the language makes me think it is not someone very sympathetic to the CJ. But, one could easily ask the same questions of The General.

The news is bad, and it gets worse. Another 22 were killed in another suicide attack in Peshawar.

The pundits here are wringing their hands as usual—what do we do? If we don't support The General, the ISI will get the nukes! Or the Islamists will get the nukes. Let me blow your mind, folks, the ISI always had the Islamists, and the ISI was always in charge of the nuclear program. Go figure.

I wanted to write a longer piece, but I am, literally, too depressed.

Tick Tock II[6]
May 30, 2007

Media rights groups have voiced growing concern over intimidation of journalists in Pakistan amid political turmoil sparked by Musharraf's suspension of Chaudhry in March that has led to mass protests by opposition parties and lawyers.

A U.S. diplomat, who was not authorized to speak for the record, confirmed last week that the United States plans to stick with Musharraf. "We are not pulling back from that relationship in any way," the diplomat said.

Tick Tock III[7]
June 4, 2007

Last night during the Democratic debate, a history professor asked the candidates what they thought of the lack of democracy in Pakistan under Musharraf. Barack Obama responded first with some baloney—something about hunting Osama bin Laden or something. Hillary Clinton followed suit and said she thinks Musharraf is doing the best he can. Only John Edwards answered him directly and stated clearly that the United States doesn't just want democracy but a particular type of democracy, and what if Musharraf goes and Islamists come to power?

Remarkable, isn't it, this tunnel vision of imperialism? Even a cursory understanding of Pakistani history can show the lack of traction the Islamists have had. Even a dubious grasp of current events can demonstrate the solid pushback by ordinary citizens against the Talibanization of Pakistan. But here we stand . . . the yin and yang of Pakistani analysis in any and all public spheres of the United States: Musharraf or Else.

A few days ago, The General issued an amendment to the Pakistan Electronic Media Regulatory Authority Ordinance (2007) "barring television networks from airing talk shows and carrying out live coverage of events relating to the judicial crisis." Today Geo TV and Aaj TV—two popular cable channels—were shut down by the state from broadcasting across the country (and specifically in major metropolitan areas). More restrictions will undoubtedly follow.

Edwards, Obama, and Clinton may not know this—or care—but the press in Pakistan has been the most vital organ of civil society throughout its existence, through Ayub or Zia or Bhutto or Nawaz. The rise of cable channels has been largely on the back of opinion and news shows anchored by strong personalities with live-studio call-in elements. These same channels carried live footage of the MQM thugs shooting and killing on May 12 as well as the police raids on the channels for attempted shutdown of the transmissions—much to the embarrassment of the spin machines.

Like I have been saying since the judicial crisis started, this is The General's endgame. He has no real moves left beside force and oppression. He has finally lost the hearts and minds of even those most forgiving souls of Pakistan's silent majority. The wise move would have been for a face-saving election, but with the blessing of freedom and liberty, Musharraf has decided to toss aside the farce of *Enlightened Moderation* and embrace his inner Mugabe.

You can see the outrage pouring from citizens and observers.

To my journo readers, this story is worth your time. I hope you can help give it some traction. I wrote off an op-ed to the *New York Times*, but since I don't have a book out, it ain't getting printed.

Tick Tock IV[8]
June 28, 2007

Griff Witte's "Musharraf's Military Reaches Deep into Pakistani Society" (*Washington Post*, June 27): "Yet in a country where the military has long been immune from criticism, its extraordinary power is now drawing open contempt from civilians. A campaign against Musharraf that began three months ago, following his suspension of the chief justice, has exploded into a full-fledged movement to oust the armed services from civilian life and send the generals back to their barracks."[9]

Carlotta Gall's "As Pakistan's Chief Looks Ahead, Army Holds the Cards" (*New York Times*, June 28): "Asked if the corps commanders might tell the general he had to go, he answered, "We may be coming to that stage.""[10]

There used to be a time when the biggest "social program" Pakistani intellectuals hammed about was defeudalization. The wave of the future: demilitarization.

Tick Tock V[11]
July 20, 2007

The Supreme Court of Pakistan, finally realizing that they can do better by not trussing up the dictatorship, reinstated CJ Iftikhar Muhammad Chaudhry and nullified the reference filed against him by Musharraf.

I find it hard to imagine how The General will survive all this. CJ Chaudhry back at the bench will surely pick up where he left off—hearing cases about the disappeared. Musharraf has lost all credibility and legitimacy since February/March. Even the Lal Masjid operation provided temporary relief. The General has already declared that there will be elections and he will run in them "in uniform"—which sounds as unhinged as anything Yahya declared in East Pakistan.

In the meanwhile, human bombs continue to blast away.

I feel like reciting some Faraz, but I will restrain myself.

Tick Tock VI[12]

August 8, 2007

Way to go, Obama!

During a state of emergency, the government can restrict the freedom to move, rally, engage in political activities or form groups as well as take a slew of other measures, including restricting the parliament's right to make laws.

It can even dissolve parliament.

Under Pakistan's constitution, the president may declare a state of emergency if it is deemed that the country's security is "threatened by war or external aggression, or by internal disturbance beyond" the government's authority to control.

If a state of emergency is to be extended beyond two months, it must be approved by a joint sitting of parliament, the Constitution says.

Kamal Hyder, *Al-Jazeera*'s correspondent in Pakistan, said the state of emergency would give the government greater control and suspend rights, such as to free speech.

See "Tick Tock V, IV, III, II, I" for how we all got here.

~~Now we start the clock on its way back.~~

Update: Musharraf decided against it. Probably because it would be a bad idea, and he is rather unpopular at the moment.

Tick Tock VII[13]

August 23, 2007

The Supreme Court has ruled that Nawaz Sharif can return to Pakistan.

Nawaz Sharif, you may recall, was the prime minister who tried to kill The General by refusing to allow The General's plane to land in Karachi and immediately succumbed to the coup soon thereafter. He then fled to Saudi Arabia, clutching a suitcase filled with gold, and agreed not to return for 10 years. That's what The General said, at least. Nawaz Sharif, on the other hand, maintains that he was ousted, forced to sign an agreement at gunpoint to stay in exile, and should not be denied his rights to return.

The Supreme Court agrees with Nawaz Sharif. Exile is bad.

In the meantime, Bhutto has given details of power-sharing discussions, which include two elections, one with The General as The General and one with Pervez Musharraf as The Artist Formerly Known as The General.

Both exiled ex–prime ministers Benazir Bhutto and Nawaz Sharif will be back in Pakistan by October and running for re-re-reelection in December. And that, gentle readers, couldn't be better news—the election (i.e., not Bhutto or Sharif in power again!). But as I have said many times, let the people choose.

What does it all mean? In terms of internal politics of Pakistan, this is tremendous news for the resurgent democratic movement in Pakistan. The full participation of the many political parties—including the Bhuttos and Sharifs—will guarantee that Pakistan starts recovering from the despotic military regime. However, that is easier said than done. The military, under Musharraf, has become the largest land-owning, asset-controlling entity in Pakistan, with ex- and current military officials serving across the civil and social landscape. How can that military be coaxed "back into the barracks"? It is quite probable that there are forces within the military eager to curtail their political vulnerabilities. The popular image of the military in Pakistani society has undergone tremendous change in recent years—from a highly valued and respected institution (the only "corruption-free" one) to a hegemonic and undesirable presence. I could argue that the military's own interests lie in withdrawing from the political realm and reburnishing its image and standing. Of course, the defense budget remains the highest expenditure in the country, and no successive civil government will change that. By and large, the military cannot lose by "giving democracy back" to the country. That was, after all, what Musharraf claimed when he took control.

In terms of the oft-mentioned "Talibanization" of Pakistan and the wider conflict with extremism, the answers are less apparent at the moment. Some certainties do exist: Any civil government will continue to fully cooperate with the U.S. efforts. In fact, the efforts in Waziristan would be strengthened by the participation of Baluchistani leaders at the federal level (Baluchistan has always been a federal/state controversy). The elections will not result in any rise-to-power of Mullah Omar in Islamabad. And a democratic Pakistan will surely be a valuable ally within the Muslim world. The uncertainties largely hinge on the nature of the elections—the participation of various groups and their freedoms to do so. It will also be a chaotic period, which can make Pakistan vulnerable to further attacks and incursions.

However, the bottom line is that Pakistan needs full and immediate U.S. support through the next six months. The United Nations should take an interest in ensuring fair elections. And the subsequent government should be cultivated and nourished throughout the full term.

Tick Tock VIII: The Emergency Plus Edition[14]
November 3, 2007

The wag will say that the nation has never left the state of emergency, but that is just being silly.

We now have a legal state of emergency in Pakistan. Actually, it is officially being called "Emergency Plus"—more than "Emergency" but less than "Martial Law." Just right.

The move is hardly surprising considering the chaos engulfing Pakistan at the moment—from political (Supreme Court deliberations on the fate of the "election") to military (the tribal/militant conflict has spread to Swat and Peshawar) to ideological (Baluchistan) to international (Rice has decided she wants democracy).

According to the Provisional Constitutional Order (PCO) declaring emergency, the steps were taken because of the recent terrorist attacks, the release of terror-suspects by the judiciary, the lack of oversight of the judiciary, and the low morale of police and army in the nation.[15]

The emergency law, Article 232 of the Constitution (summarized): The Proclamation of emergency is issued by the President if he deems that the country is threatened by internal or external violence or disturbance. The Federals can take over the Provinces, the High Court. It has to be affirmed by joint Assemblies within two months or it will automatically end. All the supreme courts in the country will have to retake their oaths to the state, and they will be barred from issuing any orders against the army or the state.

Musharraf has suspended the TV broadcasts—and prohibited any "print or electronic media discussion or analysis that hurts the national interests."

The Supreme Court, which was expected to rule on Musharraf in a few days, is currently boarded up. Cities like Sarghoda, Lahore, Karachi, and Islamabad have mobilized against suicide attacks.

Emergency Rule, maybe Martial Law, the replacement of Klashnikovs with Suicide Belts, the Vanished . . . Pakistan needed our help a year ago. It needed a genuine push for democratic processes back in March. We left unchecked, and unhindered, a megalomaniac "enlightened moderator." We keep insisting on our own interests ahead of the interests of the people of Pakistan. We remain steadfast in our belief that those people are not as developed nor as functional as we would like them to be. Pakistan needs a strong dictator. The fallacy . . . the gross oversight . . . has always been that he was never in control. He did not control Baluchistan, where a genuine call for accountability and justice was quashed by horrific military violence—including missile assassinations. Baluchistan should have been afforded our attention in 2005—but we were too busy in Iraq. It became, contiguous with Waziristan, the outpost and then the center of Taliban/extremist insurgents over the next two years. We insisted on supporting the one person who had no legitimate power to negotiate or fight for over 40 percent of territorial Pakistan. Can you imagine that?

Next up? Martial Law. More bombings. And the eventual drain of all that capital that had accumulated in the country in the past 8 years. Zimbabwe, here we come—unless, the United States and China can come to their senses and do some actual diplomacy. The status is bleak. Let us say that Musharraf resigns and leaves. The Supreme Court declares an election date, the new government solves the Baluchistan issue, the United States redeploys significant troops to Afghanistan (and keeps them there), the Pakistani military combats within cities and mountains of Pakistan. War. Chaos. Uncertainty. And this, my gentle readers, would be the best-case scenario. A more likely option is a military state somewhere between Mugabe's Zimbabwe circa 2005 and Gandhi's India circa 1976. I must be proven wrong.

For now, we have a new Chief Justice of Pakistan Supreme Court. But in an unprecedented move, only four judges have signed on to retake the oath under PCO. This is big, big news. . . .

Musharraf is to speak on "Meray Azeez Hum Watano" at 11:00 PST. Please see Aitzaz Ahsan—under arrest—being interviewed while in a toilet on the constitutional crisis by the Pakistani equivalent of Debbie Matenopoulos: "Duniya mein a kar farishtoon nay declare illegal karna hai?"[16]

Human Rights Commission of Pakistan (HRCP) Raids[17]
November 4, 2007

An email from Lahore confirms the crackdown on HRCP and other related groups:

> Today at the Human Rights Commission of Pakistan a meeting of lawyers and human rights activists (around noon) was held to discuss the present situation. A statement from Asma Jehangir, who has been detained for 90 days, was read, and subsequently the compound was surrounded by police officers in riot gear and with tear gas threatening to arrest everyone inside (around 1:45). Inside, people sang songs while the police remained outside; after some time all (as far as I know) were rounded up into buses and detained. Journalists were released. Currently, they have been taken to the Model Town police station in Lahore. I am unsure about the number of people currently detained.
>
> I have received information from my partner, a U.S. citizen, who is a research fellow (ironically researching detentions and disappearances) and who had attended the meeting at HRCP. He is also currently detained. Although they have seized most cell phones, some people have managed to keep theirs, and until recently I was receiving intermittent text messages updating me on the situation. Although they are being treated (thus far) well enough and rumor is they will be released within 24 to 48 hours, the implications seem clear—sending a strong message of intimidation to anyone who dares even discuss resistance/criticism of Musharraf.
>
> . . .
>
> Those detained were in a private meeting, inside HRCP's offices this afternoon—not staging a protest or demonstration of any kind. Among the arrested are a motley bunch who had assembled due to a shared interest in the political situation and human rights issues: students, a professor from LUMS, a professor from Punjab U, lawyers, HRCP

workers. A few have reportedly been transported elsewhere, including a staff member from HRCP, although where to is not known. Some say 40 to 50 total people are detained from the HRCP meeting, though I couldn't get this confirmed due to sporadic and interrupted phone communication with the detained.

Right now, the police are saying they may be detained from 30 to 90 days under either house arrest, in detention, or jail. We hope this is just an intimidation tactic to scare people into silence and passivity.

Black Days[18]
November 8, 2007

In Pakistan, a popular way of showing support is to wear a black armband. I would go buy a black suit, but I think I might break some Pakistan Bar Association or Johnny Cash Appreciation Society rule. So, in the meantime, just more news.

It is heartening, seriously, to see so many people putting forth so much time and effort and standing up by the side of Pakistanis. Some upcoming protests in the United States (thanks to Anil for sending word):

Washington, D.C.: Demonstration to express opposition to General Pervez Musharraf's declaration of a State of Emergency on November 3, 2007, his order to suspend the Constitution, and his subsequent actions against judges, lawyers, activists, journalists, and academics. *Where:* Pakistan Embassy in Washington, D.C. *When:* Sunday, November 11, 2007, from 1 to 3:30 p.m.

New York City: As an expression of solidarity with our beleaguered colleagues at the Pakistani bar, the New York City Bar Association, the New York State Bar Association, and the New York County Lawyers' Association, in conjunction with other organizations, invite you to attend a public rally in front of the New York County Courthouse, 60 Centre Street, on Tuesday, November 13, from 1 to 1:30 p.m.

The crude and brutal suspension of law and the legal system in Pakistan, and the repression of judges and lawyers there, require that we take a moment from our own busy schedules and demonstrate our concern.

Because the images from Pakistan show the violent repression of Pakistani lawyers wearing their customary dark suits and white shirts, we request that you appear on Tuesday in similar attire, though this is not required. What is important is a strong show of support. We hope to see you there and encourage you to distribute this as widely as you can. Thank you.

Akron, Ohio: Let's show our support. Bring yourselves (and even a sign if you wish), and come to the courthouse. Let's send this out to your/our listserv(s) to spread the word. It may be last minute, but it is a small sacrifice (infinitesimal) that we are making, compared to that which our fellow lawyers are in Pakistan.

Going Public[19]
November 12, 2007

The tide seems to be receding. The protests are not spreading beyond the lawyers and the students. The opposition parties have had no luck mobilizing. Benazir Bhutto's me-first strategy is DOA. That robust media, Aaj TV, Geo TV, ARY TV, remain inaccessible to the majority of the population. The Supreme Court justices are in house arrest. The majority of the opposition is under strict duress. The General has made a series of announcements while jiggling his Google Calendar and seems to be announcing something for January. Enough, in any case, to placate the White House.

Is it over? This nascent movement for democracy and freedom?

It is, if you conceive of it as an instant reaction to an authoritarian step—a flash of anger and frustration that is slowly simmering back down. It is, if you believe that the lawyers and the students represent rather insulated factions of the overall society who do not effect life in a significant-enough manner for "ordinary Pakistanis." There is a lot of circumstantial evidence that Musharraf's crackdown on "information" is working. He has sequestered most of the troublemakers. He has cut off any public discussion. He is threatening to try civilians in military tribunals. And the only possible alternatives look like Benazir Bhutto. These are indeed massive odds.

Yet, I do not believe that these are KwiK-E Protests that will just go away. Think back to the amazing crowds—hundreds of thousands—that mobilized for the Chief Justice. Think also of those reports about the unpopularity of Musharraf, the fall from grace of the Pakistan Army, the growing discontent about the state of affairs in Pakistan. None of that has changed. None of those miseries have gone away. The Baluchistan crisis is now the Swat and Baluchistan crisis. The Islamists have not disappeared.

These nascent protests will not go away. In fact, they have awakened a *new* segment of the civil society against The General. A fact that is abundantly clear to those inside.

CM makes an appearance in Manjeet Kripalani's Virtual Protests in Pakistan, *Business Week*, and in *Guardian*'s "Media Talk" podcast. Quaint?

Tick Tock IX: The Not Yet Nation[20]
November 15, 2007

> Several senior administration officials said that with each day that passed, more adminis-
> tration officials were coming around to the belief that General Musharraf's days in power
> were numbered and that the United States should begin considering contingency plans,
> including reaching out to Pakistan's generals.[21]

I have argued, for a while and to earlier criticisms, that the American support
for Pervez Musharraf is wrongheaded—not just in ideological terms (our self-
proclaimed call for Freedom's March across the Muslim World) but also in strategic terms (our efforts to eliminate al-Qaida and counterextremist ideologies in
Western Asia).

The support for Musharraf on ideological terms seems to me to be a rather
indefensible position, but people still manage to do it, including the White House.
The defense hinges on the "Not Yet Thesis"—freedom is good, dictators are bad,
but Pakistan is *not yet* ready for freedom and must depend on dictators to build
civic institutions, train the electorate, and, in the future, bring democracy (which
is akin to waiting for the fox to install security in the henhouse and makes perfect
sense).

We maintain that the man we know—a benevolent dictator named Pervez
Musharraf—is better than the multitudes we do not know. We fear the multitudes
on two fronts. One is that we conceive of them as masses without politics—forever
hostage to gross religious and ideological provocations. Masses who do not constitute a body politic or act with an interest in self-preservation or self-growth. Faced
with that absence of reason, we are forced to support native royals to do the job
(from Egypt to Pakistan). We justify it by stressing that we may not like these dictators, but we know that if we did not have them, the masses would instantly betray
us to the very forces of extremism that we seek to destroy. This ignores, of course,
actual historical and political realities in those countries. This disengagement
means that our knowledge remains sketchy, undifferentiated, and reliant on gross
generalizations of the "masses." It intimately links us to the gross abuses of power
that our dictators exert—with means provided by us. Second is that these masses
are Muslim. This fear grounded in our history can, at best, be understood as the
fear of the "Other" and, at worst, as the Lewis/Huntington model of civilizational
clash. Either case, it is borne out of our inherent belief in "difference." They are not
like us. They do not possess reason, etc. (Ask Dick Cheney why nuclear deterrence
worked with the Soviets but cannot work with Iranians.)

The strategic case is just as nonsensical. The fight against extremism is a fight
that ordinary Pakistani citizens have much more at stake in. It is their immediate
freedoms that are threatened by the Talibanization of their society. It is their frus-
trations that are being capitalized upon by the Islamists. The historical, political,

and social trends have always clearly shown that the Pakistani publics predominantly prefer a moderate and open society. If we really are serious, we need to *empower* the Pakistani publics and not facilitate their oppression.

The conventional wisdom, however, remains against such a reading. Take Fareed Zakaria's "Pakistan's Pinstripe Revolution" in *Newsweek*[22]—where he feels that benevolent dictators should be cut some slack and that Pakistan needs that helping hand. But Zakaria seems to misread Pakistan's judicial and political history and, at the very least, Musharraf's entire public persona. He argues that the judicial problems of Musharraf begin in 1999 when he asked—for the first time—for the Supreme Court justices to resign and retake their oaths of allegiance. What he fails to point out is that Musharraf was simply following in the footsteps of *every* dictatorial regime in Pakistan—all of whom asked the judiciary to retake their oaths—and that the judiciary acquiesced in every single case. The "new-ness" of Pakistan's recent judicial crisis is that only recently did they decide *not* to rubber stamp the military regime. . . .

Zakaria makes further dubious claims: "He turned the country's strategic orientation away from the Taliban, revived the economy with real reforms, empowered women, and spoke out against the pernicious influence of Islamic extremism." He turned the country away from the Taliban insofar as he didn't. The Taliban continue to find solace and refuge in the northwestern province, and his relationship with Karzai's regime has never gone below the boiling point. He revived the economy insofar as the United States has poured $10 billion into the Pakistani military-industrial complex since 2001. This influx of money has created the biggest land- and industry-holding entity in Pakistan's history—the Pakistan Army. Please look at Ayesha Siddiqa's *Military, Inc.* for a solid understanding of that immediate history. Empowered women insofar as he allowed the Hisba Bill to pass in NWFP, and it was only the Supreme Court that stepped in to stop it. And, finally, on that Islamic extremism front. I do not really think that publishing an editorial in the *Washington Post* about "Enlightened Moderation" qualifies as doing much if one constantly cuts deals with Islamist militants in NWFP, Swat, Quetta, and Islamist parties in Islamabad.

Another recent piece, Lee Smith's "Mixed Messages," in *Slate*,[23] is even worse. It argues not only that we should support Musharraf but that that is the only way to combat extremism. Leaving aside the Orientalist reading of history, Smith appears horribly misinformed about Pakistan. He claims, for example, "The Pakistani military, as is the case with most armed forces in the Muslim world, is the citadel of the country's modernity, its most significant secular institution and protector not only of the modern nation state but the idea of the nation state itself." I don't really know what being a citadel of modernity actually means, but the Pakistan Army has undergone a rigorous program of Islamization and faith-based militancy since Zia-ul-Haq in 1979. Whatever lingering secularism is there belongs to the older cadre of senior staff that came into the military pre-'80s. Folks like Musharraf. The main troop strength comes from rural Punjab, Baluchistan, and the Northwestern province, and no one is reading Karl Marx or Nietzsche, I assure you.

Therein lies the heart of our problems with making an ideological or strategic case for aligning with dictators. We trust and privilege the narratives they provide us. Musharraf, like Zia-ul-Haq before him, has successfully explained Pakistan and the world to us. The forces of darkness hover at the border, and only the rightfully guided leader can shepherd the nation. For Musharraf, the bugaboo is extremism; for Zia-ul-Haq, it was Communism. In both cases, we pumped amazing amounts of liquid cash and military hardware into Pakistan and waited for the eventual victory. Somehow, we still act surprised when victory doesn't materialize.

The good news is that, as I watch the Democratic presidential debate, Biden, Obama, Edwards, and Richardson are all agreeing that we need democracy in Pakistan more than we need to prop up Musharraf's dictatorship. The tide is shifting. The people of Pakistan may yet escape the *not yet.*

Tick Tock X[24]
November 28, 2007

Pervez Musharraf became a civilian today. The elections are scheduled, and candidates across the country are filing their candidacy papers—in great numbers, especially in the troubled regions. This despite great debate across the two major political parties, the Pakistan People's Party and the Pakistan Muslim League-Nawaz on whether to participate or boycott the elections. Their hesitance is understandable. Pervez Musharraf, as a civilian president, will rule under the 1973 Constitution, which has the oft-used Eighth Amendment to Article 58, enacted by the last dictator, Zia-ul-Haq, in 1985. The amendment grants the president the power to "dissolve the National Assembly where, in his opinion, . . . the Government of the Federation cannot be carried on in accordance with the provisions of the Constitution and appeal to the electorate is necessary." The amendment was used first by Zia-ul-Haq against the civilian government of Muhammad Khan Junejo, then by Ghulam Ishaq Khan against Benazir Bhutto, then by Ghulam Ishaq Khan against Nawaz Sharif, and again by Farooq Leghari against Benazir Bhutto. The last Nawaz Sharif government nullified this power of the president by passing the Thirteenth Amendment Act in 1997. In 2002, under the Legal Framework Order, General Musharraf fixed it right back.

Basically, even if these elections take place as scheduled, even if all the political parties participate, even if they are fair, open, and untampered elections (to whatever extent possible) . . . President Pervez Musharraf can, at his will, dismiss the elected government when he pleases. Historians predicting the future need only point to the past.

D-man, sitting in San Francisco, demanded: "I want a post about Sharif's impact in *CM*." Well, now. *CM* doesn't do requests, my dear friend. And, much recent evidence to the contrary, neither is *CM* a "Daily News and Commentary" blog. My passion for democratic reform and my love for all the people fighting the good fight in homistan compel me to order all of you to go read *the students and professionals in Pakistan* every day: *The Emergency Times, Rise of Pakistan, Teeth Maestro*. Seriously. Forget this desk-bound, ivory tower chained pandit in Chicago.

As for the Sharifs, I can only imagine doing a post on Tehmina Durrani and Shahbaz Sharif—but only if lapata agrees to paint their wedding photo.

People's Resistance Street Theater[25]
February 7, 2008

I do not remember if I have called to your attention the exemplary work being done for the cause of freedom and justice in Pakistan by the *People's Resistance*—"a coalition of civil society organizations that includes Karachi Women's Action Forum, HRCP, Women's Peace Commission, lawyers, journalists, and other professionals."

They have participated in marches, rallied, held candlelight vigils, and hosted banned TV shows on the streets. You can go through Abro's Flickr set to see the amazing work.[26]

It is their public theater that has intrigued me the most. The plays are the brain-child of Shahid Shafaat. This description from *Emergency Times*:

> Yesterday (Feb. 5, Tuesday), the street theatre group of PR did three chilling perfor-
> mances on sea view. It was an 8 minutes long theatre which highlighted the plight of a
> poor household, where a *chowkidaar* [security guard] takes absolute control by promis-
> ing *khushhaali* [better living] to its inhabitants. Instead of their situation getting any
> better, the family is fed-up by the *chowkidaar*'s demands for security measures in their
> home. Finally, complete chaos takes place as the situation of the family and of society in
> general goes from bad to worst. During the pandemonium, the narrator stops everyone
> and interacts with the crowd.
>
> A lot of different and interesting views were exchanged with people on the beach.
> However, probably because of my green army cap and crude Punjabi-accented
> portrayal of the *chowkidaar*, people immediately answered Musharraf as the main
> culprit for the family's plight. When asked what could be the solution for the house-
> hold's problems, many people simply suggested the removal of the army from civil-
> ian affairs, while others stated that all of us have to work together for the nation's
> betterment.

You can see pictures and also read about their first play, *Jadugar*, at Teeth Maestro as well.[27]

Inspiring.

That Election Thing[28]
February 17, 2008

The nation of Pakistan—amid bombs and terror—goes to vote tomorrow. The early reports on Urdu media are not promising about the turnout. And the recent bombings have surely dampened any and all Get-Out-the-Vote efforts.

There are over 7,000 candidates for 272 national assembly seats and 577 provincial assembly seats at roughly over 8 candidates per seat. (Akin to congressional and state legislature elections.) There are 158 women candidates.

The political parties are: Pakistan Muslim League-N (under ex–prime minister Nawaz Sharif), Pakistan Muslim League-Q (the "Musharraf" party), the Pakistan People's Party (now led by Mr. 10 Percent Zardari), Jamaat-i Islami (part of Mutahida Majlis-e Amal), MQM (the ethnic Urdu party in Karachi), Awami National Party (the ethnic Pakthon party), and the ever-lovable, Imran Khan's Tehrik-e Insaf.

You can see the TV ads for these parties, but I hear that most of the campaigning is being done by SMS/TXT messages. The snazziest TV ad belongs to PML-Q, which is the only campaign running on "record" as opposed to the cult of personality. If you are confused about the lion or the bicycle, those are the election symbols for the political parties. With a majority illiterate electorate, these symbols get stamped—often down the ballot sheet—and not names of candidates. Much political and symbolical (ahem) hay is made out of these electoral symbols. PML-Q is the bicycle, PML-N is the lion, PPP is the arrow, ANP is the lantern, MQM is the kite, JUI is the pen. The Election Commission of Pakistan has the full list to satisfy your curiosity. I have uploaded some print ads from dailies in Pakistan.[29]

These elections, fixed or not, mean little for the people of Pakistan. The facto dictatorship is still facto. I just hope that no more bombs go off at polling stations, etc. I will try and do a live blog if I can find results being announced anywhere tomorrow. Else, please point your browsers to PKPolitics.com for your election coverage. If you have any questions for me, feel free to ask.

To answer the question on every one's mind, the Islamist parties look to be heading for a national drubbing at the polls.

The Sharif Showdown Begins[30]
February 25, 2009

The stakes for the Long March are finally all on the table.

The Pakistan Supreme Court—put in place by Musharraf—has declared the Sharif brothers ineligible to stand in elections. As a direct result, Shahbaz Sharif is out as chief minister of Punjab.

Nawaz Sharif in a press conference declared that Zardari offered them a deal—drop the CJ issue, and Shahbaz Sharif can continue to hold office. Protests are planned for all of Punjab.

Long March is scheduled for March 12 to 16 to Islamabad. Its main aim is to restore the judiciary of Iftikhar Chaudhry, which was dismissed by General Musharraf. Along with the Lawyers' Movement, the three major opposition parties—Pakistan Muslim League-N, Jama'at-ei Islami, and Tehrik-e Insfat—are going to participate.

More soon.

The Long March to Justice[31]
March 12, 2009

On March 12, 1930, Gandhi marched to Dandhi—stopping in 40-plus villages—speaking about swaraj and breaking the salt laws to show their inhumanity. Satyagraha is definitely at the heart of the nonviolent demand for the restoration of the Supreme Court deposed on November 3, 2007, by Pervez Musharraf and specifically Chief Justice Iftikhar Chaudhry on March 9, 2007.

Much has happened since then. Benazir Bhutto's return in October 2007 and her assassination in December 2007. The elections in February 2008 brought a new coalition of Pakistan People's Party to power, with the swashbuckling widow Zardari taking over as president. A basic campaign promise was to solve the judicial crisis and reinstate the Supreme Court of '07.

None of the promises have been kept. Instead, the PPP regime has used the Dogar Supreme Court (cronies put in place by Musharraf) to throw out the opponent political party Pakistan Muslim League-N out of power in Punjab and restrict Nawaz Sharif and Shahbaz Sharif from electoral politics.

The Long March of March 12, 2009, leading up to a sit-in at the capital on March 16, is the only way that the people of Pakistan can produce pressure on the civilian and military regime to pay attention to justice, to accountability, and to democracy.

What shouldn't escape anyone's attention is that *this* is what democratic, nonviolent, resistance looks like. This is fine. This is normal. This is what we should expect in a society where the government and the people are out of step. This is not a coup, nor the '79 revolution.

The Zardari regime has reacted as all cornered governments do: mass arrests, police violence on crowds, implementation of laws against critical speech, etc.

The best place to follow developments is on Twitter. You should also follow the live blog on *Teeth Maestro*. You should also look over this excellent background piece entitled "The Long March—It Begins" by Madiha Tahir at *Action for a Progressive Pakistan. . . .*[32]

In solidarity.

The Silence of the Lawyers Movement[33]
April 23, 2009

Naim Sahib in *Outlook India* on the plight of Sikh families under the Swat deal: Islamic *'Adl* [Justice] in Orakzai. It is worth reading in full, and I wanted to highlight this pertinent call to the lawyers movement:

> A week has passed, but I have not seen any comment on the above in the three Urdu newspapers from Pakistan that I fairly regularly check: *Jang, Nawa-i-Waqt*, and *Daily Express*. And if the *Daily Times* or *Dawn* carried an editorial on the plight of the smallest and most powerless group of Pakistani citizens, I must have missed it. Here, I must note that while Jang failed to carry the news about the Pakistani Sikhs, it twice reported on the special arrangements made for security and hospitality for the Sikh pilgrims from India.
>
> The Pakistani lawyers who took to the streets to bring back an independent judiciary might not have read the news, busy as they must be with important matters, for none issued even a statement of regret or sympathy. As for the newly established "independent judiciary," personified by the Supreme Court of Pakistan and its Chief Justice—it took notice, *suo motu*, of the case of the whipping of a married woman and then only the other day declared that the penalty for "blasphemy" should be death in the Islamic nation—it too preferred to ignore the Sikhs. The nation's President and Prime Minister, of course, saw nothing wrong in what the Taliban had done—the two now co-share authority—and made not the slightest noise. Of course, the guardians of Islam's honour in Pakistan, the *muftis* [Sunni Islamic scholar who is an interpreter or expounder of Islamic law] and *maulanas* [religious leaders], made not the slightest protest. Most likely, they saw in the incident just one more triumph of their vision of Islam's glory in Pakistan. If anything, they showed remarkable restraint when they didn't make a public celebration of it, as they had done when President Zardari's father-in-law had the Ahmadis declared non-Muslim. Who knows but the mullahs might be planning secretly to demand that the same

shari'a [Islamic jurisprudence] should now be enforced on the equally helpless and minute population of Hindus in Sindh.

What surprises me, however, is that none of the maulanas and muftis made an issue of the exact amount of money when so many avenues of argumentation were open to them. Was the amount extorted from the Sikhs right according to all the major schools of Islamic jurisprudence? Wasn't it less? Wasn't it more? Shouldn't the amount be equivalent to the value of a certain weight in gold? And what about the requirement, according to many jurists, that the *dhimmis* [non-Muslims under Muslim rule] must additionally be publicly humiliated and made to display some distinct marker to separate them from the pure and virtuous? Shouldn't the *dhimmis* be disbarred from riding a motorbike now and limited only to riding a bicycle? So many valid questions of *fiqh* [jurisprudence] were available to the reverends for the purpose of displaying their brilliance. Further, the newspaper report does not indicate if a similar payment would be demanded again next year. Perhaps not, but then is it valid under *shari'a* to extort *jizya* [poll tax] in a lump sum? Are not the Talibans guilty of a *bid'ah* [innovation, bad] in this instance? Surely, a few *fatwas* are needed to settle that issue?[34]

Chapter Notes

1 Archived at http://bit.ly/hMcZCd.
2 Archived at http://bit.ly/fLz6PL.
3 Salman Masood, "Throngs Attend Speech by Pakistan's Suspended Justice," *New York Times*, May 7, 2007, archived at http://nyti.ms/jzNopW.
4 Archived at http://bit.ly/ew3qS9.
5 Archived at http://bit.ly/hWxE6h.
6 Archived at http://bit.ly/f3D5vE.
7 Archived at http://bit.ly/hCChpn.
8 Archived at http://bit.ly/hC33fN.
9 Archived at http://wapo.st/jTCS8M.
10 Archived at http://nyti.ms/j1SJec.
11 Archived at http://bit.ly/hN42Dy.
12 Archived at http://bit.ly/i20tqT.
13 Archived at http://bit.ly/ikpIy2.
14 Archived at http://bit.ly/g2XiIB.
15 "Text of Emergency Proclamation," *Dawn.com*, November 3, 2007, archived at http://bit.ly/mikFvU.

16 "Emergency Update—OneWorld Update 4," *PKPolitics.com*, November 3, 2007, archived at http://bit.ly/gprPjS.

17 Archived at http://bit.ly/hRooDX.

18 Archived at http://bit.ly/fdmdqY.

19 Archived at http://bit.ly/hTSZIq.

20 Archived at http://bit.ly/fKnA4S.

21 Helene Cooper, Mark Mazzetti, and David Rohde, "U.S. Is Looking Past Musharraf in Case He Falls," *New York Times*, November 15, 2007, archived at http://nyti.ms/jWj6Ju.

22 Fareed Zakaria, "Pakistan's Pinstripe Revolution," *Newsweek*, November 10, 2007, archived at http://bit.ly/mSYmtl.

23 Lee Smith, "Mixed Messages," *Slate.com*, November 5, 2007, archived at http://slate.me/lKzXMD.

24 Archived at http://bit.ly/i2MvUY.

25 Archived at http://bit.ly/emE0uc.

26 Archived http://bit.ly/eYqtdm.

27 "People's Resistance Outreach Program—Street Theater at SeaView," *Teeth Maestro*, December 26, 2007, archived at http://bit.ly/hnFWER.

28 Archived at http://bit.ly/hxUoEo.

29 Archived at http://bit.ly/gWypVF.

30 Archived at http://bit.ly/gp6OK5.

31 Archived at http://bit.ly/e3XbHt.

32 Archived at http://bit.ly/k4xNwx.

33 Archived at http://bit.ly/dFkI90.

34 C. M. Naim, "Islamic 'Adl in Orakzai," *Outlook India*, April 23, 2009, archived at http://bit.ly/eipSpX.

7
Ignore

The idea of unknowing (or deliberate ignorance) is at the heart of the empire—and arguably, specifically, the American empire. Eqbal Ahmad was one of those clear-eyed commentators, activists, and scholars who consistently demonstrated the moral and critical vacuity at the heart of knowledge production about the East. He did that by demonstrating, repeatedly, that it wasn't the "paucity" of knowledge that sustained imperialism at the center but the elision of it in policy and cultural frameworks. Edward Said's Orientalism *(1979) was monumentally successful in laying bare this collusion between knowledge and power. The posts in this chapter are bits of knowledge about Pakistan—sketches of personalities and events—which collectively remain out of purview of the empire, such that Pakistan's pasts are never more than the sum total of the immediate policy discussion.*

Imagining Pakistan I: Hali[1]
August 11, 2004

In a few days, Pakistanis (and Indians) will celebrate Independence. At midnight, August 14, 1947, the twin states of India and Pakistan were released from British dominion. Leading up to that day, I thought it worthwhile to post some signposts from the journey that culminated in 1947. In the next few days, I will post some selections from texts and intellectuals that shaped the Muslim response to British Raj in the late 19th and early 20th centuries. Today is Altaf Hussein Hali (1837–1914).

For all kinds of purposes, 1857 is the event/year that marks a profound shift in the nature of British rule, communal identity, and the idea of nation in India. In 1879, Maulana Altaf Hussein Hali sat to eulogize the state of Muslims in the world. His *Musaddas: Madd o Jazr-e Islam* (*The Flow and Ebb of Islam*) was a lament on a world gone awry where kings had turned paupers and right was crushed by might. Writing in the *marsiya* style (six-line verse with three rhyming couplets), he took to enumerate the decline of the Muslim *ummah* [global community]. The work had a profound effect on the generation of Muslim intellectuals that led the nationalist struggle against the British (the Aligarh Generation). In this poem, Hali compares contemporary Muslims with the "glorious" past of Islam:

Come! and see our abysmal decadence
See the fall of Islam without recovery
Once you see the ebb of our sea,
Never shall you believe that a flow succeeds every ebb!

Decline. It became the paradigm for conceptualizing Muslim past. By tying Islam's dominance to the political power of Muslims in India, this paradigm forced all "solutions" to the realm of the politics. All the reformists, revivalists, and revolutionists that came after Hali took as their goal the establishment of an Islamic State. Of course, colonialism had a little something to do with all that, but let's stick to the program today, shall we?

Go read a selection from Hali's *Musaddas* below the fold. Below is a hasty translation, but you can find Christopher Shackle and Javed Majeed's scholarly take at Francis Pritichett's amazing website.[2] It talks about the state of contemporary religious leaders (a topic dear to my heart). And yes, by contemporary, I mean from 2004.

The State of Religion of Islam[3]

The decrepit hall of the true faith
with its pillars shaken for a long while
is only in this world for a few days
which will never again be found by Muslims
the caretakers have removed their attention from it
now only Allah can sustain it

The Lack of Holy Men

The shrines lay in ruin
Awaiting the Dervish and the Sultan
Once the paths to hidden knowledges were open
And the Angels kept watch
Now, where are those knots of Allah's love?
Where are those Beloveds of God?

The Lack of Religious Experts

Where are the experts of legal knowledges?
Where are the commentators of Faith's record?
Where are the Principlists, those debators?

Where are the Traditionalists, those thinkers?
That gathering which was once lit up like a festival
Not a single lamp flutters there now.

The Lack of Religious Books

Where are the archives of religious books?
Where are those sites of knowledge of God?
Such a cold wind blew through this gathering
That the torches of Truth are duly extinguished
No more is any furnishing of that gathering
Nor the pitcher, nor drum, nor drummer nor cupbearer

Those Who Claim Knowledge

Many now claim to be the caretakers of the community
With their credentials attested by fools
They roam from village to village, place to place
Their eyes fixed on collecting wealth
They claim to be the leaders of today's Islam
Their take as their title, the descendants of Prophets

Many claim to be descendants of Pirs
Though they have no talent of their own
They are proud of their inheritance
That their forefathers were once celebrated
They go around with their fake miracles
Robbing their followers, and eating from them

Such are now the walkers of the Righteous paths
They who claim to be above the Law
They who say that miracles stop with them
They who claim to hold the fate of humantiy
Now, they are the leaders and they are the followers
Now, they are the Junaid and they are the Bayazid

Contemporary Theologians

Speech that incites hatred, they will make
Prose which cleaves hearts, they will write
Demeaning those who are sinners
To declare their Muslim brothers infidels
Such are the ways of our Learned
Such are the ways of our Guides

If one goes to them to with a question
Will return bearing a burden around his neck
If he dares to doubt their verdict
He earns the title of Damned from them
If his tongue utters a complaint against them
To return without harm would be difficult

At times they puff up their veins
At times they foam at their mouth
At times they call him dog or pig
At times they raise their staff to hit him
Witness these pillars of your faith
Witness these examples of the True Prophet's people

If one wants pleasure in their company
Then one must be a Muslim only
With a mark of prayer shining on his forehead
Without any deficit in his faith
With mustaches short, and beard kept long
And his trousers of the proper length

In his belief, he should mimic the Exalted
In his utterances, he parrot them
Of their opponents, he must be contemptuous
Of their followers, he must offer praise
If he does not follow, he will be damned from faith
Unfit to even meet with his Elders

The tenets of our Law were so tolerant
That Jews and Christians were our supporters
The Qur'an even gives testimony to their kindness
Even the Prophet proclaimed: Faith is Easy
But they made that Faith so difficult
That true Believer's cannot bear that burden

They give no guidance in Morals
They cultivate no cleanliness inside them
They heap such increases in outwardly rules
That not for a moment, can one escape
That Faith which was a fountain for a kind community
Is now the dirty water leftover after ablutions

Imagining Pakistan II: Jauhar[4]
August 12, 2004

There is perhaps no more quixotic a movement in Indian nationalist history than the Khilafat Movement. It started as a campaign to protect the Khilafat, and it ended with an attempt to mass-migrate Muslims of India to Afghanistan. Its most prominent leaders were Shaukat Ali (1873–1938), a young Uttar Pradesh journalist; his younger brother Mohammad Ali Jauhar (1878–1931), the editor of *Comrade*; Syed Sulaiman Nadwi (1884–1955), student of Shibli Naumani; Hasrat Mohani (1878–1951), editor of the anti-British *Urdu-i Mu'alla*; and Abul Kalam Azad (1888–1958). All of these leaders were members of what I referred to yesterday as the Aligarh Generation.

The movement failed in every respect except that it created the meme of a nationalism based on religion and proved the decisive break between Hindus and Muslims in their mutual struggle to get rid of the British.

A bit of background: In October 1918, Turkey signed an armistice agreement with the Entente Powers, and the Ottoman Empire came to an end. The Khilafat Movement was a campaign, in India, to unite Muslims across the world in an expression of anxiety over the fate of Turkey and the Khalifa (Caliph) after the war. The leaders of the Khilafat Movement wanted to preserve the role of the Khalifa. Even though it was a purely ceremonious entity in the 20th century, its existence held great symbolic value to the Pan-Islamic movements in India and Egypt. In 1918, Lloyd George had assured Indian Muslims that Britain would respect the territorial integrity of Turkey. Muslim leadership saw that as just reward for their participation in the Great War, as without Indian forces, the British would never have won the Near and Middle East theaters. Even Gandhi expressed his sympathy for their cause at the Delhi Imperial War Conference in 1918 by stating, "As a Hindu, I cannot be indifferent to their cause. Their sorrows must be our sorrows." The All India Muslim League, the same year, passed a resolution asking the British to respect the "full control by the Sultan of Turkey, Khalifa of the Prophet over the holy places and over the Jazirat-ul-Arab as delimited in the Muslim books."

Promises kept, promises broken. Gandhi distanced himself as he began to sense that the Ali Brothers wanted way more from the British. Other Hindu leaders, like Nehru and Bipin Chandra Pal, never signed on. The Muslim League distanced itself as the *'ulama* joined the Khilafat Movement in droves and started a noncooperation movement across India and issued *fatwas* to migrate. In 1922, Mustafa Kemal (Attaturk) abolished the Caliphate and all claims to the holy lands.

There is so much to say about the Khilafat Movement, but I will stop here. The concepts of *dar-ul Islam* and *dar ul-harb*, the legality of *jihad* against fellow Muslims, the relationships between nationalist movements in Egypt and in India, and the necessity of a Muslim state were all issues emerging out of the Khilafat Movement. In fact, were I to sit and write the intellectual history of Islamic revivalist movements, I would start here. Above all, though, was the split between Muslim and Hindu nationalist agendas. The Khilafat Movement was the height of cooperation, but from its ashes rose two distinct, mutually distrusting nationalisms that set a course to 1947.

Go below the fold to read the edited exchange between the prime minister of Britain, Lloyd George, and the Khilafat Delegation led by Muhammad Ali Jauhar on March 19, 1920, and, again, some very contemporary issues:

Prime minister: Now, Mr. Muhammad Ali, will you state your case?

Mr. Muhammad Ali: I have just noted down a few points, which, if you will permit me, I will amplify as we proceed, so that you will have a fair record of what we desire to present. I only want to make it clear that we have come here chiefly in connection with a religious question which is of great importance to us. With regard to this, we desire to point out what is the connection of Indian Musalmans with the Khilafat. Islam, as we understand it, is not a set of doctrines and dogmas; it is a complete outlook on life, a moral code and a social polity. It recognizes no lacerating and devitalising distinctions between things spiritual and things temporal, between Church and State. Islam recognises no ethnical, geographical, or political barriers to free human intercourse and sympathy. Islam's whole outlook on life is supranational rather than national.

Islam has always had two centers, the first is a personal one and the other a local one. The personal one is the Caliph, or the Khalifa, as we call him, the successor of the Prophet. The local center is the region known as Jazirat-ul Arab or the "Island of Arabs," the land of the Prophet. To come to our claims, Sir, the first claim that we put forward is that the Khilafat must be preserved by the entire body of Muslims at all times with adequate temporal power. Not going into the matter more fully, we would say that after the various wars in which Turkey has been engaged recently, and after the Balkan War particularly, the Empire of the Khalifa has been reduced to extremely low limits.

Prime minister: Does that mean, for instance, that you are opposed to the act of the Syrian Muhammadans who declared Amir Feisal King of Arabia?

Mr. Muhammad Ali: I hope, Sir, it will be possible for us, if we are given an opportunity, to meet with these people and reconcile them. There have been differences between Arabs and the Turks, but I hope the Emir Feisal when he looks upon this matter as a Muslim will realise that his own personal ambition and even the ambition of Arabs, can be entirely satisfied within the scheme of Turkish sovereignty.

Prime minister: Does that mean you are opposed to the independence of Arabia?

Mr. Muhammad Ali: Yes. The Muslims claim that the local center of their faith, namely the "Island of Arabia" should remain inviolate and entirely in Muslim control (through Turkey). The "Island of Arabia" includes Syria, Palestine, and Mesopotamia as well as the region commonly known to Europeans as the Arabian Peninsula. Muslims cannot acquiesce in no form of non-Muslim control, whether in the shape of mandates or otherwise, over any portion of this region. The Khalifa must be the warden of the three Sacred Harams of Mecca, Medina, and Jerusalem; and overwhelming Muslim sentiment requires that he should be warden of the holy shrines of Najaf, Kerbala, Kazimain, Samarra, and Baghdad. In this connection, Sir, I might mention one point that the Muslims cannot tolerate any affront to Islam in keeping the Khalifa as a sort of hostage in Constantinople. He is not the Pope at the Vatican much less can he be the Pope at Avignon, and I am bound to say that the recent actions of Allied powers is likely to give rise in the Muslim world to feelings which it will be very difficult to restrain, and which would be very dangerous to the peace of the world.

I think I might now turn to the Jewish claims in Palestine. The Delegation have no desire to cause an injustice to the Jewish community, and I think Islam can look back with justifiable pride on its treatment of this community in the past. No aspiration of the Jewish community, which is reasonable, can be incompatible with Muslim control of the Holy Land, and it is hoped that the Ottoman Government will easily accommodate the Jewish community in such aspirations. Some responsible propogandists of the Zionist movement with which I have conversations frankly admit: "We do not want political sovereignty there; we want a home; the details can be arranged and discussed." I asked them: "Do you mean that Great Britain herself should be the sovereign power there, or should be mandatory?" and they said: "No, what we want is an ordinary humanly speaking reasonable guarantee that opportunities of autonomous development would be allowed to us." We, ourselves, who have been living in India, are great believers in a sort of Federation of Faiths, and we cannot rule out the possibility of development in Palestine on the lines of "cultural autonomy." The Jews are, after all, a very small minority there, and I do not believe for one moment that Jews could be attracted there in such large numbers as the Zionist enthusiasts sometimes think.

May I now sum up the claims we here put forward? If the Khalifa retains his wardenship of the Holy Places, which he can very well do if the exclusive control over every part of the Island of Arabia is retained by the Khalifa himself, and if your own pledge, Sir, is redeemed in full, while the 12th point of the president of the United States, on the basis of which the Armistice was concluded, is observed, then the result will be the restoration of the territorial status quo ante bellum which Muslims claim as the irreducible minimum for the preservation of the Khalifat.

[Syed Hussain interjects]: I have only one other point to put before you, and that is in regard to feelings in India at present. As you know, this Delegation has been sent by the All India Khilafat Conference, which is not a purely Muslim organization. Besides Muslims it includes most of the foremost leaders of the Hindu community also, and I should just like to state why it is that they are with us in this matter. There has been extraordinary growth of Hindu-Muslim unity in India in recent years, and it reached its climax, if I may say so, the moment the Hindus, after realizing that this question was a matter of grave concern for Muslims, came into this movement with us.

I would just emphasize that until a decade or two back, the tradition in India was for the Hindus and Muslims to be separate. When the Indian National Congress was first founded, the Muslims were openly opposed to the whole movement, but gradually

Muslims came into the Congress and gradually this national movement has built up to this extraordinary point today.

We are on the eve of a new era in India. The British Empire is the greatest Muslim Power in the world. The world is undergoing very many phases of transformation, but if this Indo-Islamic-British unity could be achieved on a basis of reality and real contentment all around, it would certainly be a very splendid fulfillment of the destiny of the British Empire. That is all I have to say.

Prime minister: Gentleman, you have put your case with very great lucidity and with moderation, and as the head of a Government, which, as the last speaker has very well said, has to deal with an Empire which is the largest Muhammadan Empire in the world, I feel bound to listen with great care to everything that comes from our Mussalman fellow-subjects in any part of the Empire.

The second thing I want to say is this. I should like to get out of the mind of any Mussalman throughout the Empire that we are treating Turkey upon different principles to those we applied when we came to consider Christian countries. We were at war with three Christian countries and one Muhammadan country. We did not seek war with any of them. The governors of Turkey took upon themselves to wage war upon us. We have never, in my recollection, waged war with Turkey. Our quarrel was not with Turkey. Our death struggle was with Germany and the German Military Power, and we deeply regretted that the Young Turkish Party should have misled their country and brought Turkey into war with Great Britain.

Now, Turkey has been beaten. So has Germany. So has Austria, Austria has fallen to pieces. She was an Empire. What is she now? She has fallen to bits, and her fragments are scattered about. But she is not a Mussalman country. She is a Christian country. Therefore, it is no use talking about crusades. We have no crusade against Austria. She has paid the penalty of defeat. What happened to Germany? We took away Alsace-Lorraine away from Germany. The whole of Poland has been taken away. She is not Mussalman. Why should we do it? Because we are applying the principle of self-determination to there countries which oppressed subject peoples and provoked war to destroy liberty throughout the world. I do not want any Mussalman in India to think we are applying any different principle to Turkey.

The Arabs have claimed independence. They have proclaimed Feisal King of Syria. They have claimed that they should be severed from Turkish dominion. We are applying exactly the same principles in Christian places and to impose the dominion of the Sultan upon Arabia, which has no desire for it, is to impose upon Arabs something which we would not dream of imposing upon these Christian communities.

What is the other case which is put? It is the question of the temporal power of Khalifa. The question is not confined to Islam, as Mr. Muhammad Ali knows very well. It is one of the greatest controversies of Christendom too. There are Roman Catholics who believe in the temporal powers of the Pope and Roman Catholics who do not. But after the Pope was deprived of his temporal power, his spiritual power was as great and very likely greater than before. I am not going to interfere in a religious discussion where men

of the same faith take different views. I know of Muhammadans, sincere, earnest, zeal-
ous Mussalmans, who take a very different view of the temporal power to the one taken
by Mr. Muhammad Ali today. All I know is this. The Turk will exercise temporal power
in Turkish lands. We do not propose to deprive him of Turkish lands. Neither do we
propose that he should retain power over lands which are not Turkish.

All I want to say in conclusion is this. The Mussalman of India stood by the Throne
and the Empire. We gratefully acknowledge it. They helped us in the struggle. We will-
ingly and gladly recognize it. We recognize that they have a right to be heard in matter
which affects Islam. We have heard them. Not merely have we heard them, but we have
very largely deferred to their wishes in this matter. The settlement was largely affected by
the opinion of India and especially the Mussalmans of India. But we cannot apply different principles to those which we sternly applied in our settlement with the Christian
communities with whom we were also at war.

That is all I have to say, and I thank you for putting your case before me and putting
it so clearly.[5]

Imagining Pakistan III: Iqbal[6]
August 13, 2004

What can I say about Muhammad Iqbal (1876–1938)? I went to school at the
height of Islamization policies of General Zia. *Khol Ankh Zamin Dekh*, indeed. In
Zia's Pakistan, and to this day, Iqbal is the ideologue of Pakistan, the imagineer of
the Castle of Islam. We read the meagre selections in our textbooks, wrote essays
on his brilliance, and recited from memory banal verses of poetry. I never liked
him. Seemed too cold or too distant. Like the brilliant asshole who has all the
answers. Where was the pain?

I returned to Iqbal much later. Started reading his Persian works, his
Reconstruction—and I discovered the halting steps towards knowledge, the agony
over the fate of a nation, and the struggles to understand a complex Muslim past.
I appreciate Iqbal much more now. He still does not impact me like Faiz, but I
understand him. But this Iqbal is far different than what the State of Pakistan wants
its children to learn. So very different.

For example, let's take his address to the All India Muslim League on December
29, 1930:

> I have no doubt that if a federal government is established, Muslim federal state will
> willingly agree for purposes of India's defense, to the creation of neutral Indian military
> and naval forces. Such a neutral force for the defense of India was a reality in the days
> of the Mughal rule. Indeed in the time of Akbar the Indian frontier was, on the whole,
> defended by armies officered by Hindu generals. I am perfectly sure that the scheme for

a neutral Indian army, based on a federated India will intensify Muslim patriotic feeling, and finally set at rest the suspicion, if any, of Indian Muslims joining Muslims from beyond the frontier in the event of an invasion.[7]

Federated India? Joint defense forces? Don't tell Mutahida Majlis-e Amal (MMA).

Some background: Iqbal came from humble Punjabi origins. He graduated from Trinity College, Cambridge; went to Heidelberg; and got his doctorate in Philosophy from Munich and passed the Bar at Lincoln's Inn. During his stay in Europe (1905–1908) he sought to reconcile the dominance of Western civilization with the problems confronting Muslims and, akin to Hali, concluded that only a revival of fundamental Islamic principles—Equality, Self-Empowerment, Justice, Tolerance—could arrest the decline. Except it was the path of the Mystic, not the path of the *mullah*, that led to those principles.

Today's selection is chosen mainly because it highlights the same theme that Hali expounded upon—the role of *mullahs* in society. It is from *Bang-e Dara*.

Piousness and License (Zuhd aur Rindi)

I will tell you the tale of Mr. Maulvi
Though I don't want to show off my temper
He had much renown for his Sufi ways
He was praised by high and low alike
He said that Law is hidden in Mysticism
Just as Meaning is hidden in Words

Overflowing with pious wine was his heart's cup
At the bottom somewhere was total knowledge
He told of his miracles often
With which he increased the number of followers

Since a long while, he was my neighbor
The sinner and the saint were old comrades
The Exalted One enquired from a friend of mine:
That Iqbal, that dove trapped in meaning's tree
How is he in his adherence to our Commandments and Laws?
Though, in the city, his verses are thought better than Hamdani's
I hear, he thinks Hindus are not infidels
Such beliefs must be the result of Philosophy
In his nature must also be some Shi'ism
I have heard him praise Ali from his tongue
I understand Music is part of his worship
His faith is righteous, but his ways are foreign

He has no shame from sellers of beauty
That, though, is an old habit of our poets
They sing all night, and in the dawn recite Qur'an
I have yet to decipher the meaning of such conduct
But I have heard this from my followers
His youth is un-blemished like the Dawn
He is a collections of contradictions, Not Iqbal
His heart an archive of wisdom, his manner error-prone
He knows impiety, he knows our Law
If you ask him of mysticism, he is second only to Mansur
I cannot decipher the Truth of this person
He must be the founder of some new Islam

In short, he lectured on this for a while
His speech flowering for long
In this city, all talk flies to everyone
I too heard of this from my beloveds
One day, as I met the Exalted Saint on the street
That old topic came up once again
He said; that complaint was from love's lips
It is my duty to show you the path of Righteousness
I said, I have no complaint towards you
It is your right as a neighbor to chastise
My head is bowed before you in penance
My youth has aged in deference to you
If you do not know my True Self
In this, there is no fault of Hamdani
The ocean of my thoughts is indeed deep
I too am desirous to see Iqbal
I have done much pining in his absence
Even Iqbal does not know Iqbal

The Lion of Panjshir[8]
September 10, 2004

There were times when "freedom fighter" had a romantic tinge to it. Ahmad Shah Massoud, also known as "Amer Sahib" or "The Lion of Panjshir," was a "freedom fighter" in those times. He defended his home, the Panjshir Valley, from the Red Army and from the Taliban. Like Che, he became an icon and a warrior for the Afghan struggle against the USSR and, later, the Taliban. He was assassinated two days before

September 11, 2001. Today, he is on a French stamp (these French are a romantic lot, aren't they?), in an excellent documentary, in a symphony, on the new Afghani coin, and in marketplace posters, poems, and remembrances. He is a national hero in Karzai's Afghanistan and a hated figure by the Taliban and Pashtun clans.

Ahmad Shah Massoud was a Tajik, from the valley of Panjshir. The valley is a narrow pass needed by the Red Army for their supply convoys. They invaded it with division strengths seven times. Each time, Massoud's men retreated to the mountains and passes and sniped the Russians moving in and stopped them. Massoud's heroic tale was bought to the West by French Doctors Without Borders, and he became the symbol of Afghan resistance to the world—clutching his AK-47. He was the subject of Ken Follett's *Lie Down with Lions*, which I read as a youth and found terribly exciting.

After the Soviet withdrawal, Massoud's group, *Jamiat-i Islami* [Islamic Society], defeated the Soviet-left regime in 1992 and was the first group to enter Kabul. Massoud became the vice president of the Islamic State of Afghanistan led by the United Islamic Front for the Salvation of Afghanistan (or the Northern Alliance). However, the pashtun-Taliban militia came sweeping into Kabul in 1996, and Massoud retreated back to Panjshir. From there, Massoud held the Taliban off again, much as he had done against the Communists. His ideals were still intact, as he railed against the Taliban's religious extremism and their oppression of women in particular.

Of course, the Taliban and parties vested with the pashtun-Taliban opposed Massoud with wild abandon—especially the ISI. *Charlie Wilson's War* had this joke attributed to the ISI: "When a Pashtun wants to make love to a woman, his first choice is a Tajik man." There were more serious allegations against him. They say he cut deals with the Red Army and stopped attacking them, prolonging the invasion and allowing them to launch offensive in other areas. *Charlie Wilson's War* disputes much of that and blames the ISI and the CIA for the times during which Massoud was unable to continue his resistance against the Red Army.

On September 9, 2001, two journalists came to interview him. They were suicide bombers. Massoud did not survive the attempt, although the news of his death did not emerge until after 9/11. Much speculation has occurred regarding whether al-Qaida was behind this attack and whether this was a preemptive strike on a singularly important ally against the Taliban.

Ahmad Shah Massoud lives on as only genuine heroes do. He has captured the imagination of a war-torn Afghan nation. I wish someone would compile poetry written about him in Dari. I remember reading a beautiful poem sent to me last year, but I cannot locate it in my emails. His legacy lives on in the political realm as well. His friend Younis Qanuni is running against Karzai in the October election. And just from using Google to write this entry, I can see that his popularity shows no sign of abating.

State-Sanctioned Killings[9]
October 27, 2004

Yesterday, the Lower House of the National Assembly in Pakistan "banned" *karokari* [honor killings]. Specifically, the legal code will now treat such acts not as "crimes of passion" but as premeditated murders and has upped the punishment for such a crime.

I know that there are some serious reservations about the amended law, and it's all about the application anyways, but I have to applaud the Minister of Law, Wasi Zafar, who took time off from much more important business for this measure. Like any other Pakistani, I grew up hearing and reading about women killed just for glancing at someone or even just accused of glancing at someone. I place the blame squarely on the State for that. And not just Zia's Islamization efforts. Such killings are never prosecuted, because they are class crimes as well as gender crimes. Rich, powerful landholders in the villages of Sindh and Punjab are the main culprits in practicing and promoting violence against women in the context of family honor. The local *thanay dar* [constable] simply looks away unless the national media makes a stink, and, in that case, a simple FIR is registered and forgotten. If the State cannot protect its most vulnerable citizens, it cannot claim any legitimacy.

Honor. Anachronistically, a woman's body remains the locus of the South Asian family's honor. To protect the family name, you put the woman in a veil. To promote the family name, you seek marriage with a family of a higher station. To avenge the family name, you rape or kill your opponents' women.

How does one combat such practices? The first thing, obviously, is to actually *have* laws on the books that can be used by those fighting such medieval notions. In that regard, the amendment passed is a crucial step. Second, again obvious, is to actually enforce such laws. No great hope for that in the short run. But, media can play the pivotal role in this regard. It can often shame the government's hand.

But real change can only come when societal norms shift due to economic or political stimulus. In the urban communities, the economic change is happening as women constitute a growing segment of income earners in the public sphere. These professional women are more likely to assert their rights and have access to support structures outside the family. In the rural communities, the majority population where honor killings occur, women have *always* worked in the public sphere, and it has not helped them. In that context, I think change can only come through societal shifts brought about by political pressure. Religion, duh, is the obvious marker here. The State must undertake a radical and aggressive educational effort that emphasizes the rights of women in the Islamic world and back that up by cleaning up the Hudood code, doing madrasa reform, teach-ins, promoting civic NGOs, etc. I have little hope that The General is interested much in all that.

For now, let's see what the State does in this case.

The Baluchistan Issue[10]
January 13, 2005

So, what is going on in Baluchistan? Baluchistan is one of the four states/provinces of Pakistan. It constitutes roughly 40 to 43 percent of the land mass with only 5 to 7 percent share of the population. It has the richest mineral and natural resources in the country yet is the most impoverished area of Pakistan, with the lowest literacy, health, and infrastructure indices. Two days ago, "tribals" or "nationalists" or "foreign interests" launched an attack on the largest natural gas production facility in Sui, Baluchistan. This has halted the supply of natural gas to most of the country, resulting in material and economic losses. The escalation comes after ongoing sporadic violence in the region against the Pakistani military forces. The General unequivocally warned the tribal/nationalist/foreign elements that his retaliation will be swift and that "they will not even know what hit them."

This has set the stage for a showdown between Pakistan military and what the Pak media is terming "terrorist organizations," like the Baluch Liberation Front and Baluch Liberation Army. At least *Jang Daily* expressed severe doubt in its editorial about the mere existence of these organizations (which is the usual hint that India is behind it all). If they, uh, Googled it, they would know that not only do these organizations exist and have a fairly comprehensive Web presence but that their grievances are longstanding and, at least to this Punjabi/Kashmiri, fairly justified.

Let me start with a bit of history. The region was largely under Iranian kingly control and the autonomous principality of Kalat. The British wrested control away from the Khan of Kalat in the early 1840s, and it became the staging ground for the various Afghan-British wars (the Great Game) in the latter half of the 19th century. The 1876 treaty between the Khan of Kalat and Robert Sandeman accepted the independence of the Kalat as an allied state with British military outposts in the region. After the 1878 Afghan War, the British established Baluchistan as a provincial entity centered around the municipality of Quetta, with Kalat, Makran, and Lasbella continuing to exist as princely realms. The British interest in the region was largely to use it as a land-mass bulwark against Central Asian encroachments. Besides a train track, the development and settlement of British holdings excluded most of the tribal population. The administrative and legislative reforms of late-19th- and early-20th-century India overlooked Baluchistan. Around the 1930s, Baluchi nationalist parties emerged to contest for freedom from British rule. They took the princely state of

Kalat as the focal point of a free and united Baluchistan. Iqbal's vision of autonomous federation of Muslim state included Baluchistan, but the Khan of Kalat never bought into the Punjabi nationalist paradigm, arguing that the Kalat had special treaty powers. Baglar Begi Khan declared the independence of Kalat on August 15, 1947. He assured the neostate of Pakistan that Kalat would participate in the defense and infrastructure but would be autonomous. That didn't go over well at all, and the Pakistani Army entered the region to occupy the area immediately. On March 27, 1948, the Khan of Kalat gave in to the State of Pakistan and his old attorney, M. A. Jinnah. His brother Abdul Karim Baloch refused to surrender and revolted until his arrest in 1950. Baluchistan was put under Governor General control, and no elective body formed in Baluchistan until 1973.

After Partition, the threat of E. Pakistani—read Bengali—hegemony (55 percent of population at the time), forced the Punjabi military and civil elite (in 1947, Punjabis made up 77 percent of the army while being only 25 percent of the population) to constitute W. Pakistan as One Unit in the 1956 Constitution. This was done presumably to guarantee equal representation for W. Pakistan, but the measure was highly unpopular in Sindh, Baluchistan, and NWFP because it meant rule of the Punjabi over their regional interests. Separatist, subnational movements triumphing local languages and cultures and protesting Punjabi hegemony arose in all the three states. Especially in Baluchistan, the Khan of Kalat led a stringent opposition to the One Unit. But the wave of military dictatorships quashed all such designs. In 1970, Yayha Khan dissolved the One Unit to appease E. Pakistan, but the horrific damage done by the army in soon-to-be Bangladesh proved too much.

After 1971, the subnationalist movements in Sindh and Baluchistan demanded their fair share of the nationalist pie. With Bangladesh's independence, Punjab became the most populous and richest state in the country. It had 58 percent of the population, while Baluchistan had 4 percent. Led by Bhutto's central populism, Baluchistan had its first elected body in 1972. The National Awami Party (NAP) won the majority of the seats in Baluchistan and started making noises about state rights. In 1973, it was clear to the NAP that Baluchistan was the least-developed province, with the majority of civil and military bureaucracy coming from Punjab. They, quite correctly, saw this as a colonial exploitation. The discovery of natural gas reserves at Sui had made the area incredibly vital to Pakistan's and Iran's developmental programs. The refusal by the Bhutto's central government to allow NAP internal autonomy escalated a tense situation into an outright revolt. Bhutto dismissed the Baluchistan assembly and reinstituted Governor's rule. The Baluchi nationalists launched an all-out military resistance.

From 1973 to 1978, roughly 60,000 Baluchi tribesmen and militia faced off against the Pakistani Army. Iran, eager to quell any similar uprising in its bordering area, contributed air force and personnel to the Pakistani efforts. They bombarded Baluchi villages into submission. Bhutto's ouster, via Zia's military coup, forced a calm onto the situation as Zia launched into his One Pakistan Through

Islam program. The Afghanistan war, the Iranian revolution and the Zia's policies made Baluchistan into an island of outsider activity. U.S./UN aid for Afghani refugees poured into the metropolitan areas. During the '90s, the Benazir/Nawaz Sharif governments did little for Baluchistan as the Baluchi nationalist parties floundered in exile.

After The General landed into power (get it?), he tried to foster a new relationship with Baluchistan. Over the last three years, the Kachhi Canal, Mirani Dam, Gwadar Port, Makran Coastal Highway, Saindak Copper Project, and Quetta Water Supply Scheme were announced by Islamabad. Over 300 percent increase was made in the national budget for development programs in Baluchistan. Yet all these things have failed to materialize from paper into concrete.

These latest incidents emerge from the same calls for Baluchistan's equal share in the national programs and right to self-administer. The catalyst seems to be the assault on a female doctor, Dr. Shazia Khalid, by a gang of employees of the Pakistan Petroleum Limited (PPL) at Sui. The company management, along with the local police, tried to quash the issue while the central authorities ignored all pleas to intervene. This caused the initial attack on the Sui facility. Nawab Akbar Bugti, the leader of Democratic National Party Baluchistan, clearly stated that the attack was borne out of frustration on the lack of action against the employees who did the assault and was *not* a nationalist struggle for freedom by the tribals. The General, on the other hand, is going to play this as another internal/external threat to Pakistan and seems determined to carry out a military response. His pointed reference to the 1973 uprising is meant to warn the Baluchi tribals that he will not negotiate on his terms.

Today's actions by the tribals and the military response in Baluchistan can be understood within the context of the acrimonious central-regional relationship in Pakistan. The rights of states, the rights of minorities, and the rights of individuals are all negotiated within the vacuum of Islamabad military power brokers. Having no access to that, the aggrieved parties find no alternative except violent struggle. The history of MQM, of Sindh, of Waziristan, and of Baluchistan provide ample attestation to that reality. I hate to say it again, but here it goes: There is no way out except a democratically elected and constituted assembly that will reimagine Pakistan as a federation with a secular and civil Constitution at the helm.

The Ghost of Bhutto[11]
April 4, 2005

The leaders of Pakistan tend to have some aversion to natural terminations of tenure and even to natural terminations of life. On April 4, 1979, Zulfiqar Ali Bhutto, the overthrown prime minister of Pakistan, was hanged by the State of Pakistan led by the military dictator Zi-ul-Haq. Bhutto's vindictive ghost, though, haunts Pakistan in ways that Zia feared the living Bhutto would. Funny that.

He was incredibly charismatic (who can forget his address to the United Nations? [er, who remembers?]), but he was filled with contradictions. He was an intellectual who came from landed elite. He was schooled in the best of places and was bourgeoisie yet claimed to speak for the people with socialist convictions. He rose to prominence not from the mass politics but from the inner halls of bureaucratic power under the dictator General Ayub. When he became the foreign minister of Pakistan, in 1963, he wanted Pakistan on the forefront of Islamic countries and South Asia; instead, he stoked the fires in Kashmir. He hated the military, but all of his best friends were military men. He was the most trusted man Ayub had, but, in 1969, he created the political party—Pakistan Peoples Party (PPP), which toppled Ayub. He watched Pakistan break into two in 1971 to wait for his moment. The horrors of the military men turned the nation to this dapper bureaucrat who promised land reform and *roti, kapra aur makan* [bread, cloth, and house] for everyone. He became the first elected prime minister of the 32-year-old nation. He made industrial and land reform, but the only beneficiaries were landlords and industrialists. He proclaimed "Islamic Socialism," but the people never saw Islam or socialism. He gave speech after speech on the terrors of landholding exploiters of the people. He courted them as his base. He promised 18 acres of land to each peasant, and they got, well, nothing. From 1972 to 1977, he shaped Pakistan in his fractured image. More than anything, it was his death that came to symbolize the realm of political power in Pakistan.

Zia-ul-Haq led the coup against Bhutto, because the PPP had won the 1977 election. And because he wanted the address of Bhutto's Saville Row tailor. Within 90 days, Zia promised, we would have new elections that would be unmarred by the corruption that gave PPP the overwhelming majority. The detained Bhutto was charged with conspiracy to commit 30-some counts of murder. A series of white papers was released documenting the atrocities of the Bhutto regime. The Lahore High Court sentenced Bhutto to death. The Supreme Court withheld the decision.

Bhutto was a popular PM—perhaps, the most popular figure in the history of the nation. Zia hoped that a quick trial and execution would rid him of the guy forever. Right. Has that ever worked out for anyone? Just ask Pontius Pilate. All the ill will that Bhutto had fostered in his 6 years of mismanaged, authoritarian rule evaporated when the news of his death was announced on the State Radio. That announcement transformed him from a likable yet crooked politician into a martyr. PPP maintained immense rural support throughout Zia's military rule. Benazir Bhutto, the daughter, emerged as the hope of millions and the spearhead for democracy. The day she returned to Pakistan for the first time in 1986, those millions turned out to welcome her. The cult of personality that had built up around her father, herself, her brothers, her uncles, grows larger and larger to this day (husband, wives of slain brothers, mothers), stifling any hope and chance of a rebirth (there is an equal cult around Zia's ghost).

How morbid is that nation of mine?

Masses without Politics[12]
April 6, 2005

Let's continue the almost conversation about political leadership in Pakistan. Western historians often term the politics of South Asia, along with much of the developing nations, as the "politics of masses." Within this categorization hides both the fear of the masses that Hobbes expressed in his *Leviathan* ("to confer all their power and strength upon one man, or upon one assembly of men, that may reduce all their wills, by plurality of voices, unto one will") as well the subscription to Western modernity's teleological stages (brown masses are stuck in the "not yet" historical time, as Dipesh Chakrabarty wrote in his *Provincializing Europe*). Those teeming millions hover out on the streets with rallies and get manipulated by unethical leaders. They break out in riots, they burn American flags, they yell "*Allahu Akbar*" ["God is Great"]. At the head of this unseemly and frightening mass is the charismatic leader—the magical, supranatural charismatic of Weber (uncanny powers that draw on the realm of the unexplained phenomena like religion or socialism; no legal or moral framework underpinning him/her).

If one reads respected authors, like, say, Stephen P. Cohen, on the Pakistan political scene, one feels the urge to hurl on said authors some rotten fruits, so imbued are their "objective interpretations" with these prejudices. I am not going to waste time rehashing their arguments, but feel free to pick up any book that has "Pakistan" in the title and was published after 1998.

Pakistan has had exactly one type of leader: the dictator. The thing about dictators—of any stripe—is that they operate on the whole "cult of personality" philosophy. The man who really cemented the archetype in Pakistan was General Ayub (1958–1969). The self-avowed creed of "anticorruption" and "industrialization" was meant to endear him to the masses. When that failed, "Kashmir" became the rallying cry, and the 1965 war provided the rest. Bhutto (1973–1977) followed rather slavishly in Ayub's footsteps. The impermanence of power haunted him perhaps more than anyone else (the pyramid approach to governance makes coups so much easier). Zia-ul-Haq (1977–1988) played the game as well as his tired soul could. He didn't have either Bhutto's flair or Ayub's tenacity.

The triumvirate powerhouses of the military, the civil bureaucracy, and the landed elites have supplied all of these leaders (the one exception is the very intriguing Altaf Husain of the MQM). Their appeals to the masses are always the same: We will intervene directly into your life and make it better. Whether in the guise of anticorruption or modernization, the rally addresses were always about development of corner streets and neighborhood factories (anyone remember Junejo/Zia's cottage industry initiative?), of the crimes of former/current regimes, and the efforts to bring individuals to justice. Their appeals to the Americans are always the same: We will fight your proxy wars (commies or *jihadis*) if you give us money and leave us alone.

The lack of leadership on the national stage in Pakistan is inherently a representation of the lack of electoral politics and the dominance of the dictator. Those who can offer a viable alternative are quashed and sequestered. Those who toady themselves are promoted. Others abandon the field to the man with the gun.

My disgust with dictators begins and ends with the simple observation that they epitomize that particular view of the "politics of the masses." Pakistanis are forever stuck in the "not yet" time—lacking education or training or a civil society to elect governments to represent themselves. The masses are uncouth and uncivilized. "Mature" democracies, such as the United States, do not have mass rallies and tire burning after a child is killed in a road accident. "Mature" democracies elect their leaders after impassioned and logical thought as the best representing the ideals of the collective society. Pakistan has to be trained, and Condi Rice is completely devoted to the "steps towards democratization" that The General is undertaking. The pendulum of metaphors swings from "time" to "distance."

On this one, I am squarely with the Subalternists. The filthy masses of Pakistan *are* political agents, and they *are* ready for democracy. And they even have leaders. But the unsurprising reality is that the system is set to prohibit any populist challenge to the regime. The two-legged bar stool of Pakistani dictatorship is firmly situated at this moment.

At the Grown-Up Table[13]
April 13, 2005

The *Group of Four vs. the Coffee Club. India vs. Pakistan. Japan vs. China. History vs. Politics.* It plays out like a grand opera of broken trusts and rebounded relationships, but it is the very *realpolitiks* surrounding the reform and expansion of the UN Security Council. I know that this isn't the sexiest of topics and that the United Nations is as popular in the States as Kevin Federline is sincere. But, for the *rest of the world*, it remains a vital organization. So let's take a look at what is at stake.

The brief overview is that the United Nations wants to reform itself. The March 2005 report on reforms by Kofi Annan includes the provision for an expansion of the Security Council. Two competing proposals are on the table: One is to expand it by six permanent members—India, Japan, Brazil, and Germany (the Group of Four, or G-4) are championing this; the second proposal—spearheaded by Pakistan's Coffee Club coalition of 54 countries—is to add eight semi-permanent seats and divide them among across various nations of Africa and Asia. The two sides have been debating on and off the floor, with states announcing their intentions all across (Qatar supports India! Austria supports Pakistan!). All this while John "There is no such thing as the United Nations" Bolton's confirmation hearing as the UN ambassador plays out on a cable channel near you.

I will restrict myself to India's claims to the seat. It is a controversial claim in some circles. As the most populous democracy and rising economic power, India feels that it has a legitimate role to play in world politics. The detractors are wary of Indian regionalism-gone-amok. More interesting is the question, "*Why would India want this role?*" India has always had a warm but distant relationship with the United Nations. Led by the idealism of Nehru [nonalignment, anticolonial, antiaggression], India sought to project itself on a higher moral ground for most of his tenure while adhering closely to Indian self-interest. Nothing out of the ordinary in that. What was extraordinary was Nehru's firm belief that India, of all the recently minted states, belonged with the elite nations and that it was not just another "little nation." Indian delegates spoke of "the ancient land" and India's "rightful and honored place in the world." They consistently sought to present their arguments before the world audience (and for the national audience) and projected the image of global leader [especially under K. Menon '52–'62]. For Nehru's India, the only way to project more power than it possessed was to uphold moral and idealized positions without cavorting with the great powers. Kashmir, and to a lesser extent Goa, became the sticky wicket. While India itself had referred Kashmir to the United Nations, it found very little sympathy among the international community. And it had to rely on Soviet vetoes again and again. Still, with the rise of the Cold War, India consistently sought to keep the balance of influence within the Security Council. It was an ardent supporter of China's bid to be recognized even when border tensions along the Sino-Indian borders were rising.

The onset of hostilities between India and China in 1962 destroyed Nehru's idealized world view. China's aggression—a clearly political show of force—showed India that the stark reality behind its global and regional influence remained its lack of power. China took all the land it wanted and "offered" peace. It was a calculated ploy by Mao to expose the "paper tigers" of the world [Nehru and the Soviets]. Nehru's illusions were shattered [and K. Menon's career ended], and he died soon thereafter. The nonaligned nations had done nothing. Soviets had turned mum. All this led to the marked withdrawal of India from the world/UN stage. The wars of '65, '71, and the nuclear boom in '74 took any remaining shine off of International India. Things weren't so good at home anyways, so who cared? But, the '80s and '90s have slowly brought India back on the world scene.

But, just as China had once pushed India off the UN/world map, it is now putting India back by supporting India's bid for the Security Council. Wen Jiabao's recently concluded visit to India resulted in a host of agreements and pacts (The two sides declared 2006 as the "year of China-India friendship"), and China declared that it "supports India's aspirations to play an active role in the UN and international affairs." This vague statement is understood to be Chinese backing of an Indian permanent seat.

Of course, Pakistan is leading the charge against Indian acceptance to the SC. Their argument pivots on the Kashmir issue. Totally predictable. Also predictable are the Indian complaints that the U.S. position is being influenced by the Pakistani-born advisor to the president and Rice, Shirin Tahir-Kheli. Be that as it may, India does have a legitimate claim to leadership on the world stage. More than anything, the 2004 election proved that Indian democracy can play a vital and vibrant role among the totalitarian dictatorships surrounding it. I believe that they fully deserve a seat at the SC.

There is more to the Security Council story. Historical memory is at stake between China and Japan, which may endanger Chinese support of India as well. . . .

The Baluchistan Issue II[14]
January 24, 2006

Carnegie Papers just released a report on Baluchistan called *Pakistan: The Resurgence of Baluch Nationalism*, by Frederic Grare.[15] It is worth reading for a number of reasons. It strongly suggests that Baluch marginalization and dispossession are major factors in the uprising. The projects of Gwadar or Sui have not materialized as beneficial entities to the local population, who feel without a voice or participatory role. That the fruits of such programs are being siphoned off by the tribal chiefs is not addressed, though. It also clarifies that only three out of twenty-eight tribal chiefs—Bugti, Mengal, and Murri—are in open revolt against the center, which belies Islamabad's claim that this is an insurgency fueled by tribal chiefs for their benefit and points out that the revolt has spread to Makran. Lastly, there are some worthwhile observations on foreign involvements—United States, Iran, or India.

Of course, the real danger of a nationalist uprising is the fear of secession. To that end, Grare writes:

> If Pakistan is divided at some time in the future, an independent Baluchistan would become in all probability a new zone of instability in the region. Its instability would affect the interests of all the regional players. Yet, unless Pakistan changes its policy

toward Baluchistan dramatically, the possibility of Baluchistan eventually gaining its independence cannot be ruled out.[16]

And the policy that Pakistan is pursuing right now is hell bent on achieving secession: Consider Zahid Hussain's January 2006 reports of summary executions and civilian bombings in the *London Times*. I hope it isn't too futile to point to The General that the lessons of 1971 need revisiting.

All India Muslim League, 1906–2006[17]
December 30, 2006

On December 30, 1906, a group of Muslim leaders gathered in Dhaka and proposed a political association for the Muslims of India, with three aims: to protect Muslim interests, to counter Congress influences, and to support the British administration. The first meeting of this proposed entity, named the All India Muslim League, happened in Karachi on December 20, 1907. The next decades of Muslim League in Indian nationalist politics can only be described as tumultuous—as it tried to work with, against, the All India National Congress and the British. It trained, groomed, and gave a platform to generations of Muslim leaders on local, national, and international arenas. But, even as the party and its ideologies gained significance in the Indian nationalist scene, it had to go through various evolutions in its struggle to unite dueling agendas and hopes for the millions of Muslims in India.

To truly understand its impact, one would have to examine the intellectual history of the Muslim League from Syed Ahmed Khan to the two partitions—the creation of Pakistan and Bangladesh. This history of the Muslim League is of particular relevance in today's world. The oft-heard refrain about the lack of democracy and democratic practices in the Muslim world deserves a sustained critique through this 100-year history of charted and documented practice of Muslim democracy in India.

When I went through my schooling in Lahore during the '80s, we had extensive lesson plans on the All India Muslim League; we had to memorize the various resolutions and recite the points of various planning committees. All this, in practical terms, was to answer the inevitable essay question on our state board exam: Explain the Ideology of Pakistan in light of the Two Nation Theory. Ask me now to tell you what is the Ideology of Pakistan, and I will recite the mantra, *Pakistan ka Matlab Kiya? La Illaha Illal Lah* (What does Pakistan mean? No God but One). The ideology of Pakistan, in Zia-ul-Haq's Pakistan, was Islam. The narrative history of this ideology was in every history and social studies textbook post-1977 and part of every politician and leader's arsenal.

This officially sanctioned ideology of Pakistan is historically, teleologically, and, dare I say, divinely determined. There are no divergent paths or countermemories in this narrative. In this particular past, selections from the history of Muslim League exist merely to fulfill the prophecy of Pakistan. The lives and events intertwined in the history of the League appear only as counterpoints to the All India National Congress in this teleology and then only to prove the overarching truism: Hindus and Muslims were *always* two nations in India. Take, for example, this quote from a social studies textbook:

> For more than ten centuries since 711 AD Muslims, Hindus and followers of Jainism and Buddhism lived together but remained distinct in all imaginable ways of living, culture, religion and creed. It would be distortion of history to say that Indian subcontinent was and had been a cultural unity or its people lived according to agreed social codes. In his book, India (1888), Sir John Strachey observed, This is the first and most essential thing to learn about India—that there is not, and never was an India.
>
> As early as in the beginning of the 11th century, Al-Biruni observed that Hindus differed from the Muslims in all matters and habits. The speech made by Quaid-i-Azam at Minto Park, Lahore, on March 22, 1940, was very similar to Al-Biruni's thesis in theme and tone. In this speech, he stated that Hindus and Muslims belong to two different religious philosophies, with different social customs and literature. The only difference between the writing of Al-Biruni and the speech of Quaid-i-Azam was that Al-Biruni made calculated predictions, while Quaid-i-Azam had history behind him to support his argument.[18]

Note the emphatic claim to truth employed here. It may be quite easy to, historically, disprove the claims in the quote—or, even in Jinnah, Two Nation Theory—and to highlight, instead, the interdependencies and interconnectedness of Muslims and Hindus through centuries of cohabitation on the subcontinent. But the veracity of historical truths is besides the point. To engage with the history implicit in this quote is to give in to the telos of Pakistan, to imagine only a future with Pakistan or without Pakistan. Such a history already forecloses all other pasts, and all other futures.

We are forced to confront another overly determined future at the moment: the clash of civilizations, the Reformation of Islam, the telos of Terror. Since it reflects our presents just as much as those pasts, how, then, does one write a history of political Islam in South Asia? We can, for example, take a cue from Paul Ricoeur, who reminds us: "Knowing that people of the past formulated expectations, predictions, desires, fears, and projects is to fracture historical determinism by retrospectively reintroducing contingency into history." Hence, for us to consider the history and legacy of All India Muslim League is to ask of ourselves: How do we conceive of this past differently. What is the legacy of the All India Muslim League outside the teleology of Pakistan? What motivations, rivalries, and alliances prompted the creation, propagation, and demise of the All India Muslim League around the subcontinent during the past hundred years; what has been its role in the making of the nations and polities of India, Pakistan, and Bangladesh? What pasts did it engender, what present did it bring into existence, and what futures did it imagine? And, most importantly, what memories did it leave behind? As historians, we have to inhabit the past of 1906, so as to imagine the futures from 1906. To prospect, and not retrospect.

With those concerns, we held a colloquium at the University of Chicago on November 4, 2006, to note and reflect on the creation of the Muslim League, a hundred years thence. Invited were prominent scholars of the intellectual and political history of South Asia: David Gilmartin, David Lelyveld, I. A. Zilli, Sumit Sarkar, and Tanika Sarkar. We also invited graduate students who are currently working on aspects of the history of Islam in South Asia (and Muslim League): Jane Menon, Venkat Dhulipala, Maya Tudor, and Eric Beverley.

The colloquium brilliantly captured those alternative futures that we were hoping to stress. The presentations by I. A. Zilli on Shibli Naumani and David Gilmartin on British Common Law and the League were truly remarkable. But, for me, the keynote address by Naim Sahib, "A Sentimental Essay in Three Scenes," was the highlight of the whole colloquium. You can watch and listen to these sessions here.[19]

There is hope that we will continue this examination of the history of Muslim League with the construction of a Digital Archive. I am working on the prototype and hope to have more news on that front in the new year.

Histories Ahead[20]
February 8, 2008

Bush-Clinton Forever is a fun exercise is prognostication. I was just explaining that in Pakistan, the Bhutto and Sharif clans have enough heirs to keep control for the next 80 years. It helps that the military will be able to control three or four sets of 12-year increments, which is necessary for bringing about maturation in the sons and grandsons to be. Of course, the political dynasties in Pakistan are much more open to daughters-in-law, nephews, and second cousins on the father's side. Go Sonia Gandhi!

Related, I asserted to my friend raver that every chief of army staff in Pakistan *with mustaches* assumed control, while those *without mustaches* or with *slight or ineffectual mustaches* were pliable to civilian regimes. Here is the proof of this pudding.

Name	Term of Appointment	Mustache?	Martial Law?
General Sir Frank Walter Messervy	1947–1948	Yes	No
General Sir Douglas David Gracey	1948–1951	Yes	No
General Ayub Khan	1951–1958	Yes	Yes
General Musa Khan	1958–1966	No	No
General Yahya Khan	1966–1971	Yes	Yes
General Gul Khan	1971–1972	Yes	No
General Tikka Khan	1972–1976	Yes	No*
General Zia-ul-Haq	1976–1988	Yes	Yes
General Aslam Beg	1988–1991	No	No
General Asif Janjua	1991–1993	No	No
General Abdul Waheed Kakar	1993–1996	Slight	No
General Jahangir Karamat	1996–1998	No	No
General Pervez Musharraf	1996–2007	Yes	Yes
General Ashfar Pervez Kayani	2007–	No	

* *Tikka Khan is not the exception if you consider the dictatorship he wrought on the people of East Pakistan.*

Okay, I guess, this theory is as spotty as the hair I can produce on my own upper lip. But it did make me find images of these weird generals.

Priorities, People[21]
May 6, 2009

The future histories of empire will have to focus on the American penchant for building "secure embassies." Take the 2009 Supplemental Appropriations for Iraq, Afghanistan, Pakistan, and Pandemic Flu (I love that list, by the way). Pakistan gets $2.3 billion (more than Iraq, Afghanistan, or Flu). But towards what end, you ask? Well, it has $897 million for a new secure embassy and consulates in Pakistan, plus $46 million for diplomatic operations, including additional civilian staff and diplomatic security; but only $400 million for "the Pakistan Counterinsurgency Capability Fund to build the counterinsurgency capabilities of the Pakistani security forces." I mean, really? Lest you worry, the current embassy is in a happily subversive playground called "the Diplomatic Enclave," where the word "enclave" means "city within city."

Further along in the head-smacking category are the "parameters" for performances:

1. The level of political consensus and unity of purpose to confront the political and security challenges facing the region
2. The level of government corruption and actions taken to eliminate it
3. The performance of security forces with respect to counterinsurgency operations
4. The performance of intelligence agencies in cooperating fully with the United States and not undermining the security of our troops and our objectives in the region
5. The ability of the government to control the territory within their borders

Regarding points 1 and 3, how is that even measurable? And 2 is that old developmental theory canard. At least we have wiped government corruption from the United States (less Chicago). But point 5 is the best one—insofar as the word "control" leads to hysterical laughter around the world.

Here is a revolutionary idea. Put the whole $2.3 billion into building a secure U.S. embassy whose compound walls roughly parallel Pakistan's state boundaries. And then employ everyone inside for security or diplomacy. Remember, labor is cheap.

Securing Afghanistan[22]
October 9, 2009

On October 1, 1842, Lord Edward Law Ellenborough (1790–1871) issued a special proclamation from Simla, 4 years to the day after Lord Auckland had declared a war on Afghanistan:

> The Government of India directed its army to pass the Indus in order to expel from Afghanistan a chief believed to be hostile to British interest, and to replace upon his throne a Sovereign represented to be friendly to those interests, and popular with his former subjects.

In 1838, Lord Auckland had decided that a regime change was needed in Kabul—Dost Muhammad was to be replaced by the friendlier Shah Shuja. The British had kept 10,000 or more troops in Kabul to secure the new ruler. However, the uprising of 1841 in Kabul resulted in the mass killing of British troops and their families, ending the first Anglo-Afghan War in infamy.

Ellenborough's forces had gone to avenge that defeat. Ghazni, Jalalabad, and Kabul were scorched to the ground. Having done that, Lord Ellenborough saw no reason for the British to continue to stay around what precious little was left to stay around *for*.

The Governor-general will leave it to the Afghans themselves to create a government amidst the anarchy which is the consequence of their crimes.

The anarchy, which is the consequence of their crimes, indeed. It should be noted that he was installing the very tribes to power whose crimes he had come to avenge. Be that as it may, in his estimation, the mountains of northwest and the rivers of Punjab and Indus would be both a barrier to the "barbarous tribes of Affghanistan" and a "limit nature appears to have assigned to [British] empire."

But, only a few months later, in February 1843, Ellenborough endorsed the extension of the company's natural empire over the princely state of Sindh—a crucial frontier region bordering Punjab, Afghanistan, and Persia—based largely on the fears that the Mirs of Talpur were colluding with the Shah of Afghanistan against the British. This was followed by the Anglo-Sikh wars of 1845 and the annexation of Punjab. This left only the princely states of Kalat and Swat between the Afghanistan and the British.

Any and all resemblance to current events is pretty intentional.

Once More With Feelings[23]
December 8, 2009

"Yet the Army leadership is refusing to strike at the heart of the Taliban command in Baluchistan Province" declares another editorial from the *New York Times* today.[24] If only these Pakistanis would realize—*why won't they just realize*—that this is their wars, not ours.

Think back to March 2009. Then, the Taliban were on a march to Islamabad—a mere 60 miles away—and an April editorial in the *NYT*[25] chided the Pakistani Army and civilian elite for not understanding their mortal threat. "Invade Swat" became a mantra of pundits and editorials alike. After hemming and hawing—and filling up its coffers—the Pakistani Army did. It went in with guns blazing from every hilltop. It watched the million walk out of the valley with their houses gone and their livelihoods vanished. Never did the *NYT* or the administration pause to even consider what were the local histories, the local demands, the causes that would have allowed the Taliban any foothold at all in Swat. Not once was Swat's precarious constitutional structure discussed or attention paid to the Swati demands for expedient justice, equal opportunities, and resource sharing. Not once. The drums of war drown out any other voice. All the Empire seeks is immediate action. In the here and in the now.

Then, in August 2009, came the second wave. The real battle is in Waziristan, not Swat where the Taliban's real base exists. Why won't the Pakistani Army move in there already? Why are they wasting time in Swat? The timing was also good for a Pakistani "invasion" since Baitullah Mehsud had just been killed. Once again, the Army dithered until just long enough before finally launching an operation into North Waziristan. Once again, the local population fled—but this time there were no Internally Displaced People (IDP) camps and no relief efforts. Apparently as Chris Brummitt's article in the *Huffington Post* states, "most have relatives in the region."[26] Go figure that one out.

And because frontiers are "always empty," the Taliban are now going to Baluchistan. So, let us send the Pakistani Army after them. It is fun, no? This chasing. Like a global game of tag. Get serious, Pakistan Army! Get into Baluchistan, and crush those Taliban. Once again, who cares if the reality matches any of our discourse? Who cares that Baluchistan is not empty and that it already has a war?

All clear?

Step 1: NYT (representing the administration, of course) decries Pakistani Army needs to get serious on Taliban.

Step 2: Pakistani Army provides a suitable window of dithering, during which time a number of prominent pundits add their voice to the enfolding crisis.

Step 3: Pakistani Army gets more money and then moves in to the "central area" in order to combat the Talibothra.

Step 4–40: Ignore any local issues; ignore the blowback of drones; ignore the constant bomb blasts in Peshawar, Lahore, Multan; ignore any political realities. Enjoy!

Chapter Notes

1 Archived at http://bit.ly/e54ozT.

2 Archived at http://bit.ly/erPMqI.

3 Ibid.

4 Archived at http://bit.ly/ghgvrL.

5 K. K. Aziz, "The Indian Khilafat Movement, 1915–1933: A Documentary Record," 1972.

6 Archived at http://bit.ly/fYNWIJ.

7 "Presidential Address of Dr. Sir Muhammad Iqbal Delivered at the Allahabad Session of the All India Muslim League," *Kashmir-Information.com*, archived at http://bit.ly/kB1Yyh.

8 Archived at http://bit.ly/ept0TJ.

9 Archived at http://bit.ly/ePwVfs.

10 Archived at http://bit.ly/i1VZ4o.

11 Archived at http://bit.ly/ehcRnY.

12 Archived at http://bit.ly/i4T7qC.

13 Archived at http://bit.ly/fldqUZ.

14 Archived at http://bit.ly/f8omg8.

15 Archived at http://bit.ly/gnwsJ9.

16 Ibid., 12.

17 Archived at http://bit.ly/ecrOKI.

18 *Pakistan Studies XI* (Lahore: Punjab Textbook Board, 1997).

19 Archived http://bit.ly/fJAz27.

20 Archived at http://bit.ly/eyK8m5.

21 Archived at http://bit.ly/15HnMB.

22 Archived at http://bit.ly/gsL9e.

23 Archived at http://bit.ly/4KHy8l.

24 "Pakistan and the War," *New York Times*, December 7, 2009, archived at http://nyti.ms/5UtXms.

25 "60 Miles from Islamabad," *New York Times*, April 29, 2009, archived at http://nyti.ms/U8gG2.

26 Chris Brummitt, "Islamabad University Attacked, 4 Killed, as Army Presses Ahead with South Waziristan Offensive," *Huffington Post*, October 20, 2009, archived at http://huff.to/3IridX.

8
Friend

These bits of profiles, studies of persons, were often meant to introduce the American reader to the contestations over public memory and the ways in which pasts are continually erased in contemporary Pakistani politics. Such profiles are rarely found in the media, because to generate them, one needs a great amount of familiarity with the subject—and access. Imran Khan (cricketer turned politician), Benazir Bhutto (the assassinated two-time prime minister of Pakistan) and A. Q. Khan (the "father" of nuclear Pakistan), although subjects well known to the American public, retain a different narrative within Pakistan and in vernacular press. This material was my attempt to elucidate that difference.

The Curious Case of Imran Khan[1]
December 9, 2004

Yesterday, I linked to an essay by Imran Khan. Something has bothered me for a while, and I think I will hash it out here. *Why has Imran Khan failed in Pakistani politics?*

Imran Khan, from '85–'95, was Michael Jordan, Wayne Gretzky, and Joe Montana rolled into one. He retired from cricket (after winning the World Cup) and started a project to build a free cancer hospital in Lahore. For this project, he solicited donations, did fund-raisers, and gathered monies from NGOs, all to guarantee that the poor have a world-class facility. I can't even begin to describe the goodwill and cheer he accumulated through his philanthropy.

Then, he decided to enter into politics and established the *Tehrik-e Insaf* [Movement for Justice] to foster an agenda of anticorruption and development. He should have been elected prime minister in under a month. Yet he has struggled to be taken seriously by our politicians or the public. He still makes more news through his personal life than through his political one. He attacked the major parties as being corrupt and exploitative of the public, and that not only cut him out of the immense organizational structure required to engage in local politics but also made him a political pariah. The religious parties had no use for this recent playboy with a *gori* wife. He went through phases of political wranglings and compromises [even doing the *mullah* bit—for like 5 seconds], which destroyed his reputation of being a noncompromising gentleman among thieves.

His party never won any seats to speak of, and he has barely managed to get elected in the few chances he has had. After 9/11, he criticized U.S. foreign policy and has been by-and-large anti United States since the Afghanistan war. If you don't have friends in D.C. and you don't have friends in Riyadh, then you ain't got a chance in Islamabad. His latest move is to lead a XI-strong [a strong team] against The General. He is trying to emerge as the leader of a unified front—akin to the Movement for Restoration of Democracy (MRD) against Zia in '81. The thing is that Mutahida Majlis-e Amal (MMA) is doing the same thing. Chances are that Imran Khan will get sidelined, once again.

So, what does this say about the Pakistani political landscape? Why can't an immensely popular and well-liked individual take a populist platform and still fail to gather any support as a leader? Masses are malleable only to the ones in power? Or is this a unique case? In the absence of any *desire* for change, can Pakistani civil and political society realign itself against The General? Don't I have any shot at becoming the Manmohan Singh of Pakistan?

Free Mukhtar Mai[2]
June 14, 2005

In a bid to present the softer side of Pakistan, The General has restricted all movement of Mukhtar Mai—including any overseas travel. Where Musharraf is promoting the softer side of Pakistan, he does not want to promote the fact that women (like Mai) get gang-raped by community consensus [*panchaiyat* or *jirga*]—when they are not bought, sold, or killed by the same village elders. I don't even want to go into the "tradition" that allows men to barter and kill women for their honor and heritage. May the pox be on their houses.

She is an incredible woman who deserves the honor of her people. In today's *New York Times* op-ed entitled "Raped, Kidnapped and Silenced," Nicholas Kristof has some things to say as well:

> Excuse me, but Ms. Mukhtaran, a symbol of courage and altruism, is the best hope for Pakistan's image. The threat to Pakistan's image comes from President Musharraf for all this thuggish behavior.
>
> I've been sympathetic to Mr. Musharraf till now, despite his nuclear negligence, partly because he's cooperated in the war on terrorism and partly because he has done a good

job nurturing Pakistan's economic growth, which in the long run is probably the best way to fight fundamentalism. So even when Mr. Musharraf denied me visas all this year, to block me from visiting Ms. Mukhtaran again and writing a follow-up column, I bit my tongue.

But now President Musharraf has gone nuts.[3]

No. He hasn't gone nuts. He is doing what dictators do. Manage public relations. The best way to combat him is to spin this out of his hand. Send him a note. Write about this on your blogs. Write a letter to the editor. Go to the rally.

Update, June 15: Looks like the PR spun out of their hands. Salman Masood in the *NYT* reports that Shaukat Aziz ordered the lifting of travel restrictions. Great news.

Update, June 16: Saurav pointed out in the comments that the great news is not so great. BBC is reporting that her passport has not been returned and that she has withdrawn her visa application from the U.S. consulate. Quite a bad sign. Please do spread the word.

Update, June 17: June 15 press briefing from the Department of State. Mukhtar Mai has an open invitation from the United States now. Whereabouts of her passport are still unknown. I am guessing that it will be found as soon as The General gets back into town. Such a bad, bad PR move.

Update, June 18: There goes my hope that this was done by *chamchas* [cronies]. Looks like The General is making his stand.

> Musharraf said Mukhtar Mai, whose rape was ordered to punish her family for her brother's alleged affair with a woman from another family, was being taken to the United States by foreign nongovernment organizations "to bad-mouth Pakistan" over the "terrible state" of the nation's women. "She was told not to go" to the United States to appear on media there to tell her story, Musharraf told the Auckland Foreign Correspondents' Club. He said NGOs are "Westernized fringe elements," which "are as bad as the Islamic extremists."[While responding to media questions during a 3-day visit to New Zealand,] Musharraf acknowledged placing the 36-year-old on the list of people banned from leaving Pakistan.[4]

Update, June 19: Kristof has a follow-up op-ed titled "A Free Woman."[5] Nitin provides a full summary of opinion coverage. Also, do see KO's excellent post.

Update, June 21: After listening to a Rare Broadcast interview with Mukhtar Mai, it appears certain that she won't be traveling to the United States anytime soon. Meantime, there is no pressure on Islamabad, and The General is convinced that Pakistan's image got a boost from his trip to New Zealand. Saurav wrote in to remind all that there is a press conference tomorrow.

The Rosa Parks Effect[6]
June 27, 2005

Today, Mukhtar Mai appeared in front of the Supreme Court (SC) to plead the case against her rapists. Here is a very good timeline of her case[7]—including the news that her passport has been returned to her. The central decision before the SC is whether the Federal Shari'at Court (FSC) or the Lahore High Court (LHC) has juridical rights over her case. The FSC condemned six men to death for their role in her gang-rape. The LHC releases the men for lack of "substantial evidence." It is up to the SC to decide if the special-powers FSC or the civil LHC has the right to this case. The very legitimate fear is that the SC may uphold the LHC decision, and these horrid men will escape justice. We will find out tomorrow.

In Pakistan, stories of rapes and *karokari* [honor killings] blend into the cacophony of violence in the daily newspapers. They were chockfull of daughters shot, burned, or hacked to pieces by fathers, uncles, brothers, and husbands in the name of *ghairat* or *izzat* [pride or honor]—cognates of moral honor that depend on a particularly patriarchal understanding of *shame*, with nary an effort to stop and rudimentary condemnation of these abhorrent acts. Rapes are reported as brief news items. Honor killings sometimes get front-page coverage—mainly for their sensationalism—but the overall response stays the same: Honor defines independent men. The woman's body is the locus of a family's honor. It is up to the woman to protect this honor and should she fail—by getting raped or falling in love with someone else or speaking out against domestic abuse, e.g.—the men have the right to seek redress. Along with this honor comes the code of silence. Crimes against women, however unfortunate, are an understandable response from the males and should be left uncommented. The silence of outrage is mirrored in the silence of the victim. Shame dictates that a family silence their dishonor. The easiest way to accomplish this, of course, is for the victim to kill herself. The family and the community exorcize even the memory of the victim. No one remembers, except for those who committed the heinous act and those who used it as an instrument of their power. By staying out of the domain of "honor" and "shame," the state facilitates this. The lack of a police report is, in the end, the most harmful silence of all.

I will put the obvious disclaimer that this is not a situation peculiar to Pakistan or Islam or to this particular moment in history. Domestic violence or honor killings are not a culturally unique phenomenon, but they *are* a uniquely patriarchal one. One can easily find instances from Milan to Kentucky, with a layover in Dubai. If there is a difference in the rate of incidence between say, Chicago and Lahore, then it is the rule of law and effort of education that has permitted this equality and protection to women in one case and not the other. In many countries, like Pakistan, women have little recourse in law against such violence and insurmountable normative practices that sustain or encourage it. It is easy enough to start labeling Islam or South Asian/"tribal" culture as the root cause of such violence. But that would be a fundamentally flawed and disingenuous conclusion. The culprit is not Islam or South Asian culture; the culprit, undoubtedly, is the State of Pakistan.

Mukhtar Mai's bravest act is to break this lynchpin of silence. She refused to play her assigned part. It was the *imam* [prayer leader] of the local mosque who first urged the family of Mukhtar Mai to break their silence and go to the police. It was Mukhtar Mai who pressed charges against the men and pursued them in court. Neither did she disappear from the community but used her case and her court award to begin a school for girls in her village. Her act brought serious and critical scrutiny to the plight of honor killings. As a result of internal pressure from NGOs and external attention, Pakistan tightened the law against such killings—but not enough. Still, her bravery has led to mass demonstrations in her honor both inside and outside Pakistan. It has prompted others to seek justice. It has gathered hundreds of thousands of dollars for schools. Her fortitude has, in effect, crystallized a movement for women's rights in Pakistan.

The General and his trusted advisor, Neelofer Bakhtiar, treat this as a PR crisis, but one can see that they are worried. They maintain that the NGOs, in service to the international media, have trumped her up as a cause célèbre. They should be very worried. The one thing a dictatorship cannot survive is scrutiny. The other thing a dictatorship cannot survive is an internal movement for justice. Mukhtar Mai has given her country, forever mired in silences, both of those things.

The SC rules to retry the case. Good news.

Finding His Religion[8]
July 6, 2005

I have wondered about Imran Khan. In that earlier post, I quipped that he flirted with mullahs for 5 seconds. Since that post, Khan has garnered a lot of attention for his "role" in the *Newsweek*-Qur'an story . . . and accusations that his "flirting" is more than that and that he is a new strain of militant Islam. *Newsweek*, and others, pointed that it was Imran Khan who lit the spark leading to riots, etc., and that he did so for his own political purposes.

Since then, the international media has decided to take a closer look at Imran Khan. In a *Washington Post* piece, John Lancaster describes the evolution of the playboy cricketer into a political player.[9] In the piece Khan credits a Lahori mystic for his awakening to the public cause. To the critique of opportunism in his alliance with Mutahida Majlis-e Amal, he responds that it is all to keep the heat on The General. The *Daily Times* lashed out pretty harshly against the story—branding him a man crazed by mystics and used by mullahs.

In a recent interview with *American Free Press*'s Danny Kemp, Imran Khan responded to the accusation that it was his role in the *Newsweek* story that caused violence:

> "I didn't read it in Newsweek, people were calling me up. . . . Everyone now approaches me in Pakistan, they don't approach the political parties, because they are afraid to deal with such issues," he says. "Whatever kind of Muslim you are, it's the most hurtful thing you can do and to make it out as if it's the reaction of extremists is wrong," he adds. "The US are losing the war for hearts and minds. Abu Ghraib, Guantanamo, desecration of the Koran. They will create more terrorists."
>
> Khan sternly rejects suggestions that he brought up the Koran allegations to further his career. "I think that for people like me who understand both the west and Islam, it's very important for me to speak out. "If it happens again I will speak out against it."[10]

I must admit that I am still ambivalent about him. If he has spirituality or a sufi guide, that does not make him a toady for Fazlur Rahman. In fact, Rahman would frown mightily upon such mystical guidance. The key graf is later in the same story:

> His opponents—and some of his supporters—have criticised him for lacking vision about whether he wants Pakistan to be secular or Islamic, pro or anti-West, conservative or liberal. They say Khan has also wavered in his political dealings, backing Musharraf before turning on him as an American stooge, and then aligning himself with the religious right. Rubbish, says Khan, insisting his ideals are "completely coherent," focusing on *the rule of law, democracy and education in a country that is conspicuously short of all three. [emphasis added]*

Imran Khan may or may not be an opportunist. If he is, he is really bad at it. His spirituality is also his business. He remains, on the balance, a marginal figure. What does matter is that he is someone who continues to get headlines for criticizing The General. That puts him in my good book. Maybe my judgment is clouded because I am sympathetic to his social causes as well. Perhaps his calls against The General are self-serving and whatnot. I don't care. My demand is for more democracy in Pakistan—not for uniquely honest politicians.

Hrant Dink[11]
January 19, 2007

Hrant Dink, editor of *Agos*, was killed in Istanbul. Dink had been convicted by the Turkish government and given a suspended sentence in October 2005 for "insulting Turkishness." His "crimes" were an article in *Agos* and remarks after a conference wherein he reflected on being Armenian and being Turkish. You can read a summary of charges against him here.[12] If you want to know more about the background—the Turkish-Armenian strife—you can read this.[13]

Dink is not the first, nor sadly the last, of those who give their lives for the truths they hold. May he rest in peace, and may justice prevail.

DJinnah[14]
March 1, 2007

I admit that I have never been a big fan of Quaid-e Azam Muhammad Ali Jinnah. As a member of the "Generation Islam" of General Zia-ul-Haq, I have more than a passing familiarity with Jinnah's hagiography. In the fifth grade, we read essays on how he studied after dark (he used the street light!) and were asked to respond (amazing!!). In the eighth grade, we admired Jinnah's unwavering commitment to Pakistan (he was against it before he was for it!). On his birthday, we lined the streets with flowers and watched our military junta pass by. Every telecast started with *Quaid-e Azam nay Farmiya* (Quaid-e Azam said:) and some quotable quote ("Work, work, and work"). My uncle had a well-worn quip every single time: *Quaid-e Azam nay farmiya, tu chal tey main aiya* (the Punjabi speakers will get it). And so it went.

Despite the mounted portraits in every room, the newspaper articles, the speeches, the textbooks, Jinnah remained an aloof, cold patriarch for the nation of Pakistan. His fossilized and ubiquitous memory (honest, dedicated, principled, etc.) harbored very few counter-narratives. Sometimes, I would hear faint complaints about Jinnah's love for the single malt. Or questions were raised about his love for Western attire. Sometimes, even, someone would raise that highest level of critique—Quaid-e Azam Muhammad Ali Jinnah contradicted himself—though, only in a whisper.

Things have changed since the '80s, though. The nationalist hagiography has been countered by historians, such as Ayesha Jalal (the Sole Spokesman) and

Faisal Devji (forthcoming), who present a much more conflicted and uncertain leader. The State's attempt at a popular revival even floundered. A movie was commissioned by the Government under the script guidance of academics and funding by well-wishers. Naturally, the result was a truly bizarre hodgepodge of glorification and self-righteous indignation. It received a tepid response, and the State was roundly criticized for it. You can watch a music video from the movie and marvel.[15]

Since The General's ascension, the "Heroes of Pakistan" focus has shifted towards the more brazenly militant ones and the earlier generation's focus on Jinnah and Iqbal has softened considerably. Just recently, the religious party Jamaat Ulama-i Islam decided that Jinnah was no freedom fighter, because "he did nothing for Islam and Pakistan, made no sacrifice, and never went to jail." Such a public stance would have been unheard of at any previous time. This statement did receive public condemnation, and the sentiment is in no way universal—another religious party, Jamaat-e Islami, maintains a healthy respect for the Quaid—but one can begin to see another shift in the self-definition of the State of Pakistan. While Jinnah remains a restless specter in the house of Pakistan, how long before talk of exorcisms begin?

Examining the final collection of speakers for our recently held colloquium on the All India Muslim League, I realized that no one was going to speak on the Greatest Leader of the Nation. It was almost unthinkable that we would have a full day of discussions and presentations without any attention paid to him (at that moment, I was not privy to the content of Naim Sahib's keynote—which does address Jinnah's 1946 speech). And then, true inspiration struck—*CM* friend, and artist-in-residence, lapata divulged that she had done a series on Jinnah. With the extraordinary help of our dear friend Ms. Neilson, the art was framed and exhibited in the room for the colloquium. . . .

The installation was a huge success. It garnered amazing responses from everyone in the room—especially, Jinnah with Monocole and Jinnah and his sister Fatima. I overheard delightful conversations about the choice of colors and whether they reflected the perceived character of Jinnah: *Was Jinnah really blue?*[16] One distinguished guest was concerned that the artwork appeared to present a "demonic" side of Jinnah. "Is it painted by a Pakistani artist?" he asked. "Because, if it is by a Pakistani, then it is okay. If an Indian did that, it is highly inappropriate." I assured him that the art reflected the highest respect towards the nation of Pakistan. "Well, you are a Pakistani. So, I will let you be the judge," he demurred.

Well.

The Return of the Native[17]

October 18, 2007

I was going to say something but the . . .

Breaking News	Two blasts near the motorcade of former Pakistani Prime Minister Benazir Bhutto kill at least 30, officials say. Bhutto not reported hurt.

She was on her way to Jinnah's tomb. Happened around 12:15 local, over 125 dead, over 540 injured. Went off near a few police vans and PPP security cars. Benazir Bhutto was riding in a fortified, bullet-proof truck. That may have saved her life.

The twin blasts were staggered by less than a minute. GeoTV is reporting that it seemed like the combination of a suicide bomber and a car bomb. Reuters has documentation of the carnage and destruction.

There were more than a few direct threats against her.

The city has shut down. Police and rangers have closed down major ports.

The GeoTV anchor just called it *Qiyamat-i Sughra*—the Lesser Apocalypse.

Karachi Metblog has reports from the city.

Becoming Bibi[18]

October 29, 2007

Benazir Bhutto has always been less than the sum of her parts—ah, but what spectacular parts! Just go look at this amazing series on Benazir done by *CM* Chief Artist-in-Residence lapata.[19]

Perhaps no memory of my childhood in the '80s can compare to her triumphant return to Zia's Pakistan—the mantle of the anointed rested easily on her back then—all eager to be the "Daughter of the East," righteously claiming a spot at the head of the table. Sure, she had a few religious detractors, but she stopped shaking hands in public and got that *dupatta* [shawl] aligned just right and married a suitable *zamindar* [landlord]. It almost seemed like the cult of her father's personality would rub off on her. But then the reality of a neophyte outsider mired in corruption and nepotism truly blossomed on the Pakistani people, and she lost her luster. Also her seats in power. Her latest return, greeted by violence, does not lend itself to nostalgia that easily, but it continues the story of her reinventions.

In all, she has had sporadic success with trying to be a carrier of her father's legacy for the millions of Pakistan Peoples Party (PPP) followers, trying to convince the West of her liberalizing leanings, trying to convince the *mullahs* that she is not an apostate, etc. However, to my casual eye, there is only one public persona that Bibi has truly excelled at—and I do not mean this in any snarky manner—and that is the persona of a martyr's griever. One can easily psychoanalyze that to her executed father, whose ghost continues to haunt Pakistan, or her dead brothers, or the hundreds of victims of violence in the last 20 years exalted by the PPP. . . .

Benazir Bhutto, 1953–2007[20]
December 27, 2007

Benazir Bhutto was killed at a Pakistan Peoples Party (PPP) rally in Rawalpindi. At least 15 others are being reported dead in the attack. The election rally, with "foolproof security," was held at Liaqut Bagha site that had already seen the assassination of another prime minister of Pakistan, Liaqut Ali Khan.

There were earlier reports of security threats on her rally—similar reports were issued before the suicide attack on her in October.

In the nation whose history is dotted by military coups, assassinations, and hangings of public figures, this is surely the bloodiest stain. She titled her autobiography *The Daughter of Destiny*—but surely she deserved a fate other than the destiny of her father and Liaqut Ali Khan. It is truly a tragedy and a revelation of the chaos gripping the nation.

Aftermath: Riots are being reported in various cities. Rawalpindi is in chaos. Cable and cell phone services have been suspended in most of the country. Rumors are flying of curfews. No word from Musharraf yet . . . .

A rather disturbingly condescending obituary from the *New York Times*.[21] She had "grand ambition," "considerable charm," and engaged in a "dance of veils." How *Salomé* of her. I also like how she is humanized for the American readers by a scant connection to an American diplomat . . . .

Strange: The *NYT* has changed their obituary—"Benazir Bhutto, 54, Weathered Political Storm," by John Burns.[22] But get this, the earlier obituary written by Jane Perlez and Victoria Burnett has been amended to remove references to "veils" and "world's first prime leader" to "first female leader." How odd. . . .

The Benazir They Knew[23]
January 1, 2008

Once again, sitting here, I find myself instinctively examining the media coverage since December 27. Just like the JFK-inspired, home-brewed ways in which her assassination was discussed, these recent pieces all highlight some *personal* connection to Bibi, while offering their analysis. There is never a hint of any legislative or political legacy, any economic or social accomplishment. She is being remembered for who she was.

David Ignatius, "The Legacy of Benazir Bhutto," *Washington Post*: "I saw this effervescent woman many times over subsequent years, and I never lost the sense of her as an impetuous person embracing what was new."[24]

Robert Novak, "What Bhutto Was Worried About," *Washington Post*: "When I last saw Bhutto, over coffee in August at Manhattan's Pierre Hotel, she was deeply concerned."[25]

Peter Galbraith, "My Friend Died. Now Her Country May Not Make It," *Washington Post*: "I was her guest at her family home in Larkana."[26]

Ian Jack, "Born to Rule," *Guardian*: "Once I asked her if she had ever danced. 'No.' Never? 'No.'"[27]

(And this last link—not easily categorized—I cannot offer without a firm statement: Do *not* click on the author's website.)

Daphne Barak, "How Benazir Let Her Hair Down," *Daily Mail*: "We discussed girlie subjects alone and when men were present."[28]

Two exceptions—though with problems of their own.

William Dalrymple, who attempts to tie her government and her legacy to the broader socio-political phenomena: "Pakistan's Flawed and Feudal Princess," *Guardian*: "But there was something much more majestic, even imperial, about the Benazir I met."[29]

Mohammed Hanif, who provides the view from a Pakistani supporter: "How a 'Wisp of a Girl' Conquered Pakistan," *New York Times*: "I last saw her in a London flat. . . ."[30]

As I have been reading all these essays (Boy, did she have a sweet tooth!), I am struck by how utterly *unrelatable* she is deemed to appear to the vast majority of Pakistanis. Besides the most basic facts (a Pakistani-born Muslim woman), her biography is read again and again as being utterly foreign from her nation. To each of the writers above, specifically Dalrymple, she appears detached, removed, distinct, and incomprehensible to the lower or middle class. Yet those were the very classes that provided the bulwark support for her since 1985. The explanations are probably just as banal as explaining the appeal of Paris Hilton for middle Americans or of Billy Graham for political leaders, but maybe there is a lot more to it.

I know that my background (middle-class Punjabi/Kashmiri Lahori) didn't really allow a teenager to hang out with political royalty, and the best I can claim is attendance at a couple of rallies and one talk (and they call me a South Asia expert). But, perhaps, one can learn something from my own encounters with Benazir Bhutto.

1988

The elections were scheduled for November, and everyone expected Benazir's Pakistan Peoples Party (PPP) to win. She had returned home just two years earlier—April 1986—and Lahore had came out—in millions. Since then, my friends, their families, shopkeepers, slowly revealed their true colors—red, black, and green. "You support PPP too?" I would ask with an incredulous face. The biggest surprise came a month or so before the elections. Billa was the opening fast bowler for our cricket team—and hence, a person of some standing in the community. One afternoon, we were changing into our kits behind the peepal tree when I spied hundreds of tiny *Elect Chaudhry Aitzaz Ahsan* flags in his kit bag. "Are you working for the party?" He shrugged. When not bowling medium pace deliveries, but with a killer yorker in his arsenal, Billa was a "compoder" (a homegrown pharmacist) in a local doctor's shop. I had never seen him express any interest in anything besides cricket and girls. "I am going to start working for them. They pay a full *dehyari* [a day's wage], and all I have to do is put up the Arrows and take down the Bicycle." The Arrow and the Bicycle were the election symbols for PPP, led by the 35-year-old Benazir Bhutto, and the Islami Jamhoori Iteehad (IJI), led by Nawaz Sharif and Ijaz-ul-Haq, respectively. "Can I come with you when you do this neighborhood?" He didn't look all too pleased. "Okay, can you at least take me to a rally?" He never took me to the rally. Also, we lost that game. I did see Chaudhry Aitzaz Ahsan speak a couple of times.

Instead, it was another coincidence that landed me at an IJI rally near Lahore's center. I had boarded a bus going to the Mall, but IJI supporters stopped the bus and booked the driver and his vehicle for the day ferrying supporters to the rally. I figured that since I would get literally a front-row view of Nawaz Sharif, I stayed on the bus. Nawaz Sharif, an industrialist and a Lahori, was the hand-picked protégé of General Zia-ul-Haq. I had heard he told great jokes at his rally. The warm-up acts over, Ijaz-ul-Haq (son of Zia-ul-Haq) took the mic and started on a long, sexually explicit, deconstruction of Bibi's dress code. He spoke in *thaith* Punjabi and didn't even pause to hear the response to his crude one-liners. The rallying slogans, as well, turned menacingly violent. I started to make my way out of the throngs, when Nawaz Sharif took over. He began by saying that he had intelligence that Benazir was a Russian agent working with the CIA. Right.

A few days later, I was sitting with Reza, whose father was a civil bureaucrat of some high order. "You folks supporting Aitzaz Ahsan?" "I hate him, and my dad hates him. He is holding up meetings in his house, and the whole street is totally filled with stupid *jayalas* [stalwart PPP workers]." In hindsight, it is easy to figure out why a high-ranking civil servant would be wary of a PPP regime. I wasn't all that observant back then. "Well, I think it is great that we will have a woman prime minister." I tried to offer some reasons. "I heard she went to Harvard." I failed to impress him.

Bibi won the elections and became prime minister. She even had some help from the religious right—who held up the example of Ayesha (the Prophet's wife), who led a military campaign. (That it was against Ali was an irony left unexpounded.) There was an enormous amount of enthusiasm—for democracy, for breathing anew, for elections. Our neighborhood was promised paved streets and working sewage. Office holders of the local PPP chapter were sudden celebrities, and everyone wanted to take the civil service exam or get a government job. No more dreams of a military career for your middle-class son.

1996

My first trip back to Pakistan since having left in the early nineties was hard. Things were in really bad shape. There was a strange malaise. Billa, now a *jayala* [die-hard supporter], had nothing good to say about Bibi or about Pakistan. Surprisingly, he had failed to open for Pakistan International XI (the fact that he was barely 5 feet 6 inches may have had something to do with it), and his attempt to open up his own (fake) medical practice had failed dramatically at the hands of my mother. Bibi was in her second term. And the one refrain on everyone's lips: corruption. Uncles told stories of jobs taken and given to upper-level PPP supporters, people murdered for refusing to sell their property, examinations rigged, custom tariffs exploited, businesses and factories seized, immensely extravagant system of bribery codified as government practice.

We went to Shahi Qilla. Wandering around the elephant pathways, I noticed a door-shaped hole torn into the side of Sheesh Mahal. I immediately launched into a tirade over the lack of appreciation for our historical and cultural sites, but I was stopped short. "Zardari took it." "Say what?" "Well, apparently, his 10 percent of all business transactions in the country includes taking 10 percent of cool shit from historical sites." "What would he do with a 16th-century door???" "Living room decoration," they offered. I later found that the problem was far greater than that. The museums at Lahore, Taxila, and Harapa had all lost valuable artifacts to the powers-that-be. There was, of course, the usual trickle-down effect. My aunts were busy buying old doors and windows for their own houses. Retro was in.

2002

Benazir Bhutto came to speak at the University of Chicago. She defended herself against corruption ("I don't know the details of my husband's businesses, but they are all legal"). She offered that back in 1996, her government was disbanded because of Islamist threats—specifically from Osama bin Laden. He had tried to kill her, repeatedly, she claimed. It was a strange sight when the audience gave her a standing ovation. Here was a brave, secular, woman who had fought the evil and lived to tell the tale.

No questions were allowed, and so no one asked about her government's dealings with those Islamists.

I left utterly disgusted. She was pandering in the worst possible way, I thought. But, even so, I figured that at least she was providing a nonmilitary face to the American public. I had really wanted to hear her take questions. I had really wanted to see her responses.

In retrospect, what I really wanted was a democratic Bhutto. The middle class (or the lower class) in Pakistan withdrew from PPP, because those heady promises of 1988 were followed only by a deafening silence—no social progress, no economic progress happened on her watch. The past 8 years of Musharraf highlighted how removed she was from public discourse in Pakistan. The archives of the *Daily Jang* or *Dawn* or *Nawa-i Waqt* carry little about her, or by her, outside of the court cases against her and her husband. There is no commentary about her legacy or her ideologies—a reflection of how little she advanced the ideological thrust of her father.

Note this, from the Hanif piece:

> Not just any ordinary privileged heir to a political dynasty, but a girl half the nation swooned over; a sharp political operator, a speaker who even in her stilted Urdu could have a million people dance to the wave of her hand. And she was not a revolutionary by a long shot—but she could bring people to her rallies, and more important, polling stations by promising them jobs and reasonable electricity bills.
>
> On Thursday a heartbroken Bhutto-lover called and left a teary message on my voice mail. He just wanted to share his grief, but reminded me of something else: "She might have lost her political battle, but look at it this way. She raised three kids, took care of an ailing mother and still managed to stay in South Asia's most notorious arranged marriage."

In the end, she was popular because she was Bhutto. And, hence, her loss is felt—and memorialized—as the loss of a person, not a leader.

May she rest in peace.

The A. Q. Khan Corner I[31]
November 12, 2008

Pakistan's nuclear godfather has suddenly emerged from seclusion (involuntary) and penned a risible column for the *Daily Jang*.[32] It is notable, this column, for his self-aggrandizing, self-importance, and self-service. Keeping to the tradition, he sprinkles the column with bits of Urdu poetry (though not the tired old morsels) and frames himself as a "just a worker." And then he launches into a tirade against Musharraf as well as a glorification of the Bhutto family. I thought that the greater English-speaking world would want a peek into the mind of A. Q. Khan, so I translated it. Enjoy:

'Til The Dawn
—Dr. Abdul Qadeer Khan

Why ask me the cause of my silence?
There must be some reason why I remain quiet

In 1961, I was about to embark, for higher education, to the most acclaimed technical university in Berlin. I thought that I should inform the Pakistani public, especially the students, about the conditions in Germany. In those days, the office of the *Daily Jang* was on Karachi Business Road. During college (D. J. Sindh Government Science College), I would routinely walk by the office. So I went in to meet Mir Khalil al-Rahman Sahib and seek his advice. At that time, Taki Sahib was the editor, and he immediately arranged for me to meet Mir Sahib. I had heard of him, and now I knew him in person. Mir Sahib was a handsome, tall man with a commanding personality, and his intelligence was reflected in his broad forehead. He met me with great affection. He was very keen on my idea and told me to certainly keep the readers of *Jang* informed from Berlin. And thus, I left for Germany. Berlin, in those days, was the playing field for the political conflict between East and West. Only 10 days earlier, East Berlin (i.e., the Eastern Communist Germany) had erected the Wall. Innumerable Germans were running from the Communists towards West Berlin, and many were dying from the bullets of VOPOS (i.e., the East Berlin militia). In the skies, the Russian MiG fighters were daily breaking the sound barriers over the city. My hostel was roughly 15 minutes away from the Brandenburg Gate and near the Victory Column.

From there, I began to send reports to *Daily Jang* under the heading "Letters from Berlin"—which were regularly published. This continued for 2 years. In the pages of *Jang* I predicted that the mayor of Berlin, Willy Brandt, would one day become the Chancellor of Germany. And indeed, in a few years, he did. In late 1963, I shifted from Berlin to the famous technical university in Holland and stopped writing "Letters from Berlin."

Due to current affairs, I thought, why not indulge my disposition and write once again on the important matters of the country? I have always held a fondness for writing, and if there is anything important, I do write. The habit is. . . .

I cannot break this pagan habit . . .

Which is not to say that the public remains unaware of my thoughts and my emotions:

I sit quietly, but it appears
as if the whole world is telling my story

No doubt, whenever someone begins to write for the newspapers, the public tries to decipher the intent or the cause:

You may or may not be suspicious, but we

Just gain comfort from telling our painful story

We all know that Good and Evil will always battle in this world. Almighty Allah has warned us of this repeatedly in the Qur'an and declared, "Allah, protect me from the evil of the evil doers and the oppressors." Some selfish and oppressive people, purely for the sake of their self-interest, trample the rights of the people under their feet. Drunk with power, they even, God forbid, deny the existence of God and his Might. The example of Musharraf is in front of you:

In every age, humans have done evil

In every age, humans have tried to become gods

But, God forbid, the haughtiness of being a god does not make one a god. Even if such people forget entirely about God:

The oppressors now think

As if there is no god left in the world

Our bureaucracy and sycophants play a large role in making these false gods into God. Musharraf is F.A. pass [high-school equivalent], a qualification that we use to employ attendants. By a mistaken promotion, he became our commander-in-chief. It nauseated us to see such a dimwit lecture the highly educated and the experts on economics, education, foreign policy, commerce, and industry. And they would bow in front of him and wag their heads and exclaim at his intelligence. The way of an intelligent ruler (or dictator) is that he doesn't choose his companions on the basis of their flattery but on the basis of their expertise and their knowledge; he listens to their advice; and gives them all the help for the completion of important projects. There was this rumor going around about Musharraf that he complains to his army friends, "I am saddened to see that if uneducated people cannot understand my arguments, it is okay, but even educated people cannot follow me." The reason is obvious. The ability to pull the trigger of a gun and the ability to make an intelligent statement are clearly different.

Selfish and opportunist people mix heaven and Earth in false praise of such rulers and make them into Plato. These are the people, who because of such actions, weaken the foundations of the country. These people operate like Hitler and his minister of propaganda and say so many falsehoods that the ruler begins to believe them to be true and begins to consider himself intelligent. The results appear in the destruction of the country. Such was a lie spoken by Mujib ur-Rahman that the money derived from Jute sales, West Pakistan, is paving streets with gold in Karachi. It was such a big lie, it was immediately accepted.

I returned to Pakistan in the fourth week of December. This was in 1975 (i.e., nearly 33 years ago). I had returned at the request of Bhutto Sahib. Along with my wife and two daughters (ages 7 and 5½ years), I had intended to return on January 15. At the sincere request of Bhutto, and for the benefit of the country, I did not hesitate for even a moment: I left the best career, big income, and excellent facilities and stayed behind. I did not receive first salary, 3,000 rupees monthly, until 6 months later. And no other compensation from the State:

Strange is God's grant to the exalted ones

Strange are these people, who bear sorrows but keep their hearts alive

Some of the most prominent expert scientists of the country spread falsehoods in the ears of Bhutto Sahib and Ghulam Ishaq Sahib, that this young ruffian is here to make a fool out of you. He will enjoy himself for a few days and then take his leave. They explained the intricacies of the technology and the difficulties and that only three developed countries of the world (i.e., Holland, Germany, and England) have the necessary expertise—an expertise they gained after 20 years of hard work and after the expenditure of nearly $2 billion. Bhutto Sahib and Ghlam Ishaq Khan Sahib possessed the power to see the hidden truths. They had no doubts over my capacity for the truth and knew that I had not said a false word to them. Even though some people told me to declare that we will have an atomic bomb in 2 or 3 years.

I refused to tell a lie. They may have used this lie as a basis of their foreign policy and been defeated, as a result. And then some famous scientists decided that they could put some two or three thousand tons of explosive materials in some cave and then explode it and Bhutto Sahib will be satisfied and his obsession will be over. Listen. If politicians tell lies, than it is their profession, and they can, without any shame, practice their profession in front of the general simple-minded public. But it is incumbent on us scientists and engineers to always keep our profession and our conscience in mind and speak only the truth. I have always operated on this principle and never told a lie:

Truthful I am, in my word, O Ghalib God is my witness

I tell the truth when I say, I don't lie

The gist is that with the help of my colleagues, I made the impossible, possible. In only 8 short years, and for a minuscule cost, I made this depressed nation into a nuclear power. Bhutto Sahib, Ghulam Ishaq Khan, and General Zia-ul-Haq helped without fear and without regret. Any task undertaken with good intentions and with true hard work is rewarded by Allah. With the help of Honorable Benazir Bhutto, this country became a missile power. At my request, she granted me permission to seek missile technology from China and North Korea and install it here. In this, General Mirza Aslam Beg and General Abdul Wahid Kakar played key roles. It is worth thinking that even as countless selfish, bribery-prone traitors were busy tearing the country apart like hungry wolves, there remained some honest, pious, and skilled people who sacrificed their lives to keep this country on the slow path of progress. With the help of such people, by God's Will, we will make our country into a developed, welfare-based Islamic state.

I have spent the majority of my life, nearly all of my life. When I look back at my life, it is with peace and contentment, that I did my utmost to serve my dear country. I did not do any favors for my country. Instead, it is this nation that granted me all these favors, which I tried to pay back—piece by piece. I gained higher education and technical excellence in Europe for 15 years, and I wanted to use that to serve the country in important matters. In 1999, I proposed that we launch a satellite, but this high-school pass dictator did not approve my request. Still, I am proud of my service to my country. In addition to providing it with nuclear and missile power, I founded countless educational and welfare organizations. From Khyber to Gawadar, the love that exists in people's hearts is my greatest prize. One despicable, traitorous foreign agent donned the costume of presidency and tried to harm me, but he failed in his dirty deed. Instead he, himself, was evicted from the presidential house in disgrace. And now this self-styled commando cannot even set a foot in the street of this country. The public will tear him into little pieces and feed him to the eagles. My relationship is with the 170 million people, and it will always remain. No one can stop me from serving this country. We have, in our front, the golden examples of the sacrifices of Honorable Zulfiqar Ali Bhutto and Benazir Bhutto. They gave their lives but did not sell their country and became living legends. This is the reason that in "'Til the Dawn," I will reveal my thoughts, now and then:

The flame burns in every light, 'til the dawn

My thanks to Naim Sahib for bringing the column to my attention. And my apologies to him, if I messed up the translation. . . .

Imran Khan, Considered[33]
December 4, 2009

In the *Review*, I have a review of Christopher Sanford's *Imran Khan* in which I briefly consider the man. Below is what didn't make it into the review—for fairly obvious reasons—but, I thought I'd spin it here. No pun:

Much has been written on Imran Khan's transcendence from the game of cricket, but little justice has been done to his game itself. Sandford, as well, finds it hard to capture any sense of the player, even as he pays exquisitely detailed attention to life and politics on and off the field. Before we turn to all those enticing issues away from the game, let us linger, for a moment, on the game itself. Imran Khan was one of the smartest cricketers. His greatest strength as fast bowler was that he was a true batsman. He knew how to think as a batsman, which meant he made sure that the batsman played every ball he hurled at them. Consider that in his entire ODI career, he bowled 216 overs with only 18 maidens. Now most would read this as sign that he was easy to score against, but his economy rate of 3.7 runs conceded per over belies that supposition. Simply put, he bowled at the batsman. This quality, above all, not only contributed to him being one of the highest wicket takers during his career, but it ensured that his co-bowlers consistently picked up a higher percentage of wickets.

As a batsman, he had a high arch to his bat and a tendency to commit to the front foot often and early. He wasn't too orthodox in his shot selection yet had an enviably straight bat. He was also one of the best players of the short ball (a much-needed skill, since his own tendency to bowl short balls guaranteed reprisals). His hooks and pulls were always a joy to watch, and he rarely succumbed to the third-man trap.

In the field, he wasn't the swiftest or the surest. As a true embodiment of "gentleman's game," he rarely flung himself at the speeding ball. Still, he had safe hands and rarely dropped a catch. But from his long-off perch, he managed the entire field as a seasoned sea captain coordinates the crew—constantly shifting the field, swapping players, speaking with the bowler. His fields were always dynamic organisms, drawing in and out in sync with every ball that sped towards the bat.

This last was his particular strength as a captain. Unlike other team sports, the cricket captain has to act both as the heart and the mind for the team. When on field—which was the only place some of us could witness him in action—Imran Khan was a hybrid conductor and a puppeteer.

He orchestrated every movement of the other ten men on the field. He was quick with a scold as with a pat, and always in complete control. Not for nothing that Imran Khan, as the captain, was often called "the dictator."

Ghost Wars[34]
Published in the *National* (Abu Dhabi) April 16, 2010

"Pakistan was an ever-present ghost in our house. As was Zia. And Zulfikar. And Shah Nawaz. My father and I carried invisible baggage with us, both loved and feared," Fatima Bhutto writes in *Songs of Blood and Sword*. General Zia-ul-Haq was the dictator who put to death Pakistan's first elected prime minister—and Fatima's grandfather—Zulfikar Ali Bhutto in 1979. His son Shah Nawaz was found dead in Paris in 1986. Their ghosts have since been joined by those of Fatima's father, Mir Murtaza Bhutto, killed on the street in front of his home in 1996, and his sister Benazir, assassinated in 2007.

As a young woman, Fatima witnesses the violent and unnatural deaths of her dear uncle and her father. She hears whispers that her own aunt was involved—directly or indirectly—in those deaths. She grows up with the sadness of a family cleaved into factions. She writes to remember, she writes to accuse, she writes to explain. At the heart of this memoir lies the pain of a deep loss. She notes her father's perfume, his laugh, his humour and joy at living, his previous loves, his undergraduate thesis, his college friends, the music he loved, the revolutionaries he admired, the places he lived, and people he met. It is an exhaustive remembrance told reverentially, lovingly, and at times clumsily—and all the more touching as a result. She writes that she hoped, through this book, to make "my peace with my father . . . finally honouring my last promise to him—to tell his story—and then, to finally say goodbye."

Her project is a recuperative one: She wants to rescue the memory of her father, Murtaza, and to claim for him the status of a nation's saviour. She wants to tear away the skein of hagiography that now covers the memory of Benazir Bhutto, to expose her corruption, her culpability, her blind ambition. Above all, she wants to unburden herself of the sorrow of losing her father at the age of 14.

None should deny Fatima Bhutto the right to remember her loss—but that is not all this memoir aspires to. In her preface, she casts a familiar picture of Pakistan aflame, devastated from outside by drones and missiles, plundered from within by cronies and corruptions: "How have we come to this state of affairs?" she asks.

This book is her answer. But it is a simplistic, uncritical, and benighted one.

The Bhuttos, landed elite from Sindh, can claim a long and checkered history of entanglements with power—first the British colonial administration, then the new postcolonial state. Among "Sindh's largest landowners," they exerted great influence, controlling and directing hundreds of thousands of rural families. Fatima does not linger long on this early history—except to point out how "debonair," "dashing," "handsome," and "beautiful" everyone was. Her grandfather, Zulfikar Ali, is soon off to Berkeley, California, where someone mistakes him for a Mexican—this awakens in him the spirit of egalitarianism and equity. Or so it is remembered.

Zulfikar Ali's meteoric rise from Sindhi feudal to president of Pakistan is portrayed here either hagiographically or casually: At his better moments, Zulfikar Ali is remembered as being destined for greatness; during his weaker moments, he is the victim of poor advice. The most egregious omissions concern his political response to Bengali demands for equivalence in East Pakistan (which broke away to become Bangladesh after a civil war in 1971); it was the accord between the military regime of General Yahya and Zulfikar Ali's newly founded political party—the Pakistan Peoples Party—to disenfranchise the winning Awami League after the 1970 elections that sparked the conflict that led to Pakistan's repartition. Similarly, Fatima puts a naive and benign spin on Zulfikar Ali's pan-Islamic policies—ignoring the 1973 Constitution that he promulgated, which deliberately set the country on the path toward *shari'a* law, dealt a deadly blow to minority rights, and enabled General Zia-ul-Haq's subsequent Sunnification of Pakistan. Zulfikar Ali's brutal crackdown on Balochistan in 1974 is also excused: Then, he was merely a pawn of the feudals and the army. The voices of his detractors are not entirely absent, but there is no attempt to engage critically with her grandfather's legacy; true culpability always lies elsewhere.

Zulfikar Ali was deposed by General Zia in 1977; in his 1979 prison tract, *If I Am Assassinated*, he wrote, "My sons will not be my sons if they do not drink the blood of those who dare to shed my blood." After his murder in 1979, his sons Mir Murtaza and Shah Nawaz took up his call, launching a self-avowedly violent resistance against General Zia's regime—while sunning themselves in Russian-occupied Kabul. They called it *al Zulfikar* [the Sword], and Mir Murtaza rallied the support of Muammer Qadafi and Hafiz al Assad.

In March 1981, a Pakistan International Airlines flight, PK-326, was hijacked en route to Peshawar from Karachi. It was diverted to Kabul, where Mir Murtaza negotiated with the hijackers to release the women and children. The plane was next taken to Damascus, where it lingered for another week before the hijackers gave up. A *New York Times* story dated April 19, 1981, quotes Mir Murtaza saying that members of his organisation were the hijackers and that it was committed to reacting "brutally" against Zia-ul-Haq's regime. The hijackers murdered a diplomat, Tariq Rahim.

"I feel secretly proud of my father for abandoning the offer of a bland but comfortable exile in London to fight what he believed was an unjust system," Fatima writes. Her pride colours her treatment of this "phase" in her father's life; contrary to his own admission, she describes the hijackers as not having been members of al Zulfikar and says that he never admitted as much. Mir Murtaza, in her depiction, preferred the pen to the Kalashnikov—it was the younger Shah Nawaz who took on the trappings of the proto-Mujahideen.

Where Mir Murtaza does no wrong, Benazir does no right. She hovers around the edges of the text, only surfacing to have another bit of blame pinned on her silenced shoulders. She is held responsible for everything from keeping Fatima away from her father's college friends, to separating her from her cousins, to at least covering up, if not ordering, the murder of Shah Nawaz, to murdering or looking away from the murder of Mir Murtaza. There is little doubt that Benazir's governments were corrupt—and Fatima's summation of the innumerable charges against Benazir and Asif Ali Zardari is masterful. There is also ample evidence that Mir Murtaza's murder was carried out with her approval or sanctioned on her behalf. But these are matters better adjudicated by persons other than the daughter of the deceased: Here, the familial, the personal, the conspiratorial, and the legal are hopelessly indistinguishable.

The three ghosts examined—Zulfikar, Mir Murtaza, and Benazir—we must turn to Pakistan. The book is, after all, geared to an audience looking to understand Pakistan, or have it explained to them, by this telegenic representative of a troubled dynasty.

Songs of Blood and Sword can rightly be seen as the latest in a line of memoirs, like Benazir's *Daughter of the East* and Pervez Musharraf's *In the Line of Fire*—each of them devoted to uncritical presentations of their authors or their families, made to stand in for the history of an entire nation. The tale of the Bhutto dynasty, from its feudal base to its populist claims and now to the stranger-than-fiction stewardship under Zardari (where else in this world can one bequeath a political party in a will?), still deserves to be told—and told properly.

This is not that book, and it should neither be sold nor judged as such: It is merely another primary document for that unwritten history, alongside the papers of her father, grandfather, and aunt, which remain in the family home in Karachi.

In the meantime, however, the book will sell and sell: The author's criticism of Zardari's regime and of his role in her father's murder, her triumphalist Pakistani nationalism and complaints against American imperialism, and her last name are all catnip to the British, American, and South Asian media, which have already lavished considerable coverage on the book prior to its release. Fatima has stayed aloof from politics—and for that she should be commended—but this is only one branch of the family business; the perpetuation of a dynasty requires myth making as much as election victories, and her book, whatever its aims, succeeds only in draping another skein of hagiography around the Bhuttos.

Chapter Notes

1 Archived at http://bit.ly/gzHQvs.

2 Archived at http://bit.ly/hEoRhP.

3 Nicholas D. Kristof, "Raped, Kidnapped and Silenced," *New York Times*, June 14, 2005, archived at http://nyti.ms/jzZ7vZ.

4 "Musharraf Banned Travel by Rape Victim," *Rediff.com*, June 17, 2005, archived at http://bit.ly/ih39JN.

5 Nicholas D. Kristof, "A Free Woman," *New York Times*, June 19, 2005, archived at http://nyti.ms/mot1V7.

6 Archived at http://bit.ly/i1fMyp.

7 "Mukhtar Mai—History of a Rape Case," *BBC News*, June 28, 2005, archived at http://bbc.in/ebHwc1.

8 Archived at http://bit.ly/hopOsL.

9 John Lancaster, "A Pakistani Cricket Star's Political Move," *Washington Post*, July 4, 2005, archived at http://wapo.st/jeTdVO.

10 Danny Kemp, "Imran Khan on Guantanamo, Pakistan and Life after Jemima," *Daily News*, June 24, 2005, archived at http://bit.ly/mTfxUC.

11 Archived at http://bit.ly/dEakQx.

12 "Case of the Month October 2005 Hrant Dink," *English Pen*, archived at http://bit.ly/e2seON.

13 Üstün Bilgen-Reinart, "Hrant Dink: Forging an Armenian Identity in Turkey," *Open Democracy*, February 7, 2006, archived at http://bit.ly/dRbB4Z.

14 Archived at http://bit.ly/h0LzXe.

15 Archived at http://bit.ly/ZzY9z.

16 "Portrait of Jinnah in Blue," archived at http://bit.ly/iDWwTG.

17 Archived at http://bit.ly/exFged.

18 Archived at http://bit.ly/fDsH1B.

19 "The Incomparable Benazir," archived at http://bit.ly/jhSZpP.

20 Archived at http://bit.ly/i9JeYX.

21 Jane Perlez and Victoria Burnett, "Benazir Bhutto, 54, Lived in Eye of Pakistan Storm," *New York Times*, December 28, 2007, archived at http://nyti.ms/f9tmDV.

22 Archived at http://nyti.ms/m9U1h4.

23 Archived at http://bit.ly/hdx8Z4.

24 December 28, 2007, archived at http://wapo.st/m3WvbD.

25 December 31, 2007, archived at http://wapo.st/mowcBf.

26 December 30, 2007, archived at http://wapo.st/ix2wcI.

27 December 29, 2007, archived at http://bit.ly/koRJHh.

28 December 30, 2007, archived at http://bit.ly/lPjSDi.

29 December 30, 2007, archived at http://bit.ly/jib627.

30 December 30, 2007, archived at http://nyti.ms/kQWGPI.

31 Archived at http://bit.ly/dPRqxR.

32 Archived at http://bit.ly/ln7UNS.

33 Archived at http://bit.ly/5XUykT.

34 Archived at http://bit.ly/gQdmgq.

9
Wrong

The plight of the minority communities in Pakistan has been an issue since the early 1950s and is at the heart of the very ideology of this state. Most of the posts in this chapter were written after the terrorist attack on a sectarian mosque (the Ahmadi) in Lahore, which killed nearly a hundred worshippers. These same concerns, about the blasphemy, were behind the assassination of the governor of Punjab in January 2011.

Minority Wrongs[1]
May 27, 2004

Tough day today, I must say. You have Ashcroft's Seven Deadly Agents[2] roaming the streets of United States, you have Abu Hamza in London looking like an evil Captain Hook. And then you have the case of Samuel Masih in Lahore. I found out about it from an editorial in the *Daily Times*:

> A Lahore Christian of unsound mind was accused of blasphemy by the narrow-minded among us and sent to police custody. He was in a lockup when it was discovered that his general health was poor and in fact he could die while in custody. A scared SHO had him examined by a doctor who advised that Samuel Masih was in an advanced stage of tuberculosis. He was at once removed to a hospital. Then the unspeakable happened. The police constable on duty at the hospital "discovered" that Samuel was a blasphemer. He went up to his bed and smashed his head in with a steel bar.[3]

Horrific. The charge of blasphemy is brought by a gentleman who saw him spit on a mosque's wall. *Spit!*

(*Update:* Samuel Masih died from his injuries in the hospital on May 29, 2004.)

Now, the federal Shari'a Court as has only upheld *Hadd* [Islamic capital crimes] decisions in two cases (theft), which were overruled by the Supreme Court. Hence, it is fairly certain that this case will also get dismissed. But what to say about the attack? A misguided sipahi who has been trained at the Pavlovian level to hate Christians and Hindus has no rational ability to judge the veracity or strength of any claim of against the Prophet? He hears only that *Tauheen-i Risalat* [Blasphemy against the Prophet] was committed by someone, and he reacts as he has been conditioned to: with violence.

And blasphemy is not the only sword of Damocles hanging over the Christian community. In another case, Pastor Samuels and his family has been charged under the Shari'a Law for inciting a Muslim woman to marry a Christian. I am not sure about the details of this case, but it involves a Muslim woman who began a love affair with this Christian. A no-no. As the injunctions in Shari'a against a Muslim woman marrying a Christian (or other People of the Book) is much more severe compared to the relative laxity in the case of a Muslim man marrying a Christian woman.

And lest we stray into thinking that the persecution is only against Christians and only in Pakistan, this recent case in India of the tribulations of a Hindu woman and a Muslim man should dispel those notions.

Regardless, this *has* to change. Pakistan has to modify its school curriculum. It has to change the rhetoric of the *mullah*. It has to guarantee equal rights to all citizens. The *Hudood Ordinances* [Islamic capital punishment laws] instituted under General Zia-ul-Haq have got to be reevaluated. . . .

We Are All Ahmadi[4]
May 28, 2010

There is a mosque near my house in Berlin. I bike past it every time. I often stop at the light, and enjoy the minarets against the grey skies.

There is a mosque in Lahore, too.

Every attack, every atrocity, every massacre diminishes us all. This, I choose to lay at the feet of Mawdudi and his ilk, at the feet of Bhutto and his ilk, at the feet of our bearded *muftis* and their ilk. I blame those who deny citizenship to their brethren. I blame everyone who denies the freedom to practice their faith in peace.

I am afraid I have little else but rage and white hate for the perpetrators of this crime.

I am an Ahmadi.

We Are All Ahmadi III: Laws[5]
May 29, 2010

Pakistan Penal Code 298, 298-A, 298-B, 298-C, updated by Anti-Islamic Activities of Quadiani Group, Lahori Group and Ahmadis (Prohibition and Punishment) Ordinance XX 1984.

Paragraph 298-A:

Use of derogatory remarks, etc., in respect of holy personages: Whoever by words, either spoken or written, or by visible representation, or by any imputation, innuendo or insinuation, directly or indirectly, defiles the sacred name of any wife (Ummul Mumineen), or members of the family (Ahle-bait), of the Holy Prophet (peace be upon him), or any of the righteous Caliphs (Khulafa-e-Rashideen) or companions (Sahaaba) of the Holy Prophet (peace be upon him) shall be punished with imprisonment of either description for a term which may extend to three years, or with fine, or with both.

Paragraph 298-B:

Misuse of epithets, descriptions and titles, etc., reserved for certain holy personages or places:

(1) Any person of the Quadiani group or the Lahori group (who call themselves "Ahmadis" or by any other name) who by words, either spoken or written, or by visible representation;

(a) refers to or addresses, any person, other than a Caliph or companion of the Holy Prophet Muhammad (peace be upon him), as "Ameer-ul-Mumineen," "Khalifatul-Mumineen," "Khalifa-tul-Muslimeen," "Sahaabi" or "Razi Allah Anho";

(b) refers to, or addresses, any person, other than a wife of the Holy Prophet Muhammad (peace be upon him), as "Ummul-Mumineen";

(c) refers to, or addresses, any person, other than a member of the family "Ahle-bait" of the Holy Prophet Muhammad (peace be upon him), as "Ahle-baft"; or

(d) refers to, or names, or calls, his place of worship a "Masjid"; shall be punished with imprisonment of either description for a term which may extend to three years, and shall also be liable to fine.

(2) Any person of the Qaudiani group or Lahori group (who call themselves "Ahmadis" or by any other name) who by words, either spoken or written, or by visible representation refers to the mode or form of call to prayers followed by his faith as "Azan," or recites Azan as used by the Muslims, shall be punished with imprisonment of either description for a term which may extend to three years, and shall also be liable to fine.

Paragraph 298-C:

Person of Quadiani group, etc., calling himself a Muslim or preaching or propagating his faith: Any person of the Quadiani group or the Lahori group (who call themselves

"Ahmadis" or by any other name), who directly or indirectly, poses himself as a Muslim, or calls, or refers to, his faith as Islam, or preaches or propagates his faith, or invites others to accept his faith, by words, either spoken or written, or by visible representations, or in any manner whatsoever outrages the religious feelings of Muslims shall be punished with imprisonment of either description for a term which may extend to three years and shall also be liable to fine.

We Are All Ahmadis IV: A History[6]
May 31, 2010

> *Four young men ran through the streets of Gujranwala, Pakistan, trying to escape the mob rioters chasing them and reach the house of their friends. Their friends, two brothers, had already arranged to move all the women of their house and others to a nearby neighbor's home for safety. The four men reached the house of the two brothers with a trail of stone-throwing rioters behind them. The six of them climbed to the roof of the house. The stone throwers, however, had already reached the roofs of adjoining houses and began pelting the men. They were forced to come back down. The men found themselves surrounded and trapped. The rioters proceeded to beat the men with sticks and clubs and continued to stone them. While beating the men, the rioters shouted and demanded the men denounce their Ahmadi faith and "Mirza Sahib." The six men refused. The rioters then stoned the six men to death. The women of the household fought their tears and mourned quietly afterwards for fear of being heard by outsiders. The six men lay buried beneath the pile of stones for a day. No one dared approach the site of the killing out of fear of the militant perpetrators. The next day, members of the six men's religious community uncovered the bodies and discreetly buried them. Reports were filed but no charges were made by police.*
> —M. Nadeem Ahmad Siddiq, "Enforced Apostasy: *Zaheeruddin vs. State* and the
> Official Persecution of the Ahmadiyya Community in Pakistan,"
> *Law and Inequality*, December 1995

> *Sangha quoted residents as saying that the assailant*
> *threatened to not leave any Ahmadi alive.*
> —*Dawn*, Monday, May 31, 2010

Mirza Ghulam Ahmad was born in Qadiyan, a small village in Punjab in the late 1830s. He belonged to a prosperous household that had a long history of land grants and pensions from both the Mughal and Sikh courts and from the British. He worked briefly as a law clerk, but mostly his early life remains out of historical sight. In 1880, he self-published *Barahin-i Ahmadiyya*—an exegesis on prophetology, on revelation, on the conditions of Muslim society as well as an engagement with the Hindu and Christian polemical and missionary materials. It is in these pages that he first articulates his role as a *mujadid* (a millennial renewer), *muhaddath* (one in direct conversation with God), a *mahdi* (the one who will lead the apocalyptical battle), and *masih* (Jesus). There is a lot here, theologically speaking, that would rile up the orthodoxy, though much is also indebted to many strains of Sufic practices as well as theoretical explications of man's relationship to God in various philosophical schools. Ahmad continued to write in local papers, issuing pamphlets, debating everyone. Starting in 1886, he began to hold public debates with Arya Samajist—a Hindu revivalist organization, founded in 1875 by Dayanand Saraswati to defend Hindu thought and practice from Christian missionaries, with Christian missionaries; and with other Muslim scholars. In 1891, he created an organization built around himself and began the efforts to actively proselytize in the community.

His public engagement was not confined to these debates (one of them lasted for 15 days) alone. He was a prolific author, having written nearly 88 books in Urdu, Arabic, and Persian over the course of his life. In 1897, he established an Urdu weekly, *al-Hakam*, and in 1902, *al-Badr*, as well as an English monthly, the *Review of Religions*. Of his many concerns traceable in his writings and the journals, two need pointing out—Ahmadi engagement with the British regime (profoundly positive and engaged) and Ahmadi proselytizing around the world (deeply committed). Ghulam Ahmad died in 1908, leaving a will but no clarity on succession. The Ahmadiyya split into two factions—the Lahori branch and the Qadiyani branch—in 1914 along a number of issues (Ghulam Ahmad's prophethood, how Ahmadis should proselytize to non-Muslims, leadership, etc.).

Ahmadi missions began to appear in Britain and Europe (early 1910s), the United States (1920 to Michigan and Ohio), Central Asia (1921), Iraq (1922), Syria (1925), Egypt (1924), Indonesia (1926), Nigeria and Ghana (post-1918)—and along with those missions came persecution. The first deaths came in 1901 and 1903, when two Ahmadis were stoned to death in Kabul. The next wave of anti-Ahmadi violence came in 1924–1925, again starting in Afghanistan during the reign of Amir Amanullah Khan (1919 1929), when he ordered the arrest and execution of Ahmadis specifically on the grounds of apostasy. He also made being an Ahmadi a capital offense under the penal code.

The *'ulama* [religious leaders] in Delhi and Deoband agreed by publishing their own *fatwas*/exegesis on the apostasy of the Ahmadi—chief among them was Shabbir Ahmad Uthmani of Deoband, who founded the *Jamaat Ulama-i Islam*. His *fatwa* was crucial in the anti-Ahmadi riots of 1953. But the *'ulama* were not the only ones rallying after the Ahmadi. Muslim political groups, such as the *Majlis Ahrar-ul Islam*, tried to have them declared non-Muslim in the 1930s. Even the stalwart opponent of the bearded *mullah*, Muhammad Iqbal, took exception to the Ahmadi claim of a resurgent prophethood.

The Ahmadi question exposed the faith-based dysfunction in the ideology of Pakistan in 1949 (just as Bengali and Bengal were to expose the linguistic and racial dysfunctions and Baluchistan the territorial dysfunction). The *Ahrar* and various other *'ulama* began agitating for the declaration of non-Muslim status to the Ahmadi in the constitution being drafted as well as attacking the first foreign minister of Pakistan, Muhammad Zafarullah Khan (an Ahmadi). Everything from public rallies to violence shook the cities of Pakistan. . . . The fledgling government successfully resisted this pressure.

In 1951–1953, the *Ahrar* kept tremendous pressure on the government—especially the Punjab government by holding rallies (which often turned into riots) across the country. On March 5, 1953, Maulana Maududi and his *Jamaat-i Islami*, which had largely kept out of the anti-Ahmadi fervor, joined the fray. Maududi published *Qadiyani Masalah* (*The Ahmadi Problem*), using his theological know-how to structure himself at the center of the debate. This greatly intensified the public outcry as well the response of the State—which cracked down hard on the religious parties and their organs. The inquiry report issued—*The Munir Report*—is perhaps the best and only official indictment of religious parties produced in Pakistan.

The Bengal question cleaved Pakistan into two. This second partition gave rise to the first outright embrace of the process of Islamization under the leadership of Zulfiqar Ali Bhutto. From 1972 onwards, anti-Ahmadi riots spread across Punjab, with state legislatures introducing anti-Ahmadi legislations. On September 7, 1973, the State decided to amend the Constitution and added a clause requiring faith in the finality of the Prophet as a central tenant, with failure to do so to be punishable by law. The Ahmadi were finally non-Muslims and denied basic rights of citizenship. After Pakistan, similar measures were passed across the Muslim world—often linked to pressure from the Saudi Arabian regime.

1984 began another long nightmare when Zia-ul-Haq passed the Ordinance on April 26, 1984. It forbade them from declaring themselves as Muslims identifying their mosques, or using the call to prayer. Pakistan's task, to quote Zia-ul-Haq, was to "persevere in our effort to ensure that the cancer of Qadianism is exterminated."

1993 was another round of riots across Pakistan.

2000.

2010.

We Are All Ahmadi V: Erasures[7]
June 1, 2010

A picture, posted by Zackintosh on his Twitter feed, immediately arrested me. It was taken at/outside the Karachi Press Club, at a gathering meant to show solidarity of the Lahore massacre—sadly, a rather nonevent. There was a hand-written white sign in the middle, held high. The gentleman holding up the sign seems mature, and I wonder if he saw the irony—the tragic irony—of his sign. It says: "In Quaid-e Azam's first Cabinet, Foreign Minister Sir Zafarullah, was an Ahmadi." I infer that he invokes this name and this reference to point towards the tolerance and secularism interred in those early days of Pakistan. It is indeed true.

The irony is that this same sign mentioning Muhammad Zafarullah Khan—one of the closest advisors of Jinnah, who helped draft the Lahore Resolution Pakistan, served in numerous capacities, as including Pakistan's first foreign minister, president of the United Nations General Assembly, judge at Hague—would be easily found at any anti-Ahmadi rally from 1934–1954.

The *Ahrar*, as an organization, had two tenets: socialism and anti-Ahmadism. Maybe not so much on the socialism, but certainly very firm on the anti-Ahmadism. The founder Shah 'Ataullah Bukhari demanded in 1934 that Zafarullah Khan be removed from all offices. This they kept up throughout the next decade and into the 1950s. Zafarullah Khan was always the stand-in for the "secret Ahmadi control" over Pakistan (a position soon to be filled by Zionists, the United States, etc.)

From Nasr's work on Jama'at-i Islami:

> The Ahrar continued to articulate economic grievances in Islamic terms, but with a new twist; it tied the demand for economic justice to the Islamicity of the state by questioning the status of the Ahmadis. Every harangue against the government policy and demand for greater Islamicity were accompanied by complaints about the discrepancy between the wealth of the Ahmadi community and the poverty of the Muslim masses: in the homeland of Muslims, it was the Ahmadis who reaped the benefits and the Muslims who suffered hunger and hardship. The strategy was by and large successful, though it was the Ahmadis themselves who set off the final conflict.
>
> On May 17, 1952, the foreign minister turned down Prime Minister Nazimu'ddin's pleas of caution and addressed a public Ahmadi session in Karachi. By openly admitting his religion, Zafaru'llah Khan gave credence to the charge made by the Ahrar that the government was "controlled" by the Ahmadis. For the other Islamic groups and the 'ulama, who viewed the Ahmadis with opprobrium, the very presence of an Ahmadi minister in the cabinet was proof of the un-Islamicity of the state. The Ahrar and the 'ulama, infuriated by the foreign minister's actions, organized a protest march; the marchers clashed with the Ahmadis, and there was a riot.[8]

Nasr does note, elsewhere, the fact that these so-called Muslim parties were adamantly opposed to Pakistan before 1947 and un-ironically segued into becoming the sole representatives of Muslims after 1949. (But, I do find the underlying tone of that whole paragraph by Nasr highly objectionable—this insinuation that Zafarullah Khan should have kept quiet or that "Ahmadis themselves set off the conflict." Bad, bad, bad work, Nasr.)

That Zafarullah Khan's memory has been so thoroughly erased from everyday lives—where theorists often prattle on and on about the long memories of the nation-state, such intense and immediate silencings are rarely noted—is indicative of the changed narrative about Ahmadis in Pakistan—who are now simply heretics and infidels to be eliminated indiscriminately.

II.

There is another erasure on the tombstone of Dr. Abdus Salam. The word "Muslim" is scraped clean by some industrious employee of the state. I have written previously about Abdus Salam, but I didn't mention his Ahmadiyat—just that he was considered an outcast. That was another erasure.

We Are All Ahmadis VI: Community[9]
June 3, 2010

I.

Who exactly is a Muslim? It shouldn't surprise anyone that this is a question with a rather long history. Islam's first split—the Shi'a/Sunni/Kharajite—was a split over leadership and community, but the debates revolved around self-definition versus oppositional definition. Many, if not all, such schisms occurred as, participated in, or were reflected through theological prisms. Yet the doctrinal or juristical debates were rarely the sole motivators, as any passing familiarity with the fate of the Zayidis, the Alawis, the Imamis, or the Ismailis in the first 200 years of Islam can amply demonstrate.

More bluntly, theological differences were political realities and political realities were debated and encoded in communal law. For reference, see Sunni legal codes on Shi'a heresiography from any point in the 9th century onwards.

But maybe we ought to stick to more recent past and things that matter directly on the case of the Ahmadiyya in Pakistan.

The 1860s and 70s were a conflict over communal self-definition of "Muslim," over who can pray in what mosque, and behind whose "Imam." Those were the heady days of the Ahl-e Hadith versus the Hanafi/Deobandi schools. The Ahl-e Hadith considered it legitimate to physically attack the Hanafis or at the very least to reject their corrupt Muslim-ness. Riots and violence notwithstanding, the British legal system became one clear venue to contest these assertions. In a number of cases from 1884 to 1891, most notably *Queen Empress vs. Ramzan* (1885), both the lower and high courts ruled that the Muslim mosque was a public institution that did not belong to one sect or another and, hence, was open for all, whether they said the *Ameen* out loud or under their breaths. What is significant is not only that these doctrinal or ritual issues were being actively contested in British courts, by both parties, on the basis of "heresy" but also that the courts consistently refused to legalize any ritual difference as sectarian difference. The central tenets of the faith, *kalima*, were enough for the court to claim that varied rituals were minor differences, and both parties were "Mohammadan."

So when the Ahmadiyya enter this fray, not only is there a long precedent of litigation over mosques, over ritual, over heresy, but there is also established law on the books. In 1911, in Monghyr, the Ahmadis petitioned the courts to allow them to pray behind a separate imam in the same mosque. They argued that the Hanafi were denying their right to pray behind their own imam. The Hanafi counterargument was that the Ahmadi were non-Muslim to begin with.

In December 1916, the Patna High Court issued its ruling in *Hakim Khalil Ahmad vs. Malik Israfi*:

> The plaintiff alleged that they were Muhammadans and followers of Hazrat Mirza Ghulam Ahmad; that they used to offer up their prayer with other followers of their own sect in a mosque in Dillawarpur, Monghyr; that they did so up to the 2nd December, 1911, when they were illegally and maliciously interfered with and prevented from entering the mosque by the defendants' 1st party, at the instigation of defendants' 2nd party. The plaintiffs used for declaration that they had a right to offer prayers in the said mosque with the people of their own sect, and that the defendants had no right to prevent them from doing so, and that the defendants be permanently restrained from interfering with right of the plaintiffs to offer prayers in the said mosque, collectively and individually. *The Court of first instance held that the plaintiffs were Muhammadans, and that they were entitled to offer prayers individually behind the Hanifi Imam of the mosque, but that they were not entitled to form a separate congregation for prayer in the mosque.* The suit was dismissed. An appeal to the District Judge was dismissed, and he ordered it to be declared that the plaintiffs are at liberty to worship in the disputed mosque behind the recognised Imam of the mosque, in the same congregation with the defendants and other Sunnis. Both sides appealed to the High Court.[10] *[emphasis added]*

The Ahmadi counsel was Zafarullah Khan.

In 1920, the court was finally involved in adjudicating whether Ahmadi were heretical or merely sectarian. In the case *Narantakath Avullah vs. Parakkal Mammu* (1922), the court took it upon itself to "decide [it] ourselves." The judges rejected the three witnesses of the "orthodox party" as being too quick to deem everyone heretic and instead turned to the printed materials and self-descriptions of the Ahmadiyya party. In them, the judges found that there was clear adherence to *kalima*, to the finality of Muhammad, to monotheism. They found that there was some deviation on the issue of abandonment of militancy, of the relationship with the Caliph in Turkey, of Jesus's position in the theological construction and the issue of communication with God. The conclusion was that "the Ahamadiyans are in my view only a reformed sect of Mahomedans." Hence, Muslim.

This was the stable legal definition of Ahmadis under British Legal Code—the code under which Pakistan gained independence and which continues to underpin Pakistan's legal apparatus—plus, the various martial law routines. It is towards this history that I want to turn now.

II.

In a recent column, "Still No Counterterrorism Strategy," Mosharraf Zaidi had this to say:

> The religious issue of the status of the Ahmedi faith in Pakistan is further complicated because it is also a legal issue. If Pakistanis, whether they call themselves liberal or not, are interested in beating the fanatics, and making Pakistan a safe place to live for all Pakistanis, then remembering certain facts is central to the project of fixing Pakistan.
>
> The religious identity of Pakistan's Constitution was the product of a democratic discourse. It is easy to demonise Zia, particularly given his government's slavish pandering to a tiny sliver of mullahs. But frankly, reality also requires us to remember that Bhutto's own rhetoric and most of the mainstream discourse preceding Bhutto (notwithstanding Ayub's colonised vision for Pakistan) was not uncomfortable with Muslim identity. To the contrary, it had a healthy mix of political Muslimness, without any of the political Islamism that infected Pakistan under Zia.[11]

It is a patently absurd statement . . . and one that posits a completely ahistorical picture of the Ahmadi as well as the "Pakistani" public. ("There is scarcely a symbol more central to Pakistani Muslims than the life, times and person of the Holy Prophet Muhammad." O Rly?)

So about this "democratic discourse." The Islamization of Pakistan under Zulfiqar Ali Bhutto and the Sunnification of Pakistan under General Zia-ul-Haq were both top-down, constructed processes that were at odds not only with the public but with the courts and the Constitution. Before 1973, there was only the Objectives Resolution—a preamble with some general principles. The 1956 Constitution introduced Article 198, which stated that "no law shall be enacted which is repugnant to the injunctions of Islam as laid down in the Holy Quran and Sunnah," but only that a commission will make recommendation as to which laws, and how, can be conformed to Islam while enshrining minority rights. This Constitution was waylaid two years later, in 1958, so none of this had any effect on the working legal courts. The 1962 Constitution was much more restrictive in its "Islamic" hues. Pakistan became a Republic from an Islamic Republic, and Islamization procedures were dropped. An amendment, in 1963, added an Advisory Council of Islamic Ideology, which could only advise the president. The provisions in the 1973 Constitution moved the rhetorical goalpost back—

becoming, again, the Islamic Republic and enshrining Islam in the preamble and the declarative bits. But it was Zia-ul-Haq and his Hudood Ordinances that set up a parallel legal apparatus to Islamicize all of Pakistani laws. Notice now, that none of the above described processes were "democratic" in any sense of the word. There never was a mandate for any party to do Constitutional reform. See now the perniciousness of the claim that the anti-Ahmadi law represented "democratic discourse"? But, here is another damning detail—not only was this criminalization of the Ahmadi undemocratic, it was also judicial activism (well, they also gave legal sanctuary to the military coups).

Until 1974, Ahmadiyya were a religious minority within Islam—they could contest elections as Muslims, hold posts, get married, own land—their status was no different than the Sunni majority. Their status was secure in Indian legal code— as above and it was reaffirmed under *Government of West Pakistan vs. Begum Agha Abdul Karim Shorish Kashmiri* (1969), which judged Ahmadis to be citizens, to be Muslim, and to be protected under the fullness of law.

After the brutal partition of 1971, Zulfiqar Ali Bhutto sought support and sustenance in the Middle East—specifically in Saudi Arabia—and one of the channels of that ideology was Maulana Maududi's *Jamaat-i Islami*, and Ahmadiyyat was a central issue for them. They had been rebuffed in the 1950s and 1960s by sternly secular governments, but in Bhutto, though himself a nonpractitioner, they finally found a workable ally. The amendment to Article 260 of the 1973 Constitution declared Ahmadis non-Muslim, and the Second Amendment in 1974 further defined this in clause 3:

> A person who does not believe in the absolute and unqualified finality of the Prophethood of Muhammad (Peace be upon him) the last of the Prophets or who claims to be a Prophet, in any sense of the word or of any description whatsoever, after Muhammad (Peace be upon him), or recognises such claimant as a prophet or a religious reformer, is not a Muslim for the purposes of the Constitution or the law.

This was further clarified in 1983 when "any non-Muslim means a person who is not a Muslim and includes a person belonging to the Christian, Hindu, Sikh, Buddhist or Parsi community, or a person of the Quadiani group or the Lahori group (who call themselves Ahmadis or any other name), or a Bahai, and a person belonging to any of the scheduled castes."

And in 1984 came the Ordinance XX, which banned specific terms, specific practices of the Ahmadis as criminal—they could not refer to the call to prayer as *Azan*, etc. The legality of this law—and the fact that it collides with the freedom granted in the preamble to practice one's religion—was raised by a number of Ahmadi lawsuits, culminating in *Zaheeruddin vs. The State* (1993), where a number of Ahmadi were charged under the Ordinance for wearing patches inscribed with the *kalima*.

The Supreme Court rejected all the challenges and declared that Ordinance XX was not in violation of any fundamental laws in the Constitution. The majority opinion was written by Justice Abdul Qadir Chaudhry, who concluded that in an Islamic state, the court had the right to determine what is, or isn't, Islamic. The freedom to practice religion cannot supersede the desire to maintain law and order. The court was required to rule against the Ahmadi, because "if an Ahmadi is allowed by the administration or the law to display or chant in public, the Shaair-e-Islam, it is like creating a Rushdie out of him. Again, if this permission is given to a procession or assembly on the streets or a public place, it is like permitting civil war."

Martin Lau, in *The Role of Islam in the Legal System of Pakistan* (2006), explains:

> Earlier Supreme Court decisions, especially *Hakim Khan,* had rejected the claim that Islamic law could be directly applied by courts as a source of law or as a benchmark for the judicial review of legislation by arguing that only laws enacted in accordance with the provisions of the 1973 Constitution constituted valid law. The Islamisation of the legal system was, according to *Hakim Khan,* to be carried out by the elected representatives of the people and not by the High Courts or the Supreme Court. Courts were therefore barred from directly applying Islamic law so as to strike down laws which might be repugnant to Islamic law.
>
> ...
>
> *Zaheeruddin vs. The State* must be regarded as a problematic decision. Not only did it confirm the legality of the continued persecution of members of the Ahmadiyya community, which is in itself a worrying prospect, but it also attempted to establish a new interpretation of the scope and the limits of fundamental rights in Pakistan.

Therein lies the entire "democratic discourse"—from religious ideologues to craven politicians to power-hungry military dictators to judicial zealots.

We Are All Ahmadi IX: Two Poems[12]
June 6, 2010

I want to share these two poems with you. One comes from a place far from the site of the massacre and the other from its very neighborhood; one comes from within and the other from without. They are the voices everyone in Pakistan should hear.

I.

Salma A writes:

A Poem by Saqyb Zirvi[13]

When my heart rains tears in the small hours of the night,
my heart itself is visible in each teardrop.

Perhaps neither I nor this melody of life shall last till morn.
The stars are fading, and my heart is sinking.

I have been so much deceived by smiling faces, that whenever
someone bursts into laughter, my heart overflows with grief.

Neither beauty knows, nor are lovers aware of how the
heart is enthralled by an unknown face.

There are difficulties at every step for noble love. The eyes
commit the crime, and the heart feels the shame.

After all, what has the ship of love have to do with the shore?
Dashed by the billows, the heart tosses to and fro.

In love, O Saqyb, the eyes have a bad name without reason.
I have seen that the heart falls before the eyes do.

I [Salma A] have tried to comprehend the massacre in the context of who we are, as a community, as a "diaspora," and as individuals. And the gentle, noble people we have produced. I do not doubt the love many feel for their homeland, regardless of how it may feel towards them. I, sadly, do not share in this love, as I have never been, nor is it likely that I will ever be, part of that larger (and exclusive) narrative of belonging that so many take for granted. Instead, I have always tried to focus on the things that I admire about Pakistani culture in order to position myself in the world. It was the beauty of the Urdu language that kept me from feeling alienated. If we (Pakistan and I) had nothing else in common, then at least there was this contested language to bridge that gap. Urdu was adopted as the lingua franca of the Ahmadi community a long time ago. It is also the official language of Pakistan. That was my link.

This past week however, I found myself emotionally estranged from Pakistani society and culture, after years of trying to reconcile myself to it, to the point where I had lost the urge to pick up Urdu poetry again. The mind is a funny thing; it makes and forges associations between things without really "thinking."

Until I remembered that one of the greatest modern Urdu poets, Saqyb Zirvi, was an Ahmadi. This is for him, and for all those innocent bodies we lost, and their ever-living souls. And for a country I have never really known, that unimagined community.

II.

Naim Sahib posted this in a comment, but it deserves a prominent space.
Wajahat Masood writes:

In May 28 attacks, I lost some of my close friends, including the head of Lahore Ahamdiyya Jamaat, Justice (R) Munir Sheikh. He happened to be the elder brother of my life long friend, Jamil Omer, as well. So many families that I have known were personally bereaved. The Model Town attack was just 200 yards from my house. . . . My 13-year-old daughter, Kamini Masood, wrote a poem the day Jinnah Hospital (two days after Mosque attacks) was attacked and I quote:

Today my hope and pride have vanished,
That's not to be denied
Today I sunk to the floor sobbing
With my arms open wide

The power does not lie with you,
to discuss or decide
who is worthy to be alive, and who
must be made to die

Do not go out to play children,
you may not come back inside

If tear-streaked faces of broken families
begged you to stop killing their sons,
would you reflect and see your wrongs,
or would you still load your guns?

For every girl who lost a father,
every wife now a widow,
I hope you see that you have spilled,
the blood splattered on my window

You do not hear the mourning mothers,
you do not see your father cry

then it is our sons and daughters,
Not your brothers and sisters that die

Do not go out to play children
you may not come back inside

House on the Hill[14]
Original published in the Express Tribune *(Karachi), June 13, 2010*

Gaze at it however long from the outside, little makes sense. Pakistan resembles a house designed and built from the inside, piecemeal, with varied substandard materials, by perennially distracted architects.

In the unfinished basement are the "minorities"—those deemed capable of sanctuary but incapable of being seen above the surface. They are the Christians, the Hindus, the Sikhs, the Ahmadis, the Shi'as, the Queers, and the Transgendered. All must remain silent, none can be heard. Remember when a blasphemy rumour ignited Christian villages in Punjab, last year? Remember the cases of forced conversions of Hindu families? Remember the kidnapping of Sikhs? Remember the attacks on Shi'a processions and mosques? Those are the results when basement-dwellers, silenced communities are seen or heard.

There are laws that provide the infrastructure, the divisions of this house. It protects the majority by keeping the minority out of sight, uncounted and unheard. The Hindu cannot get her marriage recognised, the Ahmadi cannot call his place of worship a mosque. The Shi'a cannot fly his banner. These are the laws of the state—drafted in 1974, in 1978, in 1984, in 1992. It is this very structure which dehumanises millions of Pakistanis, every moment of every day.

There is the majority, the people who live in this house. They are always Sunni Muslim—though they are quite capable of throwing this or that "Sunni" faction out in a heart beat. They are always urban—the rural, the semi-urban lives remain out of the pale. They are always concerned with their upward mobility. They want security, prosperity, the latest electronic gadget and the fastest car. For themselves. They are never poor, never working class, never provincial but they are its consumers: they hire the poor for their housework, they buy from their carts, they embrace the diversity of fabric, the exoticness of "Sufi poetry," the colourful beads, and the regional sweets.

There is a state. It is now on Twitter even. This state, those laws, that the majority has mutually, over the last 50 years constructed a house in which none can exist save the chosen ones. This existence comes at a price. They agree to believe in the finality of the Prophet (*pbuh*) or else, cease to exist—legally and, perhaps, with the right incentive, corporally. They agree that their biggest threat are some sketches, or some Facebook fan page or some insult published in some book, in some incomprehensible language, in some faraway country. They agree to rage, to burn, to destroy their own property to represent their commitment. Who must bear their forceful self-assertion? The basement dwellers, of course, who must now be massacred, since liberty was already denied to them. They are *wajib ul-qatl* [morally and legally killable], we have already asserted.

The majority is not so secure, however. Some say Allah Hafiz and some Khuda Hafiz. Some are known to say Amen aloud in prayer and some under their breath. Some hang amulets around their necks and some don't. Some shave their beards; others grow mustaches. Some are known to skip Qur'an studies for I.T. Some practice birth control. Some take only one wife. Some actually believe in that Sufi business. Some put God in a cabinet. Some are vegetarian.

Once the Ahmadis, the Shi'as, the Hindus, the Christians were also part of the upstairs. They were also members of the house. The poor were once the founders. Slowly, they were moved down, eliminated. This is not history. This is precedent.

Dominance without Toleration[15]
November 24, 2010

1. According to the 1998 census, there are slightly more than 2 million Christians (1.59 percent of the total population) distributed roughly equally across urban and rural areas. As a minority, the Christian community in Pakistan is predominantly located in the province (state) of Punjab. Although sizable communities are found in the cities of Quetta, Karachi, and Peshawar as well.

2. The Objectives Resolution of 1949 stated that in the Republic of Pakistan, "adequate provision shall be made for the minorities freely to profess and practise their religions and develop their cultures." The Objectives Resolution was made the preamble in the 1973 Constitution. The word "freely" was removed.

3. The Church of Pakistan was amalgamated from Methodist, Presbyterian, and Anglican churches in 1970.

4. The earliest recorded attack on Christian communities was in 1952, when a family of seven was burned alive in the village of Matti. The criminals were caught, prosecuted, and hanged.

5. During the first two decades of Pakistan, Christian communities were largely integrated. They had a political party and in the 1951 and 1954 elections, they won four seats (each) in the local Punjab Assembly.

6. The 1973 Constitution of Pakistan declared that "Islam shall be the state religion of Pakistan" and restricted minority participation in government and politics.

7. General Zia-ul-Haq took over the state through a military coup in 1977 and then hung the deposed Prime Minister Zulfiqar Ali Bhutto in 1979. He also undertook a strict policy of "Islamization" through which laws and practices in the country were brought in accordance with Islamic jurisprudence. Some of the most damaging new laws fell under the rubric of "Blasphemy."

8. In 1980, he introduced Section 298-A under the Martial Law Ordinance, which criminalized derogatory remarks against the earliest leaders in Muslim history as well as the family and friends of the Prophet Muhammad. Section 298-B and C focused on disrespect to the holy book Qur'an as well as the declaration of apostasy toward the community of Ahmadis (a sect within Islam).

9. Section 298-A: Use of derogatory remarks, etc., in respect of holy personages:

> Whoever by words, either spoken or written, or by visible representations, or by any imputation, innuendo, directly or indirectly, defiles the sacred name of any wife or members of the family of the Holy Prophet or any of the righteous Caliphs or companions of the Holy Prophet shall be punished with imprisonment of either description for a term which may extend to three years, or with fine or with both,

10. Section 295-B: Defiling, etc., of copy of Holy Quran:

> Whoever willfully defiles, damages, or desecrates a copy of the Holy Quran or of an extract therefrom or uses it in any derogatory manner or for unlawful purpose shall be punishable with imprisonment for life.

11. Section 295-C: Use of derogatory remarks, etc, in respect of the Holy Prophet:

> Whoever by words, either spoken or written, or by visible representation, or by any imputation, innuendo, or insinuation, directly or indirectly defiles the sacred name of the Holy Prophet Muhammad shall be punished with death, or imprisonment for life and shall also be liable to fine.

12. Furthermore, in 1980, General Zia-ul-Haq by constitutional amendment created the Federal Shariat Court (FSC) through Article 203-D, which had the following powers:

> The Court may, either of its own motion or on the petition of a citizen of Pakistan or the Federal Government or a Provincial Government, examine and decide the question whether or not any law or provision of law is repugnant to the Injunctions of Islam, as laid down in the Holy Quran and Sunnah of the Holy Prophet, hereinafter referred to as the Injunction of Islam.

13. In 1990, the FSC concluded that the "imprisonment for life" under Section 295-B and 295-C was unjust punishment according to Islamic law. The sections were amended so that the only penalty remained was the death penalty.

14. The blasphemy laws have become the main vehicle of prosecution and persecution of non-Muslims since 1980s. And of "other non-Muslims."

15. In Gujranwala, Punjab, in 1994, three men (including a minor) were accused of writing derogatory remarks against the Prophet. The three Christians, Rehmat Masih, Manzoor Masih, and Salamat Masih, were arrested. Manzoor Masih was murdered while awaiting trial. The others were acquitted after 2 years.

16. In Faisalabad, in 1998, Dr. Bishop John Joseph publicly committed suicide. He shot himself in front of the courtroom of Justice Rana Abdul Jabbar Dogar in protest of a death sentence that had been passed out against a Christian Ayub Masih for blasphemy on April 27, 1998.

17. A series of terrorist attacks occurred in 2001 and 2002 against Christian establishments, perhaps as a result of Pakistani cooperation with the United States in the war in Afghanistan: On October 29, gunmen killed 16 Christians in the St. Dominic Roman Catholic Church near Multan. A grenade attack on International Presbyterian Church in Islamabad on March 17, 2002, killed 5 and injured 40. Unknown assailants attacked Murree Christian School on August 5, 2002, and killed six people. Unknown assailants attacked the Mission Hospital in Taxila on August 9, 2002, and killed 4 nurses, injuring 21 others. Seven Christian workers of the charity "Idara Amn-o-Insaf" were killed on September 24, 2002.

18. In November 2005, three churches, two schools and hostels, and several houses of the Christian community were burned by a mob in the city of Sangla Hill. The mob had mobilized on the rumor that someone had blasphemed against the Prophet.

19. On September 27, 2007, the missionary couple Rev. Arif Khan and Kathleen Khan was killed in their house in Islamabad on September 27, 2007.

20. In August 2009, 60 Christian homes were burned in Gojra; seven women and children were burned alive. The accused were granted bail on November 5, 2010.

21. Just on November 15, 2010, a man accused of blasphemy, upon release on bail, was shot dead by unknown assailants.

The inhumane legal treatment of so-designated "minorities" in Pakistan is starkly repugnant.

Sign your name to a petition calling for the repeal of Aasia Bibi's death sentence.[16]

Dominance without Toleration III: Guns and Roses[17]
January 8, 2011

The killer has been garlanded. Facebook fan pages, Twitter clouds of praises. For his victim, Salmaan Taseer, there are small candlelight vigils and columns bemoaning him for "going too far." How far did he go? He visited a woman who is "accused" of blasphemy, and he called the law that enables such prosecutions a *kala qanoon* [black law], meaning it was an oppressive law (implemented via coercion).

For days on end, before Taseer's assassination, TV talk shows and dailies had heightened the stakes—it wasn't one case of blasphemy, it wasn't just a law on the books, it was *Namoos-i Risalat* [the Sanctity of the Prophethood]. In everyday parlance, this and its corollary, *Tauheen-i Risalat* [Blaspheming the Prophet], have emerged as transgressions so extreme that even the accusation is enough to justify dismantling the edifice of a juridical or civil society. In practice, *Tauheen-i Risalat* has been a touchstone of Islamist parties since the 1950s and, over the years, has entered the everyday lives of hundreds of millions of Muslims as an unpardonable, unmentionable offense. The Friday sermon will invoke it, and it will insist that there is only the penalty of death, and it will intone that there is only the possibility of self-annihilation to "protect" the Prophet.

Blasphemy is, and has been since Salman Rushdie's *Satanic Verses*, a reliable apprentice to the Islamist parties. It is nonsectarian (when it comes to the Prophet), it is ahistorical, it is antiauthoritarian, and antistatist.

By nonsectarian, I mean that a Blasphemy demonstration or a Blasphemy accusation allows the Islamist party to mobilize universally. Whether by buying busloads for the demonstration or imposing arbitrary shutdowns on merchants, the Islamist party can cast the widest possible net.

By ahistorical, I mean that Blasphemy operates strictly within the purview of the modern nation-state. There is very little, and I mean that, invocation of historical precedent or understanding of either the law or the accusation. Most Islamists will be shocked perhaps to learn that at one point or another, such stalwarts of the Islamist canon as Abu Hanifa, Ibn Hanbal, Ibn Hazm, Ibn Taymiyyah, or al-Ghazzali were all accused of apostasy and Blasphemy during their lifetimes. The ignorance of such history is an advantage, since it allows the Islamist discourse to keep the issue posited as a strict binary and outside the scope of any "discussion." There is also the lack of religious historical precedent—wherein the penalty of death is considered sacrosanct, but it does not exist at all in the Qur'an and is only randomly asserted in the Hadi'th corpus.

By antiauthoritarian and antistatist, I mean that these public demonstrations, shutdowns, and vigilante acts of violence are meant specifically for the local state—insofar as it is capable of communication—or the local market. That these Islamist parties have an agenda against the State—though they be nurtured by the same state is incidental—ought not be a surprise. Even when coddled, as the Jama'at-i Islami was during the Zia regime, the Islamist parties maintain a strict anti-authoritarian and antistate rhetoric—because authority ought only to come from the power invested in them (as religious and political elite) by devout believers, and the State ought only be "Islamic" (the definition being up for debate). Blasphemy is a perfect storm, because it seemingly handicaps the capacity of the civil regime to intervene (are you against the Prophet!?) while loosening restraints on civil violence through absolution (to kill in the name of the Prophet is divine).

Ironies abound. The Prophetic tradition steeped in "I am not divine" speaks against any credulous case of Blasphemy. Yet, here we have the promoters of divinity squaring themselves in defense of someone who specifically denied himself such a status.

Many, including myself, are disheartened by the assassination of Salmaan Taseer. He had emerged, specifically through Twitter, as somewhat of a *laissez-faire* secularist. I want to stress this "Twitter" angle. Given the lack of a civil society where dialogue and discourse can transcend class boundaries, Taseer found a way to circumvent "drawing room politics," where men and women gathered on uncomfortable and ostentatious furniture to discuss "the people." I am quite willing to bet that his strident defense of secularist, pluralist policies emerged *because* of the feedback loop that Twitter provided. As a subscriber to his feed for a while, I witnessed numerous exchanges with reporters, authors, business owners, and students, where he asserted, and was pushed back on, not only government policy but a liberal worldview that needed defense, or it needed affirmation. He was abandoned by his own party and largely by the provincial government after his defense of Asiya Bibi. The Zardari regime found it best to not challenge the Islamist parties, and their reticence only exacerbated the loneliness of the Taseer and Sherry Rahman position—that the Blasphemy Laws were targeting religious minorities.

Is the death of Salmaan Taseer the death of liberal thought in Pakistan? There is no denying that the rosy days of the Lawyers Movement are long gone—buried by repeated suicide bombings, minority killings, assassinations, and a revitalized Right in Pakistan. The Afghanistan-Pakistan theatre with its unending political and military debacle has created a quicksand in Pakistan, where both the materials of war and the rhetoric of war dominate civic life. Everyone is in danger, at all times.

They have guns, and they have the roses. We have nothing except the hope that civil state will find a reason to defend its own citizenry, if only out of self-preservation instincts.

Forfeiting the Future[18]
Original published in the Caravan *(New Delhi), February 1, 2011*

A column bearing the title *"Ki Muhammad se wafa tu nay"* ["If You Are Faithful to Muhammad"] appeared on January 1 in the *Daily Jang*, the largest Urdu newspaper in Pakistan. Written by Mushtaq Ahmed Qureshi, it was quite close, in tone and in content, to an array of writing in the Urdu press commenting on the country's blasphemy laws, which have attracted considerable international attention due to the case of Asiya Bibi, a Christian woman who has been imprisoned for a year and faces a death sentence for the crime of insulting the Prophet Muhammad.

Hewing close to the conventions of Urdu column writing, Qureshi opened with the description of a social setting (a funeral) where some sober men were gathered, discussing the affairs of the day. One asked, why is the governor of Punjab giving speeches against *khatm-e nabuvat* [Finality of Prophethood]? Another, a *maulana*, replied that he did not know—but said he did know that whoever maintains that there is another prophet after Muhammad, or denies the prophethood of Muhammad, can be legally killed. It was a shame, Qureshi wrote, that even though Salmaan Taseer knew that he would die one day and be judged for his words, he was so careless. At the end of the column, Qureshi cited, with great praise, a couplet by the renowned Urdu poet Muhammad Iqbal:

> *Ki Muhammad se wafa tu nay to hum teray hain /*
> *Yeh Jahan chiz hay kiya, Loh o Qalam teray hain*
> Be faithful to Muhammad and I am yours /
> This world is nothing, the Tablet and Pen are yours.

Three days later, on January 4, Salmaan Taseer was killed—and his assassin publicly proclaimed that the murder was an answer to Taseer's efforts to amend or repeal the Blasphemy laws. Much has been written, since, about Taseer himself and about the wide approval of the assassin's act in certain segments of Pakistani society. Once again, in an echo of the aftermath of Benazir Bhutto's assassination in 2007, political commentators have depicted Pakistan facing a grave crisis, one caused by a more or less natural progression of rightist Islamic ideologies, whose dominance has erased not only liberal and secular thought but all possible futures for the nation-state.

Such ahistorical views take as given that these conservative, sectarian, and militant ideologies emerge organically from Islamic theology—and reflect, in turn, the inevitable effect of growing religiosity in Pakistan. The fault, dear Brutus, lies in the Crescent.

It is clear, of course, that a rather biased and selective understanding of the Muslim past and Islamic theology underlines the violence and fear widely on display in Pakistan. It is valid to ask what enables a columnist to make the illogical leap of equating speech against a legal principle to speech against the dominant religious truth. In a nation of over 90 percent religious conformity, why this sense of deep, abiding fear that some word, some gesture, will unravel the very fabric of belief? Why does the Prophet need Pakistan to defend him?

It behooves us to look for answers beyond the scripture and practice of Islam—for such mass hysteria is not evident among Muslims in Bangladesh or Malaysia or

Tunisia or China or America—and towards the political life of religious discourse in South Asia. What we find, in fact, is a long history of the politicisation of the Prophet in Pakistani civil society; tracing its development is critical if we are to understand what possible futures still exist for Pakistan.

In 1913, Muhammad Iqbal published his "Jawab-e Shikwa" ["Answer to the Lament"], responding to the critiques that his long poem "Shikwa" ["Complaint, or Lament"], published a year earlier, was blasphemous because of its anger and flippancy towards God. Where "Shikwa" was man addressing God ("Hear, O Lord, from the faithful ones, this lament / From those who only sign praises, a little complaint"), "Jawab-e Shikwa" reversed the narrative voice, and God answers directly—telling the beleaguered "Muslim" that it was his own lack of faith and courage that was responsible for his political and moral decline. The two poems reflect, remarkably well, the general mood of a South Asian Muslim community that saw itself under siege and at a particular nadir in historical time—colonised, devoid of political and social power, and mired in internecine and communal conflicts. Where "Shikwa" had alienated Iqbal from some of the more orthodox contingents, "Jawab-e Shikwa" was received with an ecstatic fervour. Iqbal was now the Poet of the East, and in the decades that followed his devout and mystic poetry shadowed closely his political thought that presented, in 1930, the idea of a Muslim "homeland" in the subcontinent.

Many years later, under the military dictatorship of General Zia-ul-Haq, Iqbal came to personify Pakistan itself. His verses became second only to the citations from the Qur'an as adornments in public and private spaces. It was then that the last couplet of "Jawab-e Shikwa," quoted above, emerged as the lynchpin of the Sunnification strategy of Zia-ul-Haq—a strategy that aimed to reformat both the political and cultural life of Pakistanis along "jihadi" lines.

This nonscriptural, nonritualistic, nonsectarian prescription for the ills of Muslims had some echoes in the growing corpus of praise poetry on the Prophet in the early decades of the 20th century, but it was startlingly original in its invocation of a political promise—that the Muslim, through fealty to the figure of the Prophet, could control his own destiny ("the Tablet and the Pen").

This particular prescription by Iqbal did not seem to make much of an impact in colonial India. Iqbal, of course, wasn't advocating any great shift in doctrine; Muhammad is the central figure of Islam, and his figure is revered above all. Yet after the tumultuous birth of Pakistan, there was indeed a change. Pakistan's emergence was soon connected, in narratives both political and religious, to the Prophet—he appeared in dreams to key figures to foretell the division of India, and his sayings were variously interpreted to prophesise the role of Islam in Pakistan's political life. Yet, in Zia-ul-Haq's Pakistan, the Prophet became part of the daily political life in a way that would have been unimaginable to Muslims in the 1910s. Routinely, politicians professed to receive divine sanction from the Prophet for their decisions to endorse a public platform or to run for office or to oppose the call for democratic reform; the *sunnah*—the daily habits of the Prophet—became axiomatic and emblematic rules for everyday life.

This emergence of the Prophet as a centralising and orienting *raison d'être* for Pakistan, however, was not merely an organic outgrowth of a religiously inclined society; it was a deliberate state policy, aided by Islamist parties, to mould public faith. The blasphemy riots of the 1950s, when the Ahmadi sect was violently resisted by the Jama'at-i Islami, had taught one clear lesson to the religious right: the veneration of Muhammad was great political theatre, with infinite malleability for nearly every segment of the Pakistani population. With the explicit favour of the military regime, the figure of the Prophet quickly became central to national political memory—the celebration of his birth, the *Mi'raj* [ascension], and other milestones from his life were heavily funded and carefully orchestrated events, with the massive participation of the religious elite across Pakistan. Within this discourse, the religious right and the Islamist parties constructed a categorically Sunni Pakistan (implicitly suppressing the Shi'a veneration of Ali) while projecting a nonsectarian universalism to their public lives.

Iqbal's poetry, and his concept of the Prophet as *mard-e kamil* [the Perfect Man], was a key component of Zia-ul-Haq's Sunnification politics. Even as he promoted Sunni militant organisations to wage jihad in Kashmir and Afghanistan, he pushed Iqbal's vision across school curriculums and public spheres. He even branded himself as a *mard-e momin* [Pious Man] and *mard-e haq* [Righteous Man]. However, this was not a mere appropriation of a decades-old poetical register for communal and political consumption. Zia-ul-haq, and the Islamist parties, reinvigorated the claim to Muhammad's memory by casting it in nationalist, martial terms: Pakistan was envisioned as the "Castle of Islam"—the lone defender against a world arrayed to corrupt or corrode the very foundations of Muslim belief.

Even after Zia-ul-Haq's death, the Islamist parties retained both the political theatre and the political force that the figure of the Prophet could mobilise across sectarian and class boundaries. The protests against *The Satanic Verses* in 1989 melded the defense of the Prophet, blasphemy, and virulent anti-Americanism into one heady brew—which has been feeding the Islamist parties to this day.

Even as the figure of the Prophet grew in public consumption to deified realms, it withdrew both from historical light and from political dissent. The Islamist parties, though nationalist, are also explicitly anti-statist and can effectively mobilise public sentiment against the state by invoking Muhammad—this was clearly visible in the various demonstrations against the Danish cartoons of the Prophet in 2005, graffiti from which still litters walls across Punjab.

Taseer's cold-blooded murder, and the chilling response to his assassination, reveals less about the crass "Islamicisation" of the Pakistani public and more about a deeply entrenched political program that routinely marshals potent symbols against critical voices. The evident success of this program, however, does not erase the fact that the overwhelming majority of Pakistanis battle stark poverty, high inflation, and a lack of access to basic facilities. Even as Islamist parties orchestrate demonstrations against blasphemers, every day brings another demonstration against rising electricity and gas prices and the pernicious effects of "load shedding." There are, in other words, many other potent narratives available to those in Pakistan who seek to change the cultural and political landscape. Vigilante or terrorist violence cannot be the last word in this discourse, and history itself cannot remain silent.

Chapter Notes

1 Archived at http://bit.ly/edQqFS.
2 Richard W. Stevenson and Eric Lichtblau, "As Ashcroft Warns of Attack, Some Question Threat and Its Timing," *New York Times*, May 27, 2004, archived at http://nyti.ms/j6PPdV.
3 "Editorial: Musharraf's 'Core Issue' and Realpolitik," *Daily Times*, May 27, 2004, archived at http://bit.ly/mwE98u.
4 Archived at http://bit.ly/aCR4xf.
5 Archived at http://bit.ly/ar4Ubv.
6 Archived at http://bit.ly/8Y5cro
7 Archived at http://bit.ly/cQI4BR.
8 S.V.R. Nasr, *The Vanguard of the Islamic Revolution: The Jama'at-i Islami of Pakistan* (Berkeley: University of California Press, 1994), 133.
9 Archived at http://bit.ly/daoyiQ.
10 Howard Arnold Walter, *The Ahmadiya Movement* (Calcutta: Association Press, 1918), 155.
11 Mosharraf Zaidi, "Still No Counterterrorism Strategy," *News International*, June 2, 2010, archived at http://bit.ly/9M3Kdb.
12 Archived at http://bit.ly/bLKRQ4.
13 Translated by Muhammad Abd-al-Rahman Barker, Khwaja Muhammad Safi Dihlavi, Hasan Jahangir Hamdani in "A Reader of Modern Urdu Poetry" (Montreal: McGill University Press, 1968).
14 Archived at http://bit.ly/agfE0B.
15 Archived at http://bit.ly/hfSjCO.
16 The text of the petition is archived at http://bit.ly/k4f4tj.
17 Archived at http://bit.ly/gijAYX.
18 Archived at http://bit.ly/hhT162.

10
Closers

There are two clusters of essays here. The three on Pakistan ("Pakistan Day," "Legends of the Fail," and "State of Decay") try to highlight the internal and external ways in which Pakistan is framed and curtailed. The three dealing with the United States ("The Cultural Damage of the War on Terror," "Recall America's Imperial Pasts," and "Flying Blind") form the central critique that I have tried to develop in the last year. I have tried to argue that the American imagination of its particular Other has significant blind spots even as it aggressively mounts technologically based efforts to know everything. These last few essays are meant to collect the longer pieces at the end of the book. I hope you enjoy them.

Pakistan Day 2009[1]
March 23, 2009

On March 23, Pakistan celebrates "Pakistan Day" to commemorate the Muslim League session in Lahore in 1940 at which Muhammad Ali Jinnah most crisply articulated a "Muslims are a nation" ideology. I want to highlight some sections for you. See, for example, that Jinnah builds upon twinned arguments: First that Muslims as a community had politically divergent goals and their historical specificity was inarguable. It was a strictly communitarian reading of history that forcefully argued away all notions of cohabitation, without once citing an example. Take a look at what he said then:

> We do not want that the British Government should thrust upon the Mussalmans a constitution which they do not approve of and to which they do not agree. Therefore the British Government will be well advised to give that assurance and give the Mussalmans complete peace and confidence in this matter and win their friendship. But whether they do that or not, after all, as I told you before, we must depend on our own inherent strength; and I make it plain from this platform, that if any declaration is made, if any interim settlement

is made without our approval and without our consent, the Mussalmans of India will resist it. (Hear, hear and applause.) And no mistake should be made on that score.

[[14]] Then the next point was with regard to Palestine. We are told that endeavours, earnest endeavours are being made to meet the reasonable, national demands, of the Arabs. Well, we cannot be satisfied by earnest endeavours, sincere endeavours, best endeavours. (Laughter.) We want that the British Government should in fact and actually meet the demands of the Arabs in Palestine. (Hear, hear.)

Jinnah seamlessly unites Muslims within India (remember that the 1920s and 1930s were ripe with myriad Muslim factions and political parties, from Congress to Muslim League to Unionist Party to Khaksar Tehrik to Khilafat to Mau'dudi, etc., so this "unity" is no given) with Muslims outside India by harkening the connection to Palestine. He follows that up with a call to the British Government, asking that they guarantee that no Muslim will fight in a Muslim country (in the WWII mobilization)—again, a rhetorical move that further cements the Muslim bloc as distinct on the global scale. There is a genealogy to this, of course which stretches back to debates between Afghani and Syed Ahmed Khan.

But, more interesting, was how he differentiated the Muslim community in India from all others:

> But one thing is quite clear: it has always been taken for granted mistakenly that the Mussalmans are a minority, and of course we have got used to it for such a long time that these settled notions sometimes are very difficult to remove. The Mussalmans are not a minority. The Mussalmans are a nation by any definition. The British and particularly the Congress proceed on the basis, "Well, you are a minority after all, what do you want!" "What else do the minorities want?" just as Babu Rajendra Prasad said. But surely the Mussalmans are not a minority. We find that even according to the British map of India we occupy large parts of this country where the Mussalmans are in a majority, such as Bengal, Punjab, N.W.F.P., Sind, and Baluchistan.

This notion of a "Muslim India within India" as a distinct polity had been around (primarily in Punjab) since Iqbal articulated it in 1930 and gathered steam since Rahmat Ali's 1935 Pakistan National Movement. Yet there was quite a range of options, from a federation model to separate states. Sikander Hayat, the powerful leader of the Unionist Party, was a strong supporter of the federated idea and proposed a number of resolutions to that effect in 1939. For Jinnah, who remained open to the federated model for a long while, the key argument was a distinction between "minority politics" (such as the Untouchable cause), which was local, and "Muslim politics," which was international. It is this distinction that he articulated most forcefully:

> A leading journal like the *London Times,* commenting on the Government of India Act of 1935, wrote that "Undoubtedly the difference between the Hindus and

Muslims is not of religion in the strict sense of the word but also of law and culture, that they may be said indeed to represent two entirely distinct and separate civilisations. However, in the course of time the superstitions will die out and India will be moulded into a single nation." (So according to the London Times the only difficulties are superstitions). These fundamental and deep-rooted differences, spiritual, economic, cultural, social, and political have been euphemised as mere "superstitions." But surely it is a flagrant disregard of the past history of the sub-continent of India, as well as the fundamental Islamic conception of society vis-à-vis that of Hinduism, to characterise them as mere "superstitions." *Notwithstanding [a] thousand years of close contact,* nationalities which are as divergent today as ever, cannot at any time be expected to transform themselves into one nation merely by means of subjecting them to a democratic constitution and holding them forcibly together by unnatural and artificial methods of British Parliamentary statutes. What the unitary government of India for one hundred fifty years had failed to achieve cannot be realized by the imposition of a central federal government. It is inconceivable that the fiat or the writ of a government so constituted can ever command a willing and loyal obedience throughout the sub-continent by various nationalities, except by means of armed force behind it. *[emphasis added]*

The problem in India is not of an inter-communal character, but manifestly of an international one, and it must be treated as such. So long as this basic and fundamental truth is not realised, any constitution that may be built will result in disaster and will prove destructive and harmful not only to the Mussalmans, but to the British and Hindus also. If the British Government are really in earnest and sincere to secure [the] peace and happiness of the people of this sub-continent, the only course open to us all is to allow the major nations separate homelands by dividing India into "autonomous national states."[2]

What separated Jinnah's articulation of an anticolonial, nationalist movement from other such movements around the globe was his clear break from the local Indian context:

It is extremely difficult to appreciate why our Hindu friends fail to understand the real nature of Islam and Hinduism. They are not religions in the strict sense of the word, but are, in fact, different and distinct social orders; and it is a dream that the Hindus and Muslims can ever evolve a common nationality; and this misconception of one Indian nation has gone far beyond the limits and is the cause of more of our troubles and will lead India to destruction if we fail to revise our notions in time. The Hindus and Muslims belong to two different religious philosophies, social customs, and literature[s]. They neither intermarry nor interdine together, and indeed they belong to two different civilisations which are based mainly on conflicting ideas and conceptions. Their aspects [=perspectives?] on life, and of life, are different. It is quite clear that Hindus and Mussalmans derive their inspiration from different sources of history. They have different epics, their heroes are different, and different episode[s]. Very often the hero of one is a foe of the other, and likewise their victories and defeats overlap. To yoke together two such nations under a single state, one as a numerical minority and the other as a majority, must lead to growing discontent, and final destruction of any fabric that may be so built up for the government of such a state.

. . .

Whereas under the plea of unity of India and one nation which does not exist, it is sought to pursue here the line of one central government, when we know that the history of the last twelve hundred years has failed to achieve unity and has witnessed, during these ages, India always divided into Hindu India and Muslim India. The present artificial unity of India dates back only to the British conquest and is maintained by the British bayonet, but the termination of the British regime, which is implicit in the recent declaration of His Majesty's Government, will be the herald of the entire break-up, with worse disaster than has ever taken place during the last one thousand years under the Muslims. Surely that is not the legacy which Britain would bequeath to India after one hundred fifty years of her rule, nor would Hindu and Muslim India risk such a sure catastrophe.

Muslim India cannot accept any constitution which must necessarily result in a Hindu majority government. Hindus and Muslims brought together under a democratic system forced upon the minorities can only mean Hindu Raj. Democracy of the kind with which the Congress High Command is enamoured would mean the complete destruction of what is most precious in Islam.

Jinnah ends his call with a rousing cry to "come forward as servants of Islam."

Now, one can certainly articulate the trajectory that lands Jinnah in Lahore in 1940 espousing a particular brand of "Islamic nationalism," but I'd rather skip ahead to how this "Two-Nation Theory" became the necessary condition for Pakistan's self-identity postindependence. And how it unraveled.

To restate, there are two components articulated by Jinnah. First, the transnational nature of Muslims as a community. Second, the internal coherence and distinction of Muslims within India. I think, and let me stress that I am speaking very off-the-cuff, that Pakistan's ideology until the 1965 war focused largely on that first half. Ayub Khan worked hard to forge strong pan-Islamic ties to the Nasserite Egypt. His protégé, Zulfiqar Ali Bhutto, continued this articulation of Pakistan's close ties with global Islamic community. Bhutto held an Islamic Conference in Lahore in 1974 and, also, massively courted Saudi support. The coup de grâce was delivered, of course, by Zia-ul-Haq. During his regime, he explicitly tied Pakistan's self-identity to an explicitly anti-Shi'a and Wahabi affect on the one end and a national "jihad" focused on Kashmir/Afghanistan on the other. There was also a severe curtailment of the earlier pan-Islamic position as Pakistan emerged as the "defender" of Mecca—with very close military and political ties between the two states. It may not be necessary to point out that a large proportion of the clandestine U.S. funding for the Afghan operations, at the time, were funneled through Saudi Arabia to the Pakistani military.

Jinnah's articulation of an internal coherence of Indian Muslims as a community had also died much earlier. One can peg that to the partition itself, but whatever lingered was diminished by the 1965 war (which forced an elimination of supranational contacts between the Muslim populations on either side) and it ended with the atrocities of Pakistani military on their fellow Muslims (and fellow citizens) in East Pakistan in 1970–71. As a vision of Muslim community crumbled post-1971, keep in mind the Baluchistan crisis of 1972–74, the anti-India individuation markedly grew in Pakistani foreign policy. One can say that the Pakistan two-nation theory became entirely an "oppositional" ideology built around the Kashmir issue. And the clear flag-bearer of this—in fact, the personi-fication of this—was the Pakistan Army. Zia-ul-Haq, until his death in 1986, kept these flames going. But the civilian governments that followed him (Bhutto, Sharif, Bhutto, Sharif) were just as beholden to the army and just as oppositional. The extreme effects of this are clearly perceptible in the "Islamic Bomb" saga of late 90s, Kargil, and the military standoff of 2002.

Since 2001, Musharraf's dictatorial regime sought to polish over the internal incoherence with a unified foreign front aimed primarily at operating militarily in Afghanistan, NWFP, and Baluchistan. And reaping his just rewards from the U.S. The influx of cash, some $6 billion, into the military coffers propelled it to new-found heights as the largest landlord, largest employer, largest business enterprise in the country. Musharraf's army entrenched the service track of active military service men who would retire with covetous land grants and lucrative business propositions, making them immediate "entrepreneurs." In no small part, these forces contributed to the economic growth in Pakistan since 2002.

But maintaining this new oligarchy came at a steep price for Pakistan. The two main post-2001 theaters, the states of NWFP and Baluchistan, bore the brunt of military overreach and dwindling civic engagement. In Baluchistan, since 2004, a low-grade civil war emerged after brutalities of Musharraf's regime harkening back to the Baluchi nationalist struggles of the early 70s. NWFP, which never even managed to get a proper name, remained the "frontier" both ideologically and developmentally. Besides being the military staging ground, the people were denied even rudimentary access to health care, education, or a functioning judicial system.

The issue of justice is supremely important to any understanding of either Baluchistan or NWFP. Swat, for example, was utilized as a staging ground under Zia and later as a refugee camp for Afghani victims of the Soviet war. Since then, it has been left to deteriorate. Benazir Bhutto cut a very similar deal for imposi-tion of Shari'ah in 1994. Why? Because the federal state could not provide them justice or the rule of law. A few days ago, *Daily Swat* had an account of the very first Qazi court ruling. In the district of Khwaza Khil, a Fazal Ghani entered a writ that he was owed 35,000 rupees from a Javed that he had never been able to collect. The judge called the parties to the court. Javed handed over 7,000 in court and said the rest of the 20,000 would be given in monthly installments of 5,000. The two parties signed an agreement and left the court. This was the first "Shari'a" decision under the new regime. Innocuous, yes? But that is exactly what had been missing in Swat. It is this cry for justice that has propelled ordinary Swatis to listen when warlords like Maulana Fazlullah yell into their radio broadcasts about a new system of justice. The 2007 Lal Masjid crisis may have resulted in Musharraf looking good to the U.S. establishment, but it eliminated whatever natural sympathies for the army were left in NWFP. The results are certainly predictable. In both Swat and Baluchistan, locality after locality, tribe after tribe has fallen to warlords intent on reterrorizing civilians into submission for their own causes. The two remaining states fare no better. Punjab, the largest (by population and by consumption) province, dominates the federal structure and is commonly conceived to be a resource hog. Sindh is divided along the urban/rural divide, with urban Sindh hostage to a semiseparatist movement, the Muttahida Qaumi Movement.

So we stand 62 years after independence with Pakistan a largely incoherent nation. But just as crudely as I have sketched the history of Pakistan's ideology above, let me mention the many attempts at a corrective. The 1951 Rawalpindi "Conspiracy" trial ended, by 1955, in wiping out a great segment of Leftist and Progressive thought in Pakistan. Certainly the first popular effort to wrestle back the meaning of Pakistan was Fatima Jinnah's election campaign in 1965, where she mobilized vast swathes of the population against Ayub Khan's martial law regime. Zulfiqar Ali Bhutto's initial campaign was similarly populist in its claims and wide-ranging in its appeal. The M.R.D (Movement for Restoration of Democracy) against Zia-ul-Haq. The work of citizen-poets, like Faiz Ahmed Faiz, Habib Jalib, and Ahmed Faraz. The words of Ardeshir Cowasjee. There are many, many moments at which the people of Pakistan have stood up and tried to take their country back from vested interests, singularly and collectively. In their (limited) successes and their (dramatic) failures, each of these steps was monumental in articulating an alternative vision of Pakistan to its own people.

If one is to pick a unifying theme in these contrary forces in Pakistan's short history, then Justice and the Rule of Law would be of singular importance. The movement, the so-called Lawyers Movement, which was triggered in March 2007, is, by far, the most important and most successful in Pakistan's history. It managed to remove Musharraf from military and civilian power, forced elections and, now, has reinstated the Chief Justice. It is, I think, a singular opportunity for Pakistan to undertake a serious reconsideration of its self-conception. The two-nation theory is largely incomprehensible and serves little purpose. By this I do not mean that Pakistan has lost its raison d'être or that we are back to being simplistic. Instead, we have the twin claims of Accountability and Justice for which a wide swatch of Pakistan has collectively expressed its will. It puts the focus on a properly functioning central state, which needs to provide a basic level of civic support and legal protection to its citizens.

Will Pakistan, in the coming days, attempt such a reworking of its foundational ideology? Or are the centrifugal forces too strong by now? Has the moment to "solve Pakistan" already faded? I certainly hope not.

Legends of the Fail[3]
Original published in the National *(Abu Dhabi), May 11, 2009*

Times are bleak for the state of Pakistan, if the international media is to be believed. For the past 6 weeks, the world's newspapers have charted the apparently unstoppable march of the Taliban toward Islamabad—with daily reminders that their forces are "only 100 miles" and then "only 80 miles" and then "only 60 miles" from the capital. That Pakistan is a "failed state" or "on the brink" no longer even requires elaboration: It is the universal consensus among pundits and "area experts" alike.

In the United States, the news articles have begun to game out the fall of the regime: the *New York Times*, hardly alone in its hyperventilating, has run two stories in as many weeks about America's courting the opposition leader, Nawaz Sharif, as a replacement for Pakistan's prime minister, Asif Ali Zardari. The counterinsurgency guru David Kilcullen, a former adviser to General David Petraeus, has suggested in print that the state could fail within 6 months, while Petraeus himself warns that the next 2 weeks will be decisive and that the army may have to return to power to prevent a total collapse.

The notion of Pakistan as a "failed state" has roots far deeper than the last few years; it was first deemed to have "failed" in the early 1960s, and this framework has dominated discussion of Pakistan in America from the days of the Cold War to the War on Terror. The surprisingly long history of the rhetoric of failure reveals that America's engagement with Pakistan has rarely, if ever, transcended narrow strategic aims—and that, for the United States, the solution to Pakistan's problems has always been, and will always be, the strong hand of a military ruler.

It was that under the rule of the military usurper Field Marshal Muhammad Ayub Khan that Pakistan was adopted as a Cold War ally and held up as a model "developing nation." During Khan's tenure, Pakistan was said to enjoy the benefits of a so-called developmental dictatorship—many dams were built, and much cement was poured.

The United States even helped Ayub Khan engineer an election victory in 1965. But shortly thereafter, he foolishly went to war with India; his popularity plummeted, and his flashy foreign minister, Zulfiqar Ali Bhutto, began a national campaign for a democracy based on socialist principles. Bhutto's rise ran afoul of the "domino theory" intended to check the spread of Communism; it was in this context that Pakistan was first crowned a "failed state"—giving rise to decades' worth of books and studies with titles like *The Failure of Democracy in Pakistan* (1962); *The Failure of Parliamentary Politics in Pakistan, 1953–1958* (1967); *Pakistan: Failure in National Integration* (1968); *Ethnic Conflict and the Failure of Political Integration in Pakistan* (1973); *Pakistan, Failure in Nation Building* (1977); and *Pakistan on the Brink* (2004).

By 1979, when the Soviets invaded Afghanistan, another military dictator, Zia-ul-Haq, ruled Pakistan, and the country once again became a pivotal U.S. ally, funneling arms and funds to the mujahideen across the border. The billions in U.S. military aid during that decade of armed conflict had two direct consequences for the present situation. First, the Pakistani Army became a monster on steroids, stacked against the fragile civil and bureaucratic state. And, second, the guerrilla-trained militias who ejected the Russians found themselves in charge of the country next door. But Zia's demise in 1988, and Pakistan's return to democracy, rendered it a "failed state" all over again.

The "failed state" rubric dominated the 1990s, as Pakistan became a nuclear power while stagnating economically under the burden of crippling foreign debt. But the attacks of September 11 brought Pakistan back into the American fold as a "close ally in the War on Terror," under the leadership of Pervez Musharraf, who took power in a 1999 coup. If Pakistan was on the brink of failure, few in America wanted to talk about it—at least until 2007, when Musharraf's firing of the chief justice sparked street protests that eventually led to his resignation. The exiled leaders Benazir Bhutto and Nawaz Sharif returned to contest the state's first democratic elections in more than a decade. Now the floodgates opened: A *Newsweek* cover story in October 2007 dubbed Pakistan "the most dangerous place in the world," nicely setting the tone for everything we've heard since.[4]

This decades-long tendency to reduce Pakistan's complexity to either "failure" or "stability" reflects, above all, a glaring poverty of knowledge about the real lives of 175 million Pakistanis today. Since 2007 alone, they removed a dictator from military and civilian power without firing a single shot, held the first national election since 1997—in which right-wing radical parties were soundly rejected—and launched a secular movement for justice.

None of this matters, we are told, because Pakistan is facing "an existential threat" from "violent extremists," as a State Department spokesman said on Monday. U.S. generals and media commentators are hinting that a military take-over may be the only way to arrest the imminent "failure"—to combat the "Talibanisation" of Pakistan and keep the dreaded nukes from "falling into the hands" of terrorist groups.

A comically exaggerated version of reality underpins such concerns. There are roughly 400 to 500 Pakistani Taliban fighters in the Buner region (the area deemed to threateningly close to Islamabad) and 15,000 to 20,000 operating in the region between Peshawar and the northwestern borders of Pakistan. Meanwhile, the number of active Pakistani Army personnel ranges around 500,000, supported by an annual budget of approximately $4 billion. In comparison, the Taliban in Afghanistan and Pakistan make an estimated yearly revenue of around $400 million from the heroin trade—only a fraction of which makes it to the Pakistani wing in the rural northwest of the country. As a threat to a large and diverse nation-state, 40 percent of whose population lives in urban centers like Karachi (with its 18 million residents), the rural Taliban fighters are not terribly intimidating.

Pakistan is neither Somalia nor Sudan, nor even Iraq or Afghanistan. It is a thoroughly modern state with vast infrastructure; a fiercely critical and diverse media; an active, global economy; and strong ties with regional powers, such as China and Iran. It is not a "failed state"—it even has met its debt payments to the World Bank and International Monetary Fund, at the expense of providing electricity to its citizens. It has a deeply entrenched civil bureaucracy. The "failed state" rhetoric obscures these realities. It hides the fact that religious-based parties have never garnered more than 10 percent of the seats in any election. According to its 1973 Constitution, Pakistan is an Islamic state, but it is home to multiple forms of religious expression, and the majority of Muslims in Pakistan embrace a model of Islam more syncretic than the Deobandi Salafism of the Taliban. The majority province of Punjab is ethnically, linguistically, politically, and economically far more diverse than the northwestern valley of Swat—and it is home to a well-entrenched landed elite unlikely to cede authority to the Taliban. Sindh has its own landed elite—as well as a powerful urban political party, Muttahida Quami Movement—neither of whom shows any inclination to welcome the Taliban.

Even if Pakistan is not going to capitulate to the Taliban, it does face grave dangers, and the "failed state" rhetoric—dangerous in its own right—forces our attention away from them. In Baluchistan, as a direct result of Musharraf's heavy-handed military policies, a civil war has been brewing since 2005, and there is no military solution to that unrest. At the same time, anti-Americanism is rising across the country in reaction to the campaign of missile strikes from unmanned U.S. drones, which have killed nearly 1,000 civilians since August 2008. The drones have emboldened religious conservatives who decry "U.S. imperialism" at work in Pakistan, and they are gaining strength with every tally of civilian casualties. The Tehrik Taliban-e Pakistan control in Swat is less a victory for that ragtag militia than a demonstration of the army's unwillingness to fully engage them.

The monotonous drone of "failure" implies that the fragile democracy currently in place is not worth preserving. It encourages the marginalization of the civilian government and boosts the claims of both the military and the militants. Pakistan's salvation has never been and will never be in the military's hands. The country's future lies with the millions of Pakistanis who are working to sustain democracy—and what must be defended is their resilience and strength, to prevent the self-fulfilling prophecies of failure.

State of Decay[5]
Original published in the National *(Abu Dhabi), June 12, 2009*

Pakistan ka matlab kiya? La illaha ill-allah. What does Pakistan mean? There is no God but Allah. This rallying cry boomed across India in 1945 as the struggle for independence from British rule reached its apex. Even then, that basic tenet of Muslim faith seemed an odd answer to the question posed: a declaration where one expects an explanation. This slogan has persisted through the subsequent 62 years as a readily available yell at any given gathering—from a cricket match to an anti-drone rally. Throughout these many years it has been the answer of choice—the non-answer, really—to the most fundamental question for Pakistanis: What is Pakistan? What kind of state, and for whom?

The supposedly impending "Talibanisation" of Pakistan remains a central concern for foreign observers, despite its plain improbability. While the irrational fear that the Taliban can precipitate a political or military collapse of the state has abated somewhat following the Pakistan Army's aggressive campaign in the north-west territories, the fighting has produced its own set of new problems. As a direct result of the military operation in Swat, more than a million displaced citizens are now facing a lack of food and shelter as well as a growing realization that the State has little or no plans for their rehabilitation. Adding insult to injury are political parties in Sindh and Punjab who are arguing that the Swatis cannot seek shelter in their cities—denying them the legal right of citizens to reside anywhere within Pakistan. At the same time, separatist sentiment persists among Baluchis, fired by decades of neglect, and, more recently, violent repression by the State, with the army likely to make Baluchistan its next central front.

The fear of a "Talibanised Pakistan" does not reconcile with the facts of the Islamic Republic of Pakistan. But we are still left grappling with the question: What manner of state is Pakistan? What kind of an Islamic Republic? On a continuum of Muslim-majority nations, from Saudi Arabia to Turkey, how does Pakistan define itself? Can religion, in fact, force disparate populations into political cohesion? Or is the State—as is popularly mooted—destined to disintegrate?

The early decades of the 20th century saw a number of attempts by Muslim intellectuals in India to articulate what was then termed "Islamic Nationalism." Muhammad Iqbal, a leading Muslim poet and philosopher, first posited that a federation of Muslim majority areas of India (Punjab, the North-West Frontier Province, Sindh, and Baluchistan) could form a political unit built on the principle of Muslims as contractual citizens of God's one nation. In his articulation, Iqbal was drawing on a long history—since the failed Uprising of 1857—of anti-colonial Muslim nationalist thought, which presupposed a political unity to the adherents of Islam from Cairo to Karachi. What remained unclear, however, was how Iqbal's nation would function as a state.

In 1940, Muhammad Ali Jinnah, the leading political voice of the Muslim community in India, provided the platform for the basis of the independent state of Pakistan. He argued that Muslims in India had a civilizational cohesion that remained distinct even though they had shared a thousand-year history with the Hindus. Jinnah didn't simply advance communal politics, though—he articulated a path for moving Indian Muslims from a politics of "minority rights" to one with "global citizenry." His usage of Islam as a unifying force was, then, an effort to highlight cultural affinity at the expense of political expedience. Just as he asserted the uniformity of Muslims to transcend their ethnic and linguistic diversity in India, he maintained the ability of this new state to transcend religion. In his first address to the Constituent Assembly of Pakistan in August 1947, he stressed this democratic nature of Pakistan: "Now I think we should keep that in front of us as our ideal and you will find that in course of time Hindus would cease to be Hindus and Muslims would cease to be Muslims, not in the religious sense, because that is the personal faith of each individual, but in the political sense as citizens of the State."

Pakistan, as constituted by the retreating British, was hardly a cohesive state. The two biggest provinces were themselves partitioned (Punjab and Bengal) and the fate of three princely states was undetermined—Swat, Baluchistan, and Kashmir. The country itself was divided into two unequal halves separated by India. The communal horror of Partition, which saw the displacement and killing of millions, soon gave way to the mobilization of the Army of this nascent state to redraw its borders. In fact, the actions taken then in Baluchistan and Kashmir quickly shifted the balance of power in Pakistan from the civil and the political to the military.

Still, Jinnah's hopes for a democratic state were briefly glimpsed in the first constitution, which was signed in 1956. The constitution declared Pakistan an Islamic republic but reserved minority rights and enshrined laws in the hands of a secular judiciary. But this was a short-lived achievement, and in the next several decades, dictatorial leaders would steadily erode the unity of the state through their often brutal attempts to consolidate power in Islamabad—first under the guise of modernization, and then Islamicisation, and, more recently, anti-terrorism.

The first of these, Field Marshal Ayub Khan, with the Cold War support of the United States, suspended the constitution and embarked on a decade-long military dictatorship during which he systematically broke down all progressive and democratic voices in the nation. In order to cement his military rule, Ayub Khan preyed on exactly those ethnic divisions which Jinnah had hoped to eliminate. His West Pakistani military regime deliberately marginalized the East Pakistani Bangla population. Though there were populist resisters to Ayub—most notably the political campaign of Fatima Ali Jinnah in 1965—the military dictators brokered no relief. The creation of Bangladesh in 1971—after the Pakistani military failed to recognize a legitimate national election and embarked on a systematic killing of Bengalis—spelt the end of Iqbal and Jinnah's notion that Muslims in India could form a cohesive political union. The fate of Pakistan, the state, in turn, hung in the balance.

In the aftermath of 1971, ethnic tensions flared up across Pakistan. Subnationalist movements (based sometimes on linguistic grounds, and sometimes on pre-Partition claims) emerged in Sindh, Baluchistan, Swat, and southern Punjab. The populist Prime Minister, Zulfiqar Ali Bhutto, who had campaigned on a socialist platform, responded by reasserting the Islamic nature of the state but in a manner very different from that envisioned by Jinnah. Where Jinnah conceived of a state as a democracy where the majority of citizens were Muslim, Bhutto re-defined the state itself as an Islamic state, opening the way for legal implementation of religious law. He oversaw the 1973 constitution, which declared Islam to be the official religion and curtailed the many liberties enshrined in the 1956 constitution. He also refocused Pakistan towards West Asia to forge closer ties with the global Islamic community. He held an Islamic Conference in Lahore in 1974 and worked hard to court substantial support from Saudi Arabia. Internally, he continued to escalate ethnic politics in an effort to strengthen federal powers—using the military to brutally crush Baluchi calls for justice and self-rule.

This process of Islamicisation intensified during the dictatorship of Zia-ul-Haq and became specifically a Sunnification policy. General Zia explicitly framed Pakistan's identity along two lines: one anti-Shia and Salafist, the other a national "jihad" focused on Kashmir and Afghanistan. In this, he enjoyed the specific support of the United States as it fought its proxy war against the Soviets in Afghanistan.

Twenty years of military dictatorships, under Ayub Khan and Zia-ul-Haq, cemented the rule of the few over the many. Their policies led to the emergence of specific grievances by sub-nationalist groups in Baluchistan and Sindh. In the decade of Pervez Musharraf's rule, these tensions grew dramatically and pushed the state into a greater alienation from its own citizens.

Musharraf's dictatorial regime sought to polish over any internal incoherence with a unified foreign front aimed primarily at operating militarily in Afghanistan, NWFP, and Baluchistan. The influx of cash, some $6 billion, into the coffers of the military propelled the army to newfound heights as the country's largest landlord, largest employer, and largest business. But maintaining this new oligarchy came at a steep price for Pakistan.

The two main post-2001 theatres, the states of NWFP and Baluchistan, have born the brunt of military overreach and dwindling civic engagement. It is these subnationalist discontents—and not the phantom "Taliban" threat—that pose serious problems for the unity of the state, and they cannot be answered by military escalation. In Baluchistan, since 2004, a low-grade civil war emerged after brutalities committed by Musharraf's regime, hearkening back to the Baluchi nationalist struggles of the early 1970s. NWFP remained the "frontier" both ideologically and developmentally. Besides being a military staging ground, its people were denied even rudimentary access to health care, education or a functioning judicial system. The call for Islamic law in 2008, which elicited such alarm around the world, should be seen against the backdrop of such neglect—an attempt to reassert local control and not merely an example of rampant radicalization in Pakistani society.

Rather than addressing the legitimate needs of Pakistan's various regions and groups, one government after another has, for half a century, taken power from citizens and provinces alike. If the state is indeed incoherent today, it is the consequence of decades of military rule. The greatest threat facing Pakistan today is not a ragged band of armed Pashtuns. It is what follows the deployment of indiscriminate firepower to defeat them—mass displacement and a rising toll of civilian deaths.

Strict Interpretations: A Reply to Atiya Khan[6]
Original published in Platypus Review, *February 18, 2010*

To quote Aldous Huxley and to paraphrase Atiya Khan in her *Platypus Review* article "The poverty of Pakistan's politics," I represent "a sad symptom of the failure of the intellectual class in time of crisis." In Khan's telling, it is the intellectual Left which failed (in) Pakistan, and under its sad banner now congregate blind and mute liberals such as myself. It is a strong, and harshly delivered, criticism, and I take it very seriously.

Let me begin, however, by engaging Khan on her reading of Pakistan's past. Khan posits that there was once a golden age of Left-labor politics in Pakistan, which gave the newly created state a "backbone" in the first five years of its existence. This was a time when trade unions "flourished" in industries across Pakistan, so much so, she argues, that some two hundred unions could claim over 400,000 workers as rank-and-file members by 1951. This golden age of labor curiously coincides, according to Khan, with the "failures of the Left after World War II." Though the labor unions had the organizational skills and mass appeal to push for real reform, the Left allowed those advantages to dissipate on account of the theoretical confusion and imaginative limitations born of Stalinist notions of country-based socialism. However, in her determination to shoehorn Pakistani history into a Left-labor narrative, Khan seriously misrepresents or elides actualities.

In her telling, Ayub Khan's dictatorial regime collapses not because of an all-out military revolt and a concomitant withdrawal of U.S. support, but because of labor strikes. Zulfiqar Ali Bhutto—Foreign Minister and heir-apparent of Ayub Khan and an elite landlord—becomes in Khan's piece a populist leader by seducing the labor unions and not by openly selling himself to the military brass as the only West Pakistani leader capable of holding back East Pakistani domination. Similarly, in Khan's narrative Zia-ul-Haq is the original architect of Islamization, whereas in fact the policies and practices of Islamization began under Zulfiqar Ali Bhutto as early as 1973. In fact, the constitution Bhutto pushed forward in 1973 represents the most concrete capitulation by the Pakistani state to the religious right, especially the Jama'at Islami. Zia-ul-Haq is properly considered the architect not of the Islamization, but of the "Sunnification" of Pakistan. Thus, Zia only perfected a process initiated by Bhutto. Khan stresses "Chinese opportunism" in the rise of the Afghan Taliban rather than highlighting the primary force of the Soviet invasion of Afghanistan and of joint U.S.–Pakistan efforts to train a local militia. She dismisses the Nawaz Sharif and Benazir Bhutto regimes of the late 1980s and 1990s as no more than the realization of the Taliban's agenda "to find an ally across the Khyber Pass," rather than seeing them as democratic governments (however flawed) elected by the people of Pakistan. This, of course, not only lends a far greater influence to the Afghan Taliban but also exaggerates the control those civilian governments exercised over the Pakistani military. Khan does not explain how the Taliban could set the agenda for Pakistan in the 1988 or 1993 elections when, until 1996, they were just one of a number of factions engaged in the brutal civil war then raging in Afghanistan. There are other strange lacunae buried in her narrative: She leaves unspecified who, or what, this confused and ineffective "Left" in Pakistan actually was. From what class was it drawn and in which cities? Or how did the failure to enact land reform, along with the internecine squabbling of leftist organizations and the succession of U.S.-backed military dictatorships, affect this history? The history of the Left and labor in Pakistan is certainly one of the important and largely unexamined factors in our collective efforts to understand the present. I am keen on seeing Khan make that case, but she will have to do so with far greater nuance, and with fewer liberties taken with the facts, than presented in her piece.

Yet even if Khan's various readings of Pakistani history were defensible, her tacit embrace of U.S. imperial policies in Afghanistan and Pakistan is not. She dismisses as so much belly aching my concern for the humanitarian crisis caused by the Pakistani military offensives in Swat, Waziristan, and Baluchistan as well as the political crisis caused almost daily by unmanned drone attacks. For Khan, these concerns merely provide cover to the Taliban and act as a screen for their crypto-fascism. Consequently, U.S. military strategies ought to be supported, as they are the only means available for combating the Taliban. But it is hard for me to imagine that from the scorched houses and corpses of Swat and Waziristan anything resembling an international Left could possibly appear. More likely, these policies will radicalize ever-larger segments of the population. More damagingly, the military-only strategies create new support networks for Islamist radicals and silence the voices of those who argue for a secular and progressive Pakistan. For Khan, pointing this out that makes me either a nationalist or a neoliberal.

I am interested neither in labels nor in identity politics. I consider myself a student of history. As is obvious, I am not providing apologia for the Taliban, but articulating a historically and politically precise context within which to understand the many groups uncritically labeled "Taliban." Similar efforts seem to be enjoying widespread acceptance among NATO commanders in Afghanistan, but such attentiveness to cultural and historical specificity has yet to gain popularity among political analysts of Pakistan. Still, I submit that such effort towards precision and clarity alone leads towards an understanding of how the "Taliban" emerged in Pakistan, how they currently operate, and, therefore, how they might best be combated. These contexts are utterly invisible from the drone's eye view.

A growing chorus of concerned voices now states that an uncritical embrace of U.S. military might, as it exerts itself without regards to any community, any civilian, or any local law, advance the purposes of the Taliban more than anyone else's. Yet, there are no critical voices in the larger U.S. public speaking against America's policies toward Pakistan. My op-ed for the *Nation*, to which Khan takes such exception, was just such an effort. It sought to contextualize the "Taliban are coming" hysteria, arguing that this deliberately hinders any attempt to historicize the Taliban and thus to effectively neutralize them. The Pakistani military, now being fêted with billions for fighting the Taliban, is the same Pakistani military that created the Taliban in the 1990s. The CIA that currently conducts drone missile attacks against al-Qaeda is the same CIA that in the 1980s provided the mujahideen with Stinger missiles and called them "freedom fighters." More precisely: I have little faith in the healing power of U.S. bombs.

I remain deeply troubled by the violence unleashed by these "Taliban" organizations against Pakistan's cities and inhabitants. If Khan had bothered to look beyond my short piece in the Nation, she would have found ample evidence on my blog that I have, for the past five years, consistently spoken and written against the religious extremists and for democracy and liberality in Pakistan. I have written consistently against the Pakistani military state and its corrosive politics *and* I have argued for a check on rank U.S. policies in Afghanistan, Iraq, and Pakistan. It is fair to argue that I lay too much stress on the "Taliban are coming" narrative at play in U.S. policies and media, and far less effort on denouncing every single Taliban atrocity. But it is simplistic to assume that I cannot hold the Taliban in utter contempt, and completely responsible for their terrorism while maintaining that the U.S.-Pakistani understandings of the policies based on them are misguided.

The groups now collectively labeled the "Taliban in Pakistan" are an amalgamation of various groups—from states' rights advocates in Swat to tribal warlords in Waziristan to trained militia (against India in Kashmir) in southern Punjab. More than a few are now allied with domestic antistatist organizations like the

Lashkar-e-Taiba or the international ones like al-Qaeda, and some of the local warlords now have national aspirations. Collectively, they are responsible for thousands of civilian deaths in the cities of Pakistan. To counter the threat effectively, they pose, we have to disaggregate them into their constituent parts and deal with them accordingly. Some groups will respond to political dialogue, while others can only be eliminated by force or by the civil justice system. Because they claim various political goals—and it is absolutely crucial to understand that these are "political" goals though they often change from venue to venue and from spokesman to spokesman—we have to engage them within the political realm. This is where U.S. endorsement of the rigged Afghan election, and the longer history of maintaining Karzai's puppet regime, leave us with a significant political handicap. This also means that political legitimacy must be stripped from these groups. The lingering issues of states' rights for Swat and Baluchistan require political solutions. The Pakistani military must remain under civilian political leadership and military solutions cannot be allowed to escalate into open-ended civil warfare.

The politics of the groups lumped together under the "Taliban" label is religious in its markers, its symbols, and its public face. This means that any counterstrategy must also include a public effort to "reclaim" the religious front. These groups are heavily armed and supplied in consequence of public donations, the illicit trades in heroin and electronic media, and direct funding that still comes from sources both internal (whether the continued involvement by Pakistani intelligence agencies or other social and civil groups) and external (diaspora communities as well as Saudi Arabia). The state of Pakistan must criminalize weapons possession and revoke licenses in order to start an effort to clean out the cities and stop the influx of smuggled weaponry. The recruits are overwhelmingly young, male, and illiterate. As such, they are strongly against the existing status quo, women, and education. The reform of primary and secondary education (including madrasas) should also be a priority. The state needs to enshrine the right to education within the Constitution. The gist of my *Nation* piece was this: the Pakistani Taliban lack mass appeal. There is no way in which they can overthrow the state of Pakistan. They are not a mortal threat. This is now empirically true since the Taliban were famously within 60 miles of Islamabad in March 2009 and, well, Islamabad still stands—however bloodied. We heard no more about the imminent demise of Pakistan once the Pakistani army mobilized and created a million internally displaced citizens. We heard little about the crisis of Pakistan once another front was opened up in northern Waziristan. The way I understand it, this heightening of paranoia about the Taliban was not concerned with the realities on the ground in Pakistan but rather with the ideological and political landscape in Washington D.C. and Islamabad. Absent from the discussion, and the policies, were the historical concerns of the people of the region. This, I submit, is not only shortsighted but also strategically self-defeating.

In the last year alone, 3,021 civilians were killed in Pakistan in terrorist attacks and nearly 8,000 were injured. Additionally, nearly a million were displaced due to military operations. Even for a nation of 170 million, these are devastating numbers representing real sacrifices by the citizenry. These are realities that deserve our understanding and our analysis just as much as our collective concern for the rising tide of the "Taliban." I focus on the people of Pakistan because I continue to have hope in them. I have no opinion on whether the "Left" has failed Pakistan. I do know that a broad coalition—composed of clerical and other workers, lawyers, and community activists—came together and threw out the military dictator in 2008 after a nine-year stint in power. In the election that accomplished this, the Pakistani people also roundly rejected all religious parties, embarking instead on a daring journey towards electoral democracy.

Pakistan's New Paranoia[7]
Original published in the National *(Abu Dhabi), March 11, 2010*

A new narrative is ascendant in Pakistan. It is in the writings of major Urdu-language newspaper columnists, who purport to marshal anecdotal or textual evidence on its behalf. It is on television, where the hosts of religious and political talk shows polish it with slick production values. The basic elements of the story—which has often, and erroneously, been called a conspiracy theory—are simple. Local agents (or terrorists, or soldiers, or Blackwater employees) representing a foreign power (India, or the United States, or Israel) are intent on destroying Pakistan because they fear that it will otherwise emerge as the powerful leader of the Muslim world, just as the country's past leaders had predicted. The ascendant narrative is prophetic and self-pitying, nationalist and martial; it is a way to interpret current events and a call for activism to restore the country's interrupted rise to glory.

The consumers of this narrative represent the largest demographic slice of Pakistan—young, urban men and women under the age of 30. They came of age under a military dictatorship with a war on their borders, and, more recently, almost daily terrorist attacks in their major cities. The twin poles of their civic identity—Pakistan and Islam—are under immense stress. They love Pakistan; they want to take Islam back from the jihadists. But there is no national dialogue and no vision for the state: no place, in other words, where the young can make sense of their own country. Pakistan is ideologically adrift and headed toward incoherence, unable to articulate its own meaning as either a state or a nation. To the anguished question "Whither Pakistan?" the country's leaders provide no response.

A man named Zaid Hamid, who has perhaps done more than anyone else to promote the new narrative of national victimhood, says that he has a clear answer. We are, he argues, living in the apocalyptic end-times—and Pakistan must emerge as the leader of the last struggle. Clad in his trademark red hat, he is leading rallies on campuses and in auditoriums across the country. His words—and the excited reactions of his audiences—are captured by camera crews and the footage posted on YouTube and Facebook.

In his ceremonial Urdu, laced with Qur'anic verses and English idioms, he tells the gathered that they represent a generation hand-picked by God to lead Pakistan. He warns them of the sinister forces arrayed against the blessed nation of Pakistan. He assures them that prophecies predict their victory—all they have to do is mobilize. They have to leave their seats and take back their country. Only then can they conquer India and Israel. Only then can they rebuke the United States. Only then can they fulfill the dreams of Pakistan's founding fathers. But the first step has already been taken—they came to his rally, they heard his call to action.

Zaid Hamid is the leading voice of this new Pakistani revivalism. His mysterious rise to prominence demonstrates the power of the new televised media—and the new social networks—in Pakistan, even as it provokes questions about his financial and political backers. In 2006, Hamid was a one-man think-tank in Islamabad, issuing defense and security analysis for his own company, Brasstacks. In 2007 the country, led by the Lawyers' Movement, rallied against the military regime of Pervez Musharraf and upended the established order across the nation. After the national elections of 2008, as well as the military operations in the northwest, Hamid emerged as the host of his own program on the independent channel TV One. Within the year, he became one of the biggest stars of the Pakistani punditocracy—spreading his message in columns and op-eds, on YouTube channels, and in solidly produced television documentaries.

Through each new phase in his explosive ascent to the pinnacle of Pakistan's media landscape, Hamid remained a staunchly patriotic booster of the Pakistani military, and a vicious critic of "foreign" meddling in Pakistan's affairs—usually carried out, in his account, by the American CIA or the Indian Research and Analysis Wing (RAW). He promoted a martial understanding of the Pakistani past, resplendent in the glory of jihad in Kashmir and Afghanistan. The country's army and air force, he explained, had bravely faced down threats from India, America, and Israel—but they were often undermined by their own politicians.

On his television program, which began in 2008, he turned his attention toward the more distant past, presenting hourlong documentaries on the "great heroes" of the Muslim world, the military commanders who conquered Spain or Sindh or fought the British Empire. Hamid's documentaries have a reverential—almost sacred—tone, highlighting historical documents and stressing the "authenticity" of his re-enactments. Each show ends with a solemn promise that Pakistan could one day regain its pride and fulfill its destiny.

To those unfortunate enough to have lived in General Zia-ul-Haq's militarized Pakistan, all of this is eerily familiar, and hence laden with dire portents. In the 1980s the national television channel, PTV, ritually alternated between footage of "captured" Indian agents and serial dramas glorifying the Arab warriors of the Islamic past. Zia-ul-Haq's Sunnification policies depended entirely on a turn toward the Kingdom of Saudi Arabia—from whence came both the ideology of strict sectarianism and the largesse to create madrasas and jihadist training camps. The sordid history of the U.S. proxy war in Afghanistan does not need to be told anew. What remains important is that particularly narrow definitions of history, religious practice, and national purpose were foisted upon millions of young men.

From these millions, General Zia nourished the mujahideen for the battle in Afghanistan, for Kashmir, Bosnia, and Palestine. The local and the global injustices were thus intricately intertwined for those young, hungry minds across Pakistan. The chief vehicle of dispensing such narratives was the religious history of Muslims across the world. By combining elements of Pan-Islamism with reactionary Wahhabism and layering the whole lot with a strong sense of victimhood, Zia sought to create a specific psychological profile for the Pakistani Muslim: militant and nationalist above all, angry at perceived injustices against his faith, convinced of a vast conspiratorial "other" against which one must be willing to sacrifice oneself. It was a smoldering cauldron from which both funds and personnel could always be extracted. Though these processes slowed down after Zia and though Musharraf made some gestures at changing the national dialogue—via his "Enlightened Moderation"—these are the conservative forces which continue to compel Pakistani middle class.

The genius of Zaid Hamid has been to deftly shift the role of Islam from Zia's strictly performative one to a more flexible mould. His acolytes, who call themselves *lal topis* (red hats), see a pious man who is less interested in their actual religiosity—whether they pray or not, give alms or not, wear hijab or not—and more concerned with their devotion to the idea of a resurgent, "independent" Pakistan. He calls on Islam mostly to play the role of history. He produces sayings from the Prophet Mohammad declaring victory for the Muslim armies against *al-Hind* (India) and Jerusalem. He distributes the "prophecies" of Shah Nimatullah, a Sufi poet from the 12th century. Such claims to religiously based "evidence" allow him to sidestep any direct criticisms. There are no such prophecies, of course. The traditions Hamid claims predict the conquest of *al-Hind* are spurious and were collected late in the 10th century in a book of eschatological accounts circulating along the Byzantine frontier of the 'Abbasid dynasty. The "quatrains" of Shah Nimatullah are another case of popular mythography.

What remains real, and gravely troubling, is that a quiet transformation is occurring in the cultural landscape of Pakistan. Hamid is only at the forefront of a movement that includes others like the hypernationalist columnist Ahmed Qureshi, always eager to blame India or Blackwater for each bomb blast; the televangelist Aamir Liaqat, who provides a treacly veneer of religious learning for the "Foreign Hand" theorists; the reformed rocker Ali Azmat and the fashion designer Maria B., who act as emcees at Hamid's rallies.

Like Glenn Beck, the paranoid American TV sensation, with whom he shares many traits, Hamid is channeling the deep misgivings of the middle class and offering them visions of a glorious future—one whose realization requires nothing more than blind fidelity to the supposed foundational truths of the nation. For millions of young Pakistanis, it is proving to be a heady brew. But the hangover, when it comes, will be staggering.

The Apocalypses of Zaid Hamid[8]
March 12, 2010

. . . We have been discussing Zaid Hamid here for a while—and after seeing a few hundred of his appearances on YouTube, I can offer a few bits of analysis.

Perhaps analytically most crucial is the point that he is not *merely* a conspiracy theorist. That aspect of his appeal has received the most attention, and it does resonate widely in different spheres (and for varied reasons), but he has significantly more to offer the starry-eyed. His primary appeal rests in propagating a *prophetic apocalyptic* tradition—both specific to the Prophet and symbolically linked to folks like Muhammad Iqbal. This prophetic tradition contains both an explanation of the current disasters but also a promise of restoration, of victory. From Islamic history, he takes *ahadi'th* proclaiming the triumph over India (and Jerusalem); from (what he terms) the "spiritual" realm, he takes the quatrains of Naimatullah Shah, which make exactly the same amount of sense as Nostradamus; from Iqbal and Jinnah, he takes the nationalist "prophesies." All this is amended and aided by the usual coterie of dreams, Sufi sayings, "feelings" and "emotions." This last bit is perhaps the most important to keep in mind—he argues for a "rational" argumentation (so "reports," "findings," "evidence" are prominent keywords in his speech), but it is the emotional landscape where he actually rests his case. He repeatedly calls upon his listeners to contemplate their feelings—scared, helpless, angry, righteous—and then work out how they can actively engage with them. The corrosive power of nationalist or religious slogans is most readily apparent here. I have a lot more to say about this affective turn in political punditry, but, for now, let me stick with the prophetic tradition.

In one of the YouTube exchanges, he is part of a panel interview with various military/political folks. One of the mustachioed ex-military objects to his constant claims to the "spiritual warfare," saying that his emphasis on "sufi prophecies" was rather stunted. Hamid immediately jumps back to the Prophetic *had'ith* to make the same claim. The mustachioed one has no choice but to acknowledge that the Prophet must be right. This line of reasoning—"the Prophet said"—is also deployed by his supporters to shut down the debate regarding his insane policies. . . . The response of the left/progressive/sane folks has been to mock—

to great effect. I certainly have the impulse to simply state "Bullshit" to all his stories of 110-year-old saints predicting this or that, to some random who or whom—and presto! One only needs a modicum of common sense to see through that. Yet here we are.

So, I believe we need to deconstruct his claims on historical basis—while also, I guess, stating "Bullshit."

The End-Times Narrative

To historicize his claims to these "prophetic traditions," let's start with the *hadi'th* he claims predicts a Muslim army in al-Hind. Only scattered references to al-Hind as a geographical entity exist in the *Sahih* collections.[9] The "prophetic ones" Zaid Hamid cites actually come from the accounts of *thughur al-Hind* (frontier of *al-Hind*), which were compiled in eschatological collections. Just to be clear again, they do not appear in the collectively accredited *ahadi'th*. They number around five or six (repeated). In these short accounts, *al-Hind* is one of the stages for the battle between good and evil—between *dajjal* (known as the anti-Christ in Christian eschatology) and the Muslims, at the end of time.[10] An example is this oft-reproduced tradition: "The Prophet proclaimed that two groups from my 'ummah will be protected from the fires of Hell. One is the group who will fight in the frontier of *al-Hind*, and the other group with will stay with 'Isa b. Maryam (Jesus Christ)."[11] This is the tradition repeatedly cited by Zaid Hamid.

It appears in *Kitab al-Fitan*, the compendium of eschatological traditions by Nu'aym ibn Hammad (d. 844). In a very short section entitled *Ghazwat al-Hind* (battles in *al-Hind*), Nu'aym recounts traditions that collectively tie the conquest of *al-Hind* and the capture and manumission of its Kings to the end of times. Within eschatological timeline, the conquest of al-Hind is portrayed as the penultimate step, after which both 'Isa b. Maryam (Jesus) and *dajjal* will finally emerge. For example, another tradition reported by Nu'aym presents the prophecy of the Prophet that Jesus will arrive after the conquest of al-Hind and the captivity of the kings of *al-Hind*: "*It is narrated by al-Walid who received it from Sufy'an bin 'Umar who received it from the Prophet: He said, "From my 'umma, someone will conquer al-Hind in the name of Allah and put the kings of al-Hind in chains. Allah will forgive them, and they will roam and explore Syria and they will find 'Isa b. Maryam in Syria.*[12] The motif here is certainly not "conquest" but rather "humiliation" (i.e., of seeing the King brought in chains). This emphasis on *muluk* (kings) of lands far to the East is a key motif, with kings of China also equally represented: "*There is no army greater in reward than the army going to China, then they will bring the kings of China and the kings of al-Aqaba back in chains, and when they bring them they will find that [Jesus] son of Mary has already descended in Syria.*"[13]

To properly contextualize such traditions, we have to first conclude that these traditions reflect *current* thoughts and realities—as in, localized, contemporary propaganda at the margins of an expanding empire. When one compares them to the canonical traditions—and attempts to date them—this becomes clearer:

> Historical apocalyptic traditions should be recognized, in general, to be the result of frustration and pre-conquest propaganda. Therefore, the most reasonable place to locate them would be in these intervals of inaction, especially after the major defeats of the reign of Hisham (r. 724–43). This period and the beginning of the 'Abbasid dynasty were, in all likelihood, the major periods of apocalyptic activity in Syria, which as come down to us in the form of historical apocalypses, and was mostly collected by Nu'aym two generations later.[14]

Al-Hind in these eschatological traditions is both an outlier and a rhetorical point. These traditions are focused on Byzantium—and the kings of India or China are there to serve as demonstrations of rising Muslim power as well as markers on the end time-line. These are certainly not "prophecies"—as Zaid Hamid is treating them—they are remnants of a messianic debate between expansionist and conservative cadres in the 9th and 10th centuries at the Muslim borderland with the Byzantium.

I will deal with the "Foreign Hand" and the quatrains of the Naimatullah Shah in the near future.

A Pakistan Native[15]
May 6, 2010

Associated Press gave these intriguing details in the report it carried yesterday about Faisal Shahzad, the Pakistan native who had tried (but failed) to detonate a car bomb in New York's Times Square and was arrested as he tried to leave the United States:

> "He usually walks around alone, looking lonely and kind of depressed usually," said Nejilia Gayden, 18, of Bridgeport. "Sometimes he'll mumble to himself."
> Mr. Shahzad, Mr. Chomiak said, mentioned that he wanted to grow tomatoes.
> A Pakistani man said that an acquaintance of his who was a friend of the Shahzad family told him that within the past year, Mr. Shahzad had peered critically at a glass of whiskey the friend was holding, indicating a judgmental stance typical for rigid jihadis.
> Another family friend in Pakistan, Kifayat Ali, called Mr. Shahzad "emotional" and said that he used to carry a dagger around with him as a boy.

Aliou Niasse, a street vendor selling framed photographs of New York, said that he was the first to spot the car containing the bomb, which pulled up right in front of his cart on the corner of 45th street and Broadway next to the Marriott hotel.

"I didn't see the car pull up or notice the driver because I was busy with customers. But when I looked up I saw that smoke appeared to be coming from the car. This would have been around 6.30 p.m.

"I thought I should call 911, but my English is not very good, and I had no credit left on my phone, so I walked over to Lance, who has the T-shirt stall next to mine, and told him. He said we shouldn't call 911. Immediately, he alerted a police officer near by," said Mr. Niasse, who is originally from Senegal and who has been a vendor in Times Square for about eight years.

The Cultural Damage of the "War on Terror"[16]
Original published in the National *(Abu Dhabi), September 3, 2010*

The 9/11 Commission Report, issued in May 2004, declared that a "failure of imagination" on the part of the U.S. analytical and intelligence communities was a prime reason behind their failure to prevent the September 11 attacks. One of the key recommendations by the commission, then, was to call for "routinising, even bureaucratising the exercise of imagination." But what did they mean by that word, "imagination"? In the report, it is used twice in a manner that hints towards its practical value. Once, when discussing the "principal architect of the 9/11 attacks," Khalid Sheikh Muhammad [KSM]: "highly educated and equally comfortable in a government office or a terrorist safe house, KSM applied his imagination, technical aptitude, and managerial skills to hatching and planning an extraordinary array of terrorist schemes." Second, when commenting on the foresight of the National Security Council member Richard Clarke, the only person in the administration concerned about the danger posed by hijacked aircraft. Here the commission notes that his concerns came not from intelligence briefings but from "Tom Clancy novels."

In the first case, it reads more like "cleverness" or "ingenuity" than imagination (the report praises KSM's acquired skills and his adaptability, not his "creativity"). But in the second case, we have a meaning slightly closer to the conventional usage: the "imagination" of Tom Clancy, the writer of fictional thrillers, which supposedly provided clues to the possibility of an attack like that of September 11. Yet the intelligence community failed to grasp the value of this novelist's imagination. That the novelist can grasp truths about the terrorist that cannot be accessible to the trained and the skilled seems, on the face of it, a bizarre claim. So, perhaps, the commission meant that the novelist could better imagine Khalid Sheikh Muhammad himself—to understand, that is, what choices, what turns, and what histories collided to make him possible? And that it was this capacity, which needed to be routinised: the capacity to imagine this Other, to give them an interiority, a mindfulness, an agency, a history.

Six years later, the commission's hopes seem to have been misplaced: The years since September 11 have not provided us with many examples of "the exercise of imagination" when it comes to fictional representations of the Terrorist. When imagined in literary fiction, would-be perpetrators of terrorist violence cleave to a by-now-familiar set of stereotypes: as rigid, sexualised "outsiders" possessing already articulated ideologies. John Updike's 2006 novel *Terrorist* sets out its cardboard characterisation from its very first lines: "Devils, Ahmad thinks. These devils seek to take away my God. All day long, at Central High School, girls sway and sneer and expose their soft bodies and alluring hair." Another type of truncated imagination is at display in the work of numerous other American writers who have addressed terrorism in fiction but constrained themselves almost entirely to the perspective of their American protagonists.

These failures of imagination, in fact, are symptomatic of a uniquely American engagement with the figure of the Terrorist—one that has both a cultural and political impact. Culturally, the Terrorist appears as a "known unknown" (to use Donald Rumsfeld's haiku)—predetermined along the matrix of "Radical Islam" and its understood components, which grant a specific age, a specific geography, and a specific profile.

The Terrorist in this cultural milieu can act as a simple marker for forces that are themselves incomprehensible to many—Islam or Pakistan—that allow civilisational arguments without even the rhetorical need to invoke facts, history, or local knowledge. One simply has to assert known unknowability—as in the most recent case of the so-called Ground Zero Mosque, where the word "mosque" is, in itself, a provocation, and the Muslims bear the burden of proving beyond unreasonable doubt their patriotism, their good intentions, or even the basic fact that they are American. In effect, once understood as Muslims, the planners of the Islamic community centre in Lower Manhattan automatically become "outsiders"—and they are presumed, therefore, to harbour heinous desires and nefarious intentions.

But the political impact of this imaginative failure is even more pernicious and devastating. It renders the policies for punishing or fighting the Terrorist also unknowable. The practices of the state are, it is assumed, the only viable possibilities of a response to terrorism—an example being the tortured explications of torture itself that were peddled by the media, in which the overwhelming consensus was that whatever actions the state deemed necessary were the correct ones. It demands an unwise degree of trust in the institutions of power; it gives their narrative all the agency, all the truth. It gives us a world where only the degree of torture is debated and not the morality of it, where incarceration without even a charge is merely an electioneering issue and not a constitutional crisis, and where indiscriminate surveillance is routinely defended with the argument that if you have nothing to hide you have nothing to fear.

On this highly limited and highly corrosive cultural and political terrain, the figure of the Terrorist enjoys a surprisingly uncomplicated public life in America—devoid of any complexity and bestowed with nearly universal consensus as to its motives, designs, and actions. This may not come as a surprise, but it should. The practice of terrorism is certainly not new to the world (nor to America, for that matter), and, over the course of its own history, it has never before been viewed in such simplistic terms. The Terrorist is, after all, an intimate to the European and has always been imagined with complexity and nuance: with the capacity to act against the state, to target individuals for assassinations, and to trumpet ideologies, while standing opposed to but also within society.

English received the word from the French *terreur*, and the earliest proud self-proclaimers of the label "Terrorist" were the French Jacobins in the 1790s. The assassinations and bombings by anarchists and saboteurs that occurred in the late 19th and early 20th centuries were amply covered in fiction, defined in legal terms, philosophised and theorised. Works like Dostoevsky's *The Devils* (1872), Joseph Conrad's *The Secret Agent* (1907), André Malraux's *La Condition Humaine* (1933), Arthur Koestler's *Thieves in the Night* (1946), and Albert Camus's *The Just Assassins* (1949) represented the best in the realm of Europe's cultural imagination; at the same time, the actions of colonial powers, like Spain in the Philippines, Britain in India and Malaysia, and France in Algeria, represented the worst of the political realm.

Between 1980 and 2001, the world's highest concentration of terrorist attacks was in India, where the Sikh Khalistan Movement and the Liberation Tigers of Tamil Eelam were responsible for the assassination of two prime ministers. The Kashmiri, the Assamese, and the Naxalite separatist movements and the communal riots between Hindus and Muslims provided even more political turmoil from the 1970s onwards. As had been the case in Europe, India's response to terrorism was both politically draconian and imaginatively complex. Indira Gandhi's imposed suspension of the constitution during the Emergency (1975–1977), or the military crackdown in Kashmir in the 1990s, co-existed with the intimate portraits of the Terrorist in popular cinema and arts—Mani Ratnam's 1998 *Dil Se* being a particularly evocative example: a love story enveloping the tale of a young female suicide bomber who is put on this path as a direct result of atrocities committed by the Indian Army. So what accounts for the American blind spot, the failure of imagination in conceiving of the Terrorist as anything other than exceptional, foreign, and prone to the basest sexual and ideological provocations?

It is worthwhile to note that, in American formulations, terrorism remains a uniquely non-Western phenomenon and one that comes from a time other than our own; the ideology of its exponents is often casually described as medieval and, hence, in direct conflict with the modern. To construct such an understanding, one has to necessarily forget the European genesis of terrorism, and one has to necessarily make the Terrorist a figure outside of comprehensibility—an alien, an outsider. The template for the Terrorist, in the American imagination, is rigid and historically dated. It is the template of the Old Man of the Mountain.

"And in this manner the Old Man of the Mountain got his people to murder any one whom he desired to get rid of." So reads Marco Polo's travelogue, a hodge-podge of Crusade histories and circulating eyewitness accounts of the East as well as myths, marvels, and legends. Polo was not the first to introduce Christian Europe to the 12th-century Islamic sect known as the Assassins, but he certainly gave the legend its fullest form and fixed it in the Western imagination for centuries to come. They are a community of *mulahid* [heretics] living in remote mountains, who believe that the "Shaykh al-Hashishim" is their prophet, and they do whatever he asks of them, even at the cost of their lives. Shaykh is translated as the "Old Man" and, presumably, the hashashin as "assassin." To these earlier sketches, Marco Polo had added new colour: a secret paradise, filled with beautiful and willing maidens, somewhere high in the mountains, where the kidnapped youth first opens his eyes and gazes at rivers of milk and honey. Here he stays, engorging himself on all the delights, being indoctrinated, taught the skills of evasion and of murder. Then, he is drugged once again, and this time, he awakens to find himself in front of the Old Man, his prophet, who now asks him to do his bidding, the killing of a rival, and the reward would be the return to the Paradise.

It may not be an accident that George W. Bush, in his utterances immediately after September 11, invoked the Crusades. For one of the earliest and most influential advisors to the White House on matters Islamic was Bernard Lewis, the "doyen of Middle East historians" and one of the main proponents of the "Clash of Civilisations" thesis, a darling of Bush and Cheney, and the chief-explicator of Islam to the rest of America. He was also the author of the most popular scholarly work about the Assassins, his 1967 study, *The Assassins: A Radical Sect in Islam.*

The Crusades and the Assassins were central to Lewis's understanding of Muslim terrorists. In his framing, the figure of the Terrorist remains perpetually fixed to the 12th century: The Terrorist is an outsider, the Terrorist is brainwashed and beholden to an incomprehensible ideology, the Terrorist is a young sex-crazed man, the Terrorist is an automaton bent on destroying Western civilization. It mattered little to this account that the historical "Assassins" were a secret sect who called themselves *fedayeen* (self-annihilators), operating in the mountains of Alamut, in northern Iran. Theologically, they were Nizari Ismai'ili—a subsect within the Shi'a tradition—but their cause was political: They were intent mainly on carving out a space for themselves against the declining Seljuk empire and the Egyptian Mamluks. Hence, they were responsible mainly for assassinations of Mamluk officials and other Muslim notables. There are no credible reports that they ever took hashish—only the Mamluks referred to them, derogatorily, as the *hashashin* [those who consume hashish and, some claim, the origin of the word "assassin"]—or that they ever had a secret paradise.

Lewis's Assassins/Terrorists model, which has come to dominate the American discourse on terrorism, is clearly ahistorical, but it also has a geographical component: The place of the Terrorist, in this view, is always "outside." Recall that one of the rationales for the invasion of Iraq was the so-called fly-paper theory, which posited that as long as we were killing terrorists "over there," they couldn't come and kill us "over here." This geography of exclusion can be seen most starkly in the realm of law, where the Terrorist is deprived of the protections and rights that apply to "domestic" space: confined at Guantanamo Bay, stripped of constitutional rights, subject to "extraordinary renditions."

The failure of these policies, of course, has been widely observed and fiercely argued. But the confluence between the political and cultural understandings of the Terrorist in America has gone almost entirely unremarked: This single framework renders all Muslim Americans politically suspect and culturally incomprehensible. What's more, that they are politically suspect makes them more culturally unknowable; their cultural foreignness, in turn, makes them more politically suspect.

It is among the accomplishments of Amitava Kumar's new book, *A Foreigner Carrying in the Crook of His Arm a Tiny Bomb* (Duke University Press, 2010), that it refuses to separate the cultural and the political means by which the War on Terror has been waged. Kumar's slim volume begins in India, with the wrongful arrest of terror suspects—and with the observation, by a poultry farmer in Walavati, that "What the Americans were doing in Abu Ghraib, they learned from our policemen here." As he traces the ordeals of the "ordinary men and women whose lives are entangled in the War on Terror," Kumar endeavours to connect not only the tortuous practices common to states fighting terrorists but also the ways this "war" has been imagined. He covers the cases of three convicted terrorists, in their own words, and in the words of their loved ones. The three men were all caught in sting operations and accused of planning crimes, or expressing the desire to commit crimes, against the United States: one convicted of purchasing a rocket launcher, another of wanting to detonate bombs in the New York City subway, and the last of funding Sikh terrorists in India.

Alongside his personal encounters with these terrorists, Kumar shows the haphazardly constructed legal cases, the government witnesses, and the clash of half-digested cultural understandings. He peels back the stories that we only know by headlines—the Lackawanna Six, the American Taliban—with a novelist's eye and a reporter's doggedness. Kumar is not out to rehabilitate these characters nor to act as their apologist. He keeps a studied distance, a knowing diffidence—but not just to the terrorists: to the prosecution, to their evidence, to the informants used by the U.S. government to provoke the defendants into convictable speech and acts.

It is when he widens his gaze from the terrorists to the arts, to public speech and to advocacy, in order to highlight the efforts of artists to observe, catalogue, and explain—and the efforts of the state to control, coerce, and regulate—that his book becomes a truly horrific indictment of post-September 11 "failure of imagination." He correctly identifies "all of us" as participants in the state's war on terror—sanctioning the drone attacks, extrajudicial assassinations, and extraordinary renditions. By focusing on the banality of the state's cases against the old, the infirm, the misfits, the ill-suited, Kumar reminds us that the war raging far from our doorsteps is also all around us. He wants to bring that war closer, and to make its consequences visible, by exposing the inequities of domestic counterterrorism prosecutions. It is a hard case to make, especially in a country that is yet to face up to the realities of the war it rages far away, in Afghanistan and Pakistan. But it is an essential case, and a moral one, and he makes it powerfully in the vacuum that has been left by the failures of fictional and historical imagination.

Kumar makes both a political and legal argument, but also a cultural one. It is to his credit that, while writing a nonfiction book, he acknowledges the power of the imagination—of art—to wrestle into view that which politics works to hide from us. Kumar's work demonstrates that the Terrorist is not a "known unknown": He is both ordinary and comprehensible. So what does it really mean to imagine the Terrorist? One answer can be found in the work of the American artist Daisy Rockwell, whose paintings exemplify an effort to humanise the other, to shift the gaze of Americans inward rather than outward, and to force a dialogue with the "known unknowns." Rockwell is the granddaughter of Norman Rockwell, the painter of iconic America. In her paintings of terrorists and militants—Osama bin Laden, Mullah Omar, John Walker Lindh, Umar Farouk Abdulmutallab, Mohamed Mahmood Alessa, Veerrappan—they are depicted gazing directly at the viewer, based on photographs that are disconcertingly ordinary. It is a humanising and an intimate gaze, which disarms the viewer—one unaccustomed to seeing these figures surrounded in bright colours or dazzled in sparkle. But out of this seemingly jarring contrast emerges the most pertinent question—what exactly are we looking at? Who exactly are we viewing? After all, the central conceit of the Assassin/Terrorist paradigm is to deflect such questions and to shroud them in darkness. Rockwell, instead, locks the Terrorists into a silent conversation with us, where they inhabit the space between the canvas and our imagination, utterly knowable and completely fragile.

In the aftermath of September 11, Rockwell was teaching South Asian literature at a university in Chicago. She remembers the shocked, confused eyes of her Pakistani-American Muslim students—who confessed that they felt they had suddenly been made outsiders, that they now hovered irreversibly at the edges of an American life that had not been easy to negotiate to begin with. Those eyes seem to follow us in Rockwell's paintings of John Walker Lindh, the so-called American Taliban, or of Umar Farouk Abdulmutallab, the Nigerian underpants bomber.

Kumar writes that one of his key concerns was to find out "how artists and writers, those conventionally regarded as imaginative, would help us disturb the algebra of hate." Certainly, his own book is a clear challenge to the ossified discourse on terrorism in the United States. Paintings like Rockwell's are perhaps even more fundamentally disruptive. They grant that the terrorist might look like one's uncle, one's student, someone who can potentially be understood, someone who resolutely belongs to this time, this space, and this history.

Flying Blind: U.S. Foreign Policy's Lack of Expertise[17]
Original published in the National *(Abu Dhabi), March 4, 2011*

"I am sitting you next to Secretary Clinton at dinner. Say exactly what you think. If you don't, I never—ever—want to hear you criticise the policy again." So said Richard Holbrooke, the U.S. special representative to the Af-Pak region, barely a week after assuming his new position under the Obama administration. He was talking to Rory Stewart, and Stewart told the anecdote on the *Huffington Post* after Holbrooke's sudden death in 2010.

Holbrooke, Stewart remembered, praised his acumen regarding Afghanistan, and listened to him, even though Stewart disapproved of the emerging policy of General Petraeus. To Holbrooke, Stewart was the expert who dared disagree but whose disagreement still needed to be heard in the halls of power.

Stewart is widely considered an expert on Afghanistan. Currently a member of Parliament in Britain, he sits on the influential Foreign Affairs Select Committee. Previously, he was the Ryan Family Professor of the Practice of Human Rights at the Harvard Kennedy School. Before that, in 2003–04, he worked in southern Iraq with the American administration. And prior to that, in 2002, he walked 6,000 miles—partly across Afghanistan. This last bit, his walk in Afghanistan, became the fulcrum of his 2004 book, *The Places in Between*, which was a bestseller in the UK and the United States. The website for his book declared that he survived his walk because of "his knowledge of Persian dialects and Muslim customs" and a grounded knowledge of the entire region.

Now, as an elected politician, Stewart has moved out of that nebulous region of policy experts into policy makers, but his credentials in the field continue to dominate his public persona. A sure sign of his biographical and political heft was Ian Parker's recent profile in the *New Yorker*, which frankly assessed his chances of becoming prime minister.

Parker notes that Stewart "speaks some Dari and no Pashto" and had only limited exposure to the country, having lived, on and off, in Kabul. Yet, the very fact of his "walking" had transformed a recent college graduate with fantasies of becoming the next T. E. Lawrence (who tried to engineer the birth of a new Arabia during the First World War) or Wilfred Thesiger (who walked over the Empty Quarter of Arabia and became known for his sparse travelogues of the Middle East) into the "real thing." Unlike his heroes, however, Stewart's main competence was not in navigating the desert but knowing D.C. He isn't the only person who has managed to merge a personal narrative implying site-specific knowledge, avowedly ethnographic in nature, with a deep engagement with the political and analytical clusters of the American and British military.

In July 2010, the *New York Times* reported on the popularity of Greg Mortenson's 2006 memoir *Three Cups of Tea: One Man's Mission to Promote Peace . . . One Man's Mission to Fight Terrorism and Build Nations . . . One School at a Time* among the U.S. military high command. The report described General McChrystal and Admiral McMullen using the text as a guide to their civilian strategy in Pakistan. Mortenson's book quickly became required reading in military academies (the report hinted at the role played by the wives of senior military brass in promoting the title), and Mortenson has since spoken to the U.S. Congress and testified in front of committees. Mortenson himself, though a selfless worker for the most disenfranchised of Pakistan's northwestern citizens, possesses no deep knowledge of the region's past or present and is avowedly "nonpolitical" in his local role. Still, his personal story, his experiences, and the work of his charity are now widely considered to be a blueprint for U.S. strategy in the Af-Pak region.

Both Stewart and Mortenson illustrate one particular configuration of the relationship between knowledge and the American empire—the "nonexpert" insider who can traverse that unknown terrain and, hence, become an "expert."

Even a cursory examination of the archive dealing with the American efforts in Iraq, Afghanistan, and Pakistan demonstrates that there has been no related growth in specific scholarly knowledge about those sites of conflict. The knowledge of Arabic, Urdu, or Pashto remains at extremely low levels in official corridors. There is, one can surmise simply from reading the back-and-forth sway of military and political policy in Afghanistan, very little advancement in understanding of either the text or context of that nation.

In America's imperial theatre, Stewart and Mortenson exemplify a singular notion of "expert." We can build, based on the profiles of other specimens— Robert D. Kaplan, Fareed Zakaria, Robert Kagan—a picture of what the ideal type looks like from the official point of view. Such an "expert" is usually one who has not studied the region and especially not in any academic capacity. As a result, they do not possess any significant knowledge of its languages, histories or cultures. They are often vetted by the market, having produced a bestselling book or secured a job as a journalist with a major newspaper. They are not necessarily tied to the "official" narratives or understandings and can even be portrayed as being "a critic" of the official policy. In other words, this profile fits one who doesn't know enough.

At the same time, there are greater claims, and greater efforts, towards satellite cameras and listening devices; drones that can hover for days; databases that can track all good Taliban and all bad Taliban. Yet who can decipher these data? When one considers the rise of "experts," such as Stewart or Mortenson, against the growth of digitised data, which remains elusive and overwhelming, one is left with a rather stark observation—that the American war effort prefers its human knowledge circumspect or circumscribed and its technical knowledge crudely totalised.

IT WASN'T ALWAYS THIS WAY. In 1879, when the U.S. Congress created the U.S. Geological Survey to chart and measure the American West, it simultaneously established the Bureau of American Ethnology. Funded directly by the Congress, this body was chartered to record the languages, habitations, folktales, and oral histories of Native American tribes. It ought to be noted that these efforts to "know" occurred in direct relationship with the opening up of the American West to Eastern capital, labour, and settlement.

The decade following the Second World War saw the creation of Area Studies departments across universities in America. These had an explicit charter to study those countries and regions that had remained "hidden" from American purview but that were now considered the frontline in the emerging Cold War: China, India, Japan, the Middle East. Whether they were funded by the Department of State or Defense, or via external, "independent" sources, such as the Social Sciences Research Council, the Ford Foundation, or the Carnegie Mellon Foundation, conferences and publications were established to serve the interests of the American state. These developments saw the rise of the "Kremlinologist" and the "East Asianist," both within and outside the academy.

If there was ever a situation in which linguistic, cultural, and historical expertise were privileged in American foreign policy, then the period between the Vietnam War and the end of the Cold War fundamentally altered it. The academy grew critical of American foreign policy and tried to distance itself. At the same time, the activities of U.S. academics became the subject of official scrutiny. Various scholars were investigated by the House Un-American Activities Committee for secret Communist sympathies or for having "gone native." The realignment of expertise under Kissinger, and later the Clinton administration, eliminated those career foreign services officers who had lifelong attachments to the regions they covered. The rise of postcolonial and poststructuralist critiques of the relationship between power and knowledge further complicated the terrain.

This widening gulf between the corridors of power and the halls of academia came with the unintended consequence that, barring a few notable exceptions, any knowledgeable critique of American foreign policy gradually vanished. It is this vacuum that is filled by Stewart and Mortenson, who combine accessibility with a whiff of "on-the-ground" expertise. A very similar role is played, in a popular culture hungry for "authentic" voices from the conflicted sites, by the fictions of Khaled Hosseini or Daniyal Mueenuddin.

YET THESE PUNDITS ARE ONLY PART OF THE STORY. The more troubling aspect is the change from human expertise to technical knowledge. The *Washington Post* noted recently that the U.S. Air Force is rolling out a satellite-based observation technology called "Gorgon Stare." A triumphalist quote described the programme thus: "Gorgon Stare will be looking at a whole city, so there will be no way for the adversary to know what we're looking at, and we can see everything."

This "everything" dominates most tech-based strategies, which are regularly puffed in the media. Some mention databases of tribal affiliations and sympathies down to each inhabitant of a given street, neighbourhood, city, and district. This database is then placed at the fingertips of U.S. military personnel via their hand-held electronic devices, letting them bring up the dossier on each Afghan they encounter.

This peculiar urge to know and then unknow remains a central conundrum for all empires. A very similar teleology is visible in the history of the British Empire in India. The earlier colonisations were accompanied by a bevy of East India Company employees who assiduously studied languages, learnt the local customs, and became—to use the term popularised by writer William Dalrymple—"White Mughals." That is, they "went native." But just as the colonial efforts to map and know India picked up steam—in the 1830s and 1840s—the company administration began to raise concerns that British officers were losing their loyalty to their own country.

Lord Ellenborough, who led the British invasion of Afghanistan, was famously sceptical of British officers, such as Richard F. Burton or James Outram, who were regarded with suspicion for being too good with languages, travelling in disguise among the natives. Before he became a renowned traveller and Orientalist, Burton served in Karachi and wrote the following regarding the conduct of his fellow officers: "The white man lives a life so distinct from the black, that hundreds of the former serve through what they call their 'terms of exile,' without once being present at a circumcision feast, a wedding, or a funeral."

The "mutiny" of 1857 fully cleaved this ruling elite from the ruled masses—as the British coloniser retreated from civic space, creating segregated communities, thoroughfares, and establishments. Linked to this withdrawal, however, was the most extensive and descriptive effort to count, catalogue, and tabulate the vast populations of India. The 1870s and 1880s were, as in the case of the American West, decades of prodigious ethnographic output where geographies of caste, lineage, tribe, language, and settlements were carefully and explicitly mapped through survey teams headed by colonial administrators and staffed by legions of local knowledge brokers. By the turn of the century, however, British high imperialism, once again, changed the character of knowledge gathering and the relationship of colonial power to the Indian landscape. The description gave way to the table.

One particularly pertinent example of this process is the geographical surveys and census of the North West Frontier Provinces. First conducted in 1904, and again, in 1910, they produced reams of maps, alongside came the Gazettes, which gathered lore, history, ethnographies. By 1930, this had progressed to the creation of databases—or registers, as they were then called—on individual people.

In a register produced in December 1930, to give one quick example, titled—"List of leading Mullas on the border of the North West Frontier Province"—the following categories of information are listed: "Name," "Parentage," "Year of birth," "Caste or sect," "Residence," "Whether influential. If so with which tribes or sections," "Attitude towards Government as far as known," and "Remarks." Remarkably close in conception and execution to the databases maintained by the United States in Afghanistan, this register shows the progression from the ethnographic narrative to the data table, as the instrumentalisation of political and colonial power began to converge explicitly into a brute-force stratagem.

Whether by the use of anthropologists and social scientists in the Human Terrain System or the reliance on the ethnographic "expert," the American Empire has often held the British example as a template (most likely at the behest of other scholar-combatants, like Niall Ferguson or Bernard Lewis). Implicit in their critique, as in that of Rory Stewart, is the express desire that America must do a better job at being an empire.

Even superficially this is, of course, a categorically illogical thing to assert. There is no better way to do empire. The condition of asserting political and military will over a distant population is one that cannot sustain itself in any modern, liberal society. The efforts to understand will inevitably lead to the understanding that the people of Afghanistan or Pakistan or Iraq desire the power to make their own decisions—without the imposition of governments or militaries sanctioned and placed from afar.

The knowledge of languages and expertise will inevitably expose the lie that there is widespread support for unilateral military escalations. The hope of a civilisational mission (which sustained the likes of Lawrence or Burton in their critiques of the failure of the British to do empire better) does still glimmer in some eyes—those of Fouad Ajami or Thomas Friedman or George W. Bush.

This hope, being irrational and racist, actually requires blindness to the immediate and the real. Notice simply the befuddled faces of area experts when confronted by Tahrir Square. Notice simply that it isn't the masses in the street that confound but the lack of explicit violence from the masses and the lack of religiosity of the masses.

The appeal of the drone's eye is precisely that it does not see everything, because it carries no understanding of the things it records. The experts who are required to imagine Afghanistan or Pakistan traverse those spaces in a manner similar to the drones, on their own preprogrammed missions, where every little thing becomes a target on which to pin their policies.

Chapter Notes

1 Archived at http://bit.ly/eP7V6i.

2 *Address by Quaid-i-Azam Mohammad Ali Jinnah at Lahore Session of Muslim League, March, 1940* (Islamabad: Directorate of Films and Publishing, Ministry of Information and Broadcasting, Government of Pakistan, Islamabad, 1983).

3 Archived at http://bit.ly/fOxxkR.

4 Ron Moreau, "Where the Jihad Lives Now," *Newsweek*, October 20, 2007, archived at http://bit.ly/ajQ3zd.

5 Archived at http://bit.ly/e5vzXw.

6 Archived at http://bit.ly/afdELI.

7 Archived at http://bit.ly/fHtuHL.

8 Archived at http://bit.ly/9EDXYn.

9 Those would be Muslim, al-Bukhari, al-Tirmidhi, Ibn Maja, al-Nasa'i, and Abu Da'ud.

10 On al-Dajjal and Christ in Muslim eschatology; see Neal Robinson, "Antichrist," in *Encyclopaedia of the Qur'an.*

11 Sunan Nasa'i, *Bab Ghazwat al-Hind.*

12 Nu'aym ibn Hammad, *Kitab al-Fitan* (Mecca: Maktabah al-Tajar'iah, 1991), 252–253.

13 Ibid.

14 David Cook, *Studies in Muslim Apocalyptic* (Princeton: Darwin Press, 2002).

15 Archived at http://bit.ly/9iCfJP.

16 Archived at http://bit.ly/fD7XJw.

17 Archived at http://bit.ly/dZCJi8.

Epilogue

Early in the morning of Monday, May 2 (Pakistan time), 2011, a helicopter-borne team from the U.S. Special Forces entered Abbottabad in northern Pakistan and killed Osama Bin Laden after a brief firefight with some of his guards. They took his body, sought and won near-certain confirmation of his identity, and then flew it out to sea, where they gave it a deep-water "burial."

At Sea[1]
May 4, 2011

I.

> *Rudolph says to the sheriff,*
> *"For five long years you've tried.*
> *And you can search as long as you like,*
> *you can try with all your might,*
> *but I'll see you in the sweet bye and bye.*
> *I'll see you in the sweet bye and bye."*

> *Sheriff says to Eric Rudolph,*
> *"Through caves and abandoned mines,*
> *We'll search through scraps and the old feed sacks.*
> *In every old place you could hide."*
> —"Ballad of Eric Rudolph", Michael Holland (2008)

> *For a time, Mr. Rudolph's success as a fugitive reframed the conflict,*
> *from criminal vs. the law to local boy vs. federal intruders. It made him*
> *a celebrated underdog, with T-shirts being sold bearing the phrases*
> *"Run Rudolph Run" and "Hide and Seek Champion."*
> —*New York Times*, April 9, 2005

Eric Rudolph disappeared for five years in the United States. He planted bombs and killed civilians at the 1996 Atlanta Olympic Games, family-planning clinics, and a gay club in 1998, and then he went on the run. It was hard to believe, sitting in the United States, that someone could disappear like that. We were all in the known universe. I don't believe that, at his capture, much was made of him. John Ashcroft called him "the most notorious American fugitive." This was in 2003. The coverage, which I followed, didn't make any connection between Rudolph and terrorism or between the plausibility of local help and Rudolph's long evasion. Rudolph belonged to some other America—not the one where, on May 1, 2003, George W. Bush had declared "Mission Accomplished" and where John Ashcroft was busy busting potheads. Rudolph was some lingering story—one about battles long over. His acts, his flight, his evasion, or his capture had little to offer us.

II.

Long before, he had become a hero in much of the Islamic world. . . .
—*New York Times*, May 2, 2011

It is wrong to claim that Osama bin Laden was irrelevant long before he was killed. He wasn't. He represented, and represents, hundreds of thousands of lives lost since December 2001, when U.S. forces reportedly failed to capture or kill him. He disappeared for the next decade, but that absence was filled with wars in Iraq and Pakistan—wars waged on the heads of civilians, among urban centers, and at the cost of trillions. Just the technological developments of killing from the skies accomplished in this decade are numbing to the mind or any sense of morality. No, Osama bin Laden was never irrelevant, and he was never off the script. Sure, George W. Bush or Pervez Musharraf told us that the battle was now bigger, the stakes higher, and the cost greater, but they were empty words. The deaths of September 11, 2001, and the destructions that followed hold us accountable—to remember that the cost of those lives began in a bid for this one life. Let us also not forget that the road from Tora Bora to Abbottabad is strewn with over 100,000 civilian bodies. So, we must deal with that life and the narratives it spawned. The *New York Times* claims that he was a "hero in much of the Islamic world." The obituary moves on, and we are left with that "fact." What are we to make of it? Heroes, after all, were gods and immortals.

III.

The code name for Bin Laden was "Geronimo."
—*New York Times*, May 2, 2011

I recently spoke at a conference in Chicago about teaching South Asia critically and I concluded with this:

To tell the story of America's tangled history with South Asia is the first and most basic step in teaching South Asia critically. Elihu Yale, who lived and worked in India for nearly three decades with the British East India Company (1670–1699), donated to the Collegiate School of Connecticut three bales of goods—Madras cotton, silk, and other textiles from India—laying the financial foundation for their first building. The first seated chair of Sanskrit emerged at Yale. In 1800 when Alexander Dow negotiated yet another treaty with the Sindhi Mirs to establish ports and harbors on the Arabian Sea, he specifically noted that Americans were to be kept out of Sindh. The 1856 Guano Islands Act passed by Congress claimed for the United States any "unclaimed" island with sufficient supplies of bird waste (to be used as fertiliser by American farmers) by any American entrepreneur and mandated that this annexation should be defended by the U.S. Navy. The list of island territories annexed, claimed, or contested—Cuba, Puerto Rico, Guam, Hawaii, the Philippines, and so on—is long and scattered around the globe. But that act of Congress is also part of the legal framework that created Guantanamo Bay and that enables drone assassinations in "remote frontier" regions of Pakistan, where there "is no rule of law." The opium trade network that sustained the East India Company's coffers in the mid–19th century by supplying Bengal-raised opium to China was remitted through American cotton, and that money seeped right into the Southern slave economy.

These entanglements disrupt the teleologies of postcolonial study in the United States, and they complicate the relationship of the academic to the funding bodies, to the region, and to the student. The politics of provincializing Europe are all too evident, but the necessity to provincialize America bears laying out. We must look at the war the U.S. government waged on the Native American populations—decreed explicitly by the post–Civil War Congress. We need to look at the Barbary Muslim pirates, in pursuit of whom American power first went to the Mediterranean Sea. We need to look at the American imperial gaze that stretched out towards the West and called it the Open Frontier and sought to settle it, sought to categorize its people and its histories and to build ethnographic portraits of the "good Indians" and the "bad Indians." It is of utmost importance to our understanding of the American engagement with "the tribe" post-2005 that we recall the work of John Wesley Powell and the Bureau of American Ethnology. We need to pay as much attention to Locke, Jefferson, Whitman, Turner, Wilson as we do to Hegel or Heidegger or Bentnick or Curzon.

The "Indians" or the "hostiles" as they were once named remain an indelible part of our national myth. The myopia we extend out to the caves of Afghanistan and Pakistan exists in North Carolina, Alabama, and Oklahoma. We have programmed forgetfulness into our civic and political lives. We have enabled our academic lives to nonentities in the public sphere.

IV.

I go myself, as agent of the British Government, to a Court of the language and manners of which I am utterly ignorant, and to accomplish that of which the most sanguine have no hope. It is simply a matter of duty.
—James Abbott, *Narrative of a Journey from Heraut to Khiva, Moscow and St. Petersburgh* (1843)

Abbottabad was named to memorialize the service of Sir James Abbott, commissioner of the Hezara region. One can say that he became immortal.

V.

So I would have no objection if we picked out a country that is a likely suspect and bombed some oil fields, refineries, bridges, highways, industrial complexes, airports, military bases, and anything else that is of great value but doesn't shelter innocent civilians. If it happens to be the wrong country, well, too bad, but it's likely it did something to deserve it anyway. Or would in the future. And its leaders, as well as other troublemakers, would get the message: Terrorism is too costly a game.

President Clinton says we should be cautious about placing blame or taking action. OK. But when the time comes for punishment, it wouldn't be an eye for eye. That's just a swap. We should take both eyes, ears, nose, the entire anatomy. That's how to make a lasting impression.
—Mike Royko, *Chicago Tribune*, April 21, 1995

Salman Rushdie wrote on May 2 that he wants Pakistan to be declared a terrorist nation and expelled from the "comity of nations." To Rushdie, a 6 foot 4 inch man wandering around a country of 5 foot 8 inch plebeians without getting noticed is inconceivable, and, hence, the entire 180 million must pay the price. They were all in the know. Keeping mum even as drones kept killing their lots; even as the Taliban kept blowing up hotels, police compounds, intelligence agency offices, shrines, and hospitals; even as the United States kept endorsing and supporting dictatorial power over them; even as the United States kept funding their military to the tune of tens of billions while "nonhumanitarian aid" was pegged to a billion or so; even as an earthquake and a flood shook their geography loose. The millions of Pakistan kept their quiet, maybe giggling in anticipation of whenever Uncle Sam would catch them in the act. Now they have been caught! The ISI knew! This validates all the drones and their missiles! It means *more drone missiles!* Yeah. That is what it means. They were all in it, Rushdie. Every stinking lying one of them.

Royko wrote what I quote above after the Oklahoma City Bombing. I remember that morning. I was ironing my clothes for my night shift at the restaurant. I remember Connie Chung breathlessly telling me that men of Middle Eastern hue had been seen fleeing the scene. She was literally out of breath: The war in the

Middle East has finally come to the United States. Royko was similarly shocked and convinced. It wasn't important that almost immediately the call went out to look for white Caucasian suspects. Later, in October 2001, we kept hearing that Timothy McVeigh got his training or his weapon or something from Iraq. Royko's wish came true—we got both ears, nose, the entire anatomy. Maybe Rushdie's wish would come true as well. Who remembers Geronimo anyways?

Epilogue Note

1 Archived at http://bit.ly/mE9SdB.

Glossary

Acronyms

a.k.a.: also known as

BJP: Bharat Janata Party

CJ: chief justice

CM: Chapati Mystery

CW: conventional wisdom

EIC: East India Company

FSC: Federal Shari'at Court

HRCP: Human Rights Commission of Pakistan

HVT: high-value target

IJI: Islami Jamhoori Iteehad

INC: Iraqi National Congress

ISI: Inter-Services Intelligence

JI: Jama'at-i Islami

JS: Jon Stewart

LHC: Lahore High Court

LUMS: Lahore University of Management Sciences

MEK: *Mujahedin Khalq*

MQM: Muttahida Quami movement

NGO: nongovernmental organization

NWFP: Northwest Frontier Province

NYT: The *New York Times*

PCO: Provisional Constitutional Order

U.S. AID: U.S. Agency for International Development

WaPo: The *Washington Post*

WSJ: The *Wall Street Journal*

WMDs: weapons of mass destruction

Terms

'adl: justice

al Zulfikar: the Sword

bid'ah: innovation, bad

chowkidaar: security guard

chamchas: cronies

dehyari: a day's wage

dhimmis: non-Muslims under Muslim rule

dupatta: shawl

fatwa: legal pronouncement in Islam about a specific topic, issued by a religious law specialist

fiqh: jurisprudence

imam: prayer leader

izzat: pride or honor

jizya: property tax levied on conquered populations

kala qanoon: black law

karokari: honor killings

khatm-e nabuvat: Finality of Prophethood

khushhaali: better living

madrasa: building, including a mosque, used for teaching Islamic theology and religious law

mahdi: the one who will lead the apocalyptical battle

mard-e haq: righteous man

mard-e kamil: perfect man

mard-e momin: pious man

marsiya: six-line verse with three rhyming couplets

masih: Jesus

maulanas: religious leaders

Mi'raj: ascension

muftis: Islamic scholar who is an interpreter or expounder of Islamic law

muhaddath: one who transmits a tradition

mujadid: a millennial renewer

mullah: Muslim religious figure

Namoos-i Risalat: the Sanctity of the Prophethood

Pakistan ka Matlab Kiya? La Illaha Illal Lah: What does Pakistan mean? No God but One.

Peccavi: confession of sin

roti, kapra aur makan: bread, cloth, and house

shari'a: Islamic jurisprudence

sunnah: words and deeds of the Prophet

Tauheen-i Risalat: Blaspheming the Prophet

Tehrik-e Insaf: movement for justice

'ushr: annual tax on Muslim

zamindar: landlord

CPSIA information can be obtained at www.ICGtesting.com
Printed in the USA
LVOW100218280513

335586LV00001B/98/P